STUFFED ANIMALS

From Concept to Construction

Abigail Patner Glassenberg

LARK

Asheville

CONTENTS

STUFFED
ANI

'ease return/renew this item by the last date shown.
` may also be renewed by the internet*

·ry.eastriding.gov.uk

↲ PIN will be required to access this service
↲ obtained from your library

LARK CRAFTS

An Imprint of Sterling Publishing
387 Park Avenue South
New York, NY 10016

ISBN 978-1-4547-0364-8

Library of Congress Cataloging-in-Publication Data

Glassenberg, Abigail Patner.
  Stuffed animals / Abigail Patner Glassenberg. -- First Edition.
    pages cm
  Includes index.
  ISBN 978-1-4547-0364-8
  1. Soft toy making--Patterns. 2. Stuffed animals (Toys) I. Title.
  TT174.3.G586 2013
  745.592'4--dc23
                              2012020872

Distributed in Canada by Sterling Publishing
c/o Canadian Manda Group, 165 Dufferin Street
Toronto, Ontario, Canada M6K 3H6
Distributed in the United Kingdom by GMC Distribution Services
Castle Place, 166 High Street, Lewes, East Sussex, England BN7 1XU
Distributed in Australia by Capricorn Link (Australia) Pty. Ltd.
P.O. Box 704, Windsor, NSW 2756, Australia

For information about custom editions, special sales, and premium and corporate purchases, please contact Sterling Special Sales at 800-805-5489 or specialsales@sterlingpublishing.com.

Email academic@larkbooks.com for information about desk and examination copies.
The complete policy can be found at larkcrafts.com.

Manufactured in China

2 4 6 8 10 9 7 5 3

larkcrafts.com

INTRODUCTION

Sewing stuffed animals, or softies as they are often called, is a wonderful way to explore your creativity.

With just a few scraps of fabric and some stuffing, you can create something soft, fun, creepy, or hilarious—a huggable stuffed friend for someone special. There are many softie patterns available in books and magazines and online that you can turn to when you want to create a toy, but wouldn't it be cool to come up with your own design? Drafting your own softie pattern is wonderfully satisfying. It can take a few tries to get things just right, and you will probably need to edit the pattern along the way, but once you have something that works, an original pattern can take you far. You could create dozens, or even hundreds, of softies with it and give them away, or sell them. Or you could draw out the pattern template and write up the sewing instructions and sell the pattern online or to a publisher to have it printed in a book. Your original pattern—or patterns, because I hope you won't stop at just one—can lead you in all kinds of new pleasurable and profitable directions.

And you don't need to be an artist to do it! My goal with this book is to show you step by step how to design and create your very own soft-toy patterns, from a simple sketch to a completed, stuffed toy ready to give or sell.

When I first began making softies I went to the library in search of pattern books. At that time most of the books were very dated, but the patterns had a vintage charm that appealed to me, and the instructions were still valid and informative. I taught myself to sew and to design toys by reading those books and experimenting with those patterns.

Over time, I wanted to sew toys not just as a hobby but as a business, too. To do this, I needed to develop my own, original patterns. For many years since then, I have had a successful small business selling my toys, and I often get requests for my patterns. I have published patterns in various books, magazines, and websites over the years, and I wrote a book of fabric bird patterns that was published in 2011, but gnawing at the back of my mind every time someone requested a pattern from me was the idea that it would be even better to teach readers to create their own original patterns.

The patterns in this book are organized from easiest to most complex. Each pattern is followed by a series of lessons in which I have broken down how I designed that particular pattern, shown you a variety of options for other ways I could have gone about the design process, and given you various ways to finish the toy.

If you are just beginning to sew toys, I recommend that you begin with the first pattern. Read the lesson to learn the basic skills of toy design, and then sew the toy using my pattern to practice those particular skills. Then, get started designing your own first toy by employing some of those skills. If you have already designed soft toys but would like to learn some new pattern-drafting techniques, look through the toys I have presented here and select one that employs an element you may be unfamiliar with. Have you worked with joints? Have you used darts? Do you find designing a head gusset intimidating? Read through the lesson that demonstrates a technique that is new to you, sew the pattern, and then try to use that technique in a new softie pattern of your own design.

Some people come to softie making with a lot of sewing experience. If you've sewn garments or items for your home, or if you've been a quilter for years, you already know quite a bit about how to choose, cut, and sew fabrics, but for many people making a softie is their very first sewing project. The desire to create a cute teddy bear or a silly monster is often what motivates crafters to dust off their machines and start sewing. Even for the most experienced sewist, there are aspects of the craft of softie making that require you to treat fabrics and create patterns in ways that you may not have done in other sewing projects. And perhaps drafting your own patterns for a project is new to you. For these reasons, this book begins with a look at the tools and materials that will be most helpful to you in your work, an introduction to softie-pattern drafting, and an overview of the basics you'll need to know to sew and stuff a softie.

Where do the ideas for toys come from? Keep your mind open to inspiration whenever and wherever it may appear. Children in your life may request a particular toy from their imagination, from a trip to the zoo or the farm, or from a book they've read. Or you may want to bring one of your own illustrations to life in fabric just for the joy of making something new. As you dream about your new design, think about your subject's distinguishing characteristics. A red breast makes a bird a robin, but done in all black it could be a crow. A horse pattern made up in black and white stripes is a zebra. Just pulling out my bins of fabric and looking through them is often enough to spark an idea for a new stuffed animal.

Dig in and enjoy! Make a new toy and make yourself smile!

Part 1:

GETTING

STARTED

LEGEND

1 Large scissors
2 Scissors for paper
3 Ruler
4 Circle templates

5 Hemostats
6 Measuring tape
7 Sliding gauge
8, 9, 10 Sketching materials

11 Seam ripper
12 Craft knife
13 Freezer paper

14 Awl
15 Small sewing
(embroidery) scissors

TOOLS & MATERIALS

To design and sew a stuffed animal you only really need basic sewing tools like pins, scissors, thread, a marking pen, and a sewing machine. However, as with any fine craft, specialized tools can make the process easier, quicker, and more refined. On the following pages you'll find a comprehensive list of the tools and materials that I keep in my design studio. Most of them are inexpensive and easy enough to find. Having the right tool for the job makes the process of designing and sewing a stuffed animal markedly easier. It's worth it to invest in good tools!

Sketching Materials ● All of my softie designs begin in some way within the pages of an 8 1/2 x 11-inch (21.6 x 27.9 cm) sketchbook that I like to keep on my desk, along with a sharpened pencil and a good eraser, to record my ideas. I try not to be intimidated by the blank white page and instead just give myself the freedom to sketch without judgment or pressure.

Image Library ● Build an inspiration library consisting of nature books and magazines, toy catalogs, illustrated children's books, and other visual references that suggest a toy idea to you. Get in the habit of clipping images that inspire you and posting them on an inspiration board or gluing them into a notebook. This sort of thing can also be useful when you need to examine details, such as how a dolphin's fin is shaped or how a horse looks in full gallop.

Ruler ● A standard 12-inch (30.5 cm) school ruler, or even better, a clear acrylic ruler, is a handy tool when drafting patterns. If you know you want a toy to be a certain size overall, you can measure and mark that size on your pattern-drafting paper to begin with and then draw the pattern.

Basic Sewing Tool Kit

Every project requires slightly different tools and materials, but there are some basic tools that you'll use over and over. Here's a list of what I suggest you keep on hand.

- Ruler
- Sliding gauge
- Flexible measuring tape
- Circle templates
- Freezer paper and pencil
- Scissors for cutting paper
- Large scissors for fabric only
- Small embroidery scissors
- Pinking shears
- Craft knife
- Muslin
- Pincushion and pins
- Sewing machine and needles
- Needles for hand-sewing
- Seam ripper
- Iron and ironing board
- Disappearing fabric marker, fabric pencils, and chalk
- Craft glue
- Glue stick
- Hemostats

Sliding Gauge ● Use a sliding gauge to easily add a seam allowance to pattern pieces before cutting them out if you aren't comfortable eyeballing it. Set the gauge to a $1/4$ inch (6 mm), then run it along the edges of your pattern pieces, using a disappearing fabric marker or chalk to mark the seam allowance onto the fabric with a small dot every $1/2$ inch. Connect the dots to create an even $1/2$-inch (6 mm) seam allowance around the pattern piece.

Flexible Measuring Tape ● A flexible measuring tape is useful for calculating the circumferences of a pattern piece because you can wrap the tape carefully along the edges as they curve inward and outward. Most retractable measuring tapes are $1/4$ inch (6 mm) wide, so another way to easily add a $1/4$-inch (6 mm) seam allowance (see above) is to simply run a measuring tape along the edge of the pattern, marking the fabric as you go.

Circle Templates ● Circle templates can be as important as a ruler. Let's face it: drawing a perfect circle is difficult! You can also use them for drawing arcs and partial circles that may become haunches, teddy bear ears, snouts, or other body parts. And they are an invaluable tool for making eyes. I bought my circle template at an office supply store.

Enlarging/Reducing Photocopier ● I like to work on new patterns based on sketches in my sketchbook, but sometimes I want the toy itself to be either larger or smaller than my initial sketch. I go ahead and draw my pattern based on my sketch and then either enlarge or reduce the pattern pieces on a photocopier.

Freezer Paper and Other Options for Pattern Templates ● I buy freezer paper by the roll at the grocery store in the aluminum foil aisle. Freezer paper saves you multiple steps because you can draft your pattern on it, cut it out, and iron it to your fabric without having to retrace or pin it. (For more information, see Using Freezer Paper for Creating, Cutting, and Sewing Patterns on page 19.) If freezer paper is not available in stores near you, you can buy sheets of it online through doll-making supply sites. You can also draw your patterns on tracing paper, blank newsprint, or thin cardboard, and then either pin or trace them onto the fabric.

Scissors ● Small sewing scissors, sometimes called embroidery scissors, are an essential softie-making tool. I have several pairs that I keep in various places in my sewing room—they're perfect for cutting little pieces from fabric, clipping curves, and snipping threads.

Use a pair of standard scissors for cutting out larger pattern pieces from fabric and for cutting yarn. Never cut paper, or anything else for that matter, with your fabric scissors or they will quickly become dull. You may want to mark them with tape or ribbon to differentiate them from the other scissors. And remember to get your scissors sharpened regularly. It makes a big difference in the accuracy of your cutting!

You also should have a third set of scissors for cutting paper. Use these scissors when you are cutting out your paper pattern pieces and if you need to cut anything else, like tape or cardboard.

Craft Knife ● A craft knife is useful for cutting intricate shapes from felt, for cutting small slits in fabric, and for clipping curves. Be sure to change the blade frequently to keep it sharp.

Pincushion and Pins ● I use three types of pins. Glass-head pins are great because they will not melt if you accidentally iron over them. Appliqué pins are about half the length of a standard pin and have a very small head. These are very useful for pinning small softie pieces. And standard pins with round, black plastic heads are great for testing eye placement on a softie before sewing on the eyes. Throw out any bent pins because they will not hold your pattern pieces together accurately.

You can never have too many pincushions. I keep one next to my machine, one on my cutting table, and one on the ironing board. And I like to keep a fourth pincushion just for my appliqué pins because they are small and tend to get lost in the other three pincushions!

LEGEND

1 Perle cotton
2 Clear thread
3 Extra strong thread
4 All-purpose polyester thread
5 Glue stick
6 Craft glue
7, 14 Eyes and noses
8 Pincushion and three types of pins
9 Buttons
10 Embroidery floss
11 Doll needles
12 Needles for hand sewing
13 Yarn
15 Disappering fabric marker
16 Chalk

Sewing Machine with an All-Purpose Presser Foot ● I prefer to do most of my softie sewing on my sewing machine. Machine-sewn seams are neat, strong, and quick to make, giving me good results with less effort, especially on larger toys and toys that will get a lot of wear and tear. You don't need a fancy machine to sew beautiful softies; a machine that performs basic stitches is enough. I use an all-purpose presser foot almost all the time. If your machine has an adjustable needle position, allowing you to move the needle all the way to the right, you'll find it useful for sewing pattern pieces with narrow seam allowances. And if you want to create a toy with a zipper, like the Dinosaur with the zippered mouth on page 158, you'll need a zipper foot.

Sewing Machine Needles ● Before you begin a new softie project, make sure that your sewing machine needle is fresh. Changing your needle regularly cuts down on frustration because small softie pieces are less likely to get pulled down into the machine if the needle is sharp and free of burrs. To test your needle, remove it and drag the shaft across your fingernail. If it makes a scratch, it has a burr and should be thrown out.

SEWING MACHINE NEEDLE SIZE CONVERSIONS

	AMERICAN	EUROPEAN
lightest	8	60
	9	65
	10	70
	11	75
	12	80
	14	90
	16	100
	18	110
heaviest	19	120

Select the right sewing-machine needle for the fabric you are sewing with. Machine needles come in various sizes with European and American annotation systems. Both numbers may be listed, but the order makes no difference (12/80 is the same as 80/12).

If you use a machine needle that is too heavy for the fabric, like a 19/120 on lightweight cotton, you will create unnecessarily large holes in the fabric with every stitch. In softie making, the fabric is stuffed, and the stuffing can leak out of those holes. The fabric will be weakened along the stitching line, too, and is likely to pull apart. A machine needle that is too light for the fabric, like an 8/60 on wide-wale corduroy, is likely to break during sewing, and the eye will not be able to accommodate extra-strong thread that may be needed for sewing thicker fabrics. If you are sewing a softie from denim, choose a special jeans/denim needle. These needles have extra-sharp points and a stiff shaft and come in sizes from 10/70 to 18/110. They are also useful for sewing through many layers of fabric at once. For leather or other heavy nonwoven fabrics choose a leather needle. These needles have wedge-shaped points and come in sizes from 11/75 to 14/90. If you are not sure whether the needle is the right size for your fabric, make a test seam on a scrap first.

Needles for Hand-Sewing ● I recommend buying a variety pack of the standard sewing needles, called sharps. Sharps are medium-length needles with a rounded eye. They are numbered 1 through 10, indicating the diameter of the needle, with size 1 being the thickest. If you are working on a very small softie, or one made with more delicate materials, you may want to hand-sew details with a quilting needle. These needles, called betweens, are shorter and have smaller eyes than those of sharps.

Embroidery needles are essential if you want to embroider features on your softie. These needles are similar to sharps, but with a larger eye to accommodate thicker thread like floss or perle cotton.

A curved upholstery needle is especially useful for sewing yarn onto your toy. These needles have large eyes to accommodate yarn and are sturdy enough not to bend or break while you are working. Their curve makes it easy to create stitches that are closely spaced.

Beeswax ● I keep a piece of beeswax next to my needle book. When I am ready to hand-sew, I thread a needle, then drag the thread along the edge of the beeswax so that it is coated. Before I sew, I run the thread between my fingers just to set the wax and brush off any excess. The wax helps the thread pass smoothly through the fabric, strengthens the thread, and prevents tangles. Beeswax is also useful for waxing embroidery floss or perle cotton to create stiff whiskers. You can find beeswax online or with the notions at the fabric store.

All-Purpose Polyester Thread ● I generally use all-purpose polyester thread for machine-sewing softies. Sometimes called sew-all thread, it will not shrink when washed and is very strong, so it will stand up to firm stuffing. Invest in good-quality thread! Bargain-bin thread frays and breaks easily and will only lead to frustration. When choosing a thread color, look for a shade lighter than the fabric you are using. Lighter-colored stitching is less likely to show than stitches made in thread that is darker than your fabric.

Extra-Strong Thread ● I find extra-strong (or heavy-duty) thread to be a most useful item. There is nothing more frustrating than carefully ladder-stitching an opening closed only to have the thread snap on the last stitch! Once I started using extra-strong thread to close openings, I eliminated this problem. Now I always have extra-strong thread on hand in a variety of colors to use not only for closing openings but also for ladder-stitching tails, ears, muzzles, horns, or any other small part to a softie's body.

Extra-strong thread is sold in fabric and quilt shops right next to the standard-weight threads. It is sometimes referred to as topstitching thread; upholstery or button-twist thread also works well. When sewing with extra-strong thread, use an embroidery needle because the larger eye accommodates the wider width of the thread.

Seam Ripper ● Mistakes are part of the creative process. The wonderful thing about stitching mistakes is that they are entirely removable! Use a seam ripper to safely and efficiently unpick stitches when you make a mistake. Avoid reaching for embroidery scissors for this task because, although they will cut the stitches, they may also cut the fabric! I keep my seam ripper right next to my sewing machine so that it's handy whenever I make a stitching mistake.

Muslin ● It is important to make a prototype for any new design before you sew it from your chosen fabric. You can buy muslin fairly inexpensively at the fabric store and use that for making prototypes, but I like to use old bedsheets. That way, if I need to make several before I have a pattern that works, I don't feel badly about wasting fabric!

Fabric Stash ● Softies can be sewn from all sorts of fabrics. You can buy new fabrics or reuse fabrics you already have. Because softie pattern pieces are usually small, making softie projects is a perfect way to use up your treasured fabric scraps.

Trim Stash ● Making softies is a wonderful way to use bits and pieces of trim left over from other projects. All kinds of trim can be incorporated into a softie design, including rickrack, braid, pompoms, tassels, cord, lace, bias tape, fringe, and ribbon. Thrift stores and rummage sales are great places to find very affordable trim, and you might just stumble upon some vintage trim that is really special. I keep all my trims together in a shoebox and pull them out when I'm looking for something to make a softie extra special. And when I'm feeling uninspired, sorting through all the textures and colors found in my box of trim helps me feel creative again!

Iron and Ironing Board ● A steam iron and an ironing board are essential for any sewing project. I always tell my students, if you're sewing, you're ironing! If possible, prewash your fabric and always press out any wrinkles before cutting.

Disappearing Fabric Marker, Fabric Pencils, and Chalk ● A fabric marker is very handy for transferring markings from pattern pieces onto fabric. The marks made with a water-soluble fabric marker will disappear when you mist them with water from a spray bottle. The marks made with some water-soluble fabric markers will reappear as a brown residue if the toy is machine washed, so read the fine print before purchasing one. The marks made with air-soluble fabric markers disappear on their own after a certain period of time, typically 24 hours. If you are using a darker fabric, or one with a pronounced texture, such as corduroy, nothing works better than simple school chalk. It's inexpensive, is easy to find, and shows up well on fabric. Simply rub off the marks when you no longer need them.

Craft Glue ● There are times when it makes more sense to glue a detail onto a softie's body than it does to stitch it in place. I keep a good craft glue on hand for just that purpose. If I am applying it to a tiny area, I bend a paper clip and use the tip as an applicator for the glue. Hold pieces in place with pins until the glue dries.

Glue Stick ● Glue sticks are great to temporarily adhere two layers of fabric together before stitching. I use them most often when creating layered eyes by rubbing the glue stick over the back of each layer and sticking the layers together. With the layers fused it is much easier to create neat, even stitches and to make two identical eyes.

Fiberfill Stuffing ● I stuff almost all of my toys with polyester fiberfill because it is readily available at most fabric and craft stores, is relatively inexpensive, and allows my toys to be washed in the washing machine. Fiberfill is made by extruding liquid polyester through miniscule holes. The fibers dry and are either coated with silicone or left uncoated. The coated fibers result in high-loft fiberfill, which feels slippery between your fingers and creates a squishy toy. The uncoated fibers become firm-pack fiberfill, which feels rougher and, just as the name implies, can be packed very firmly into a cavity. I generally prefer firm-pack fiberfill because I usually like to stuff my toys very firmly, but for a squishy, huggable toy (such as the Hippo on page 152), high-loft stuffing is perfect. Most of the time there is no information on a bag of fiberfill indicating whether it is high loft or firm pack. You may want to experiment with different brands until you figure out how each behaves.

Almost all fiberfill is white, which works for most projects. Occasionally you may find that, when working with dark, looser-weave fabrics, the whiteness of the fiberfill shows through. Black fiberfill does exist, although it is currently very difficult to find. If you are stuffing only a small area, try black wool roving as an alternate stuffing material.

Doll Needles ● Doll needles are long needles that are especially useful for toy making because they can be inserted into one side of a toy's body, go through the stuffing, and come out the other side—which may be several inches away. Doll needles are commonly found in 3-inch (7.6 cm), 5-inch (12.7 cm), and 7-inch (17.8 cm) lengths. I find that at the 5-inch (12.7 cm) doll needle is the one I use most often.

Hemostats ● Hemostats are surgical forceps. They resemble scissors, but the ends are not sharp, so they cannot cut. Instead, the tips are used to grasp hold of small parts and can then be clamped shut so that the grasp will not release while you are using them. I find that it is most useful to have a smaller, 5-inch (12.7 cm) pair of hemostats with curved, ridged inner tips for turning and stuffing tiny pieces, and a larger 7-inch (17.8 cm) pair, also with ridged inner tips, for stuffing larger toys.

Awl ● A ball-point awl has a graduated shaft that begins with a tiny circumference and widens as it nears the handle. The ball point slips between the weave of the fabric, allowing me to create a hole without cutting any of the fibers and thereby weakening the fabric. I use my ball-point awl to create a hole to insert safety eyes and joints. And the shaft of the awl is nice and strong, making it a perfect tool for tugging on fur caught in a seam and freeing it for a more seamless look on a finished toy. Note that this awl is a specialty sewing tool and not the type used in woodworking and leatherworking.

Buttons ● I have a huge button collection sorted by color and size, and I use buttons in many different ways when I make softies. Tiny 1/4-inch (6 mm) buttons, often sold as "doll buttons," are perfect for eyes on very small toys, or for use on softie clothing. Look for pairs of 1/2-inch (1.3 cm) brown and black buttons that you can use as eyes for larger toys. You can even layer a smaller button on top of a larger button to create a pupil. Pretty decorative and vintage buttons make great hair and shoe accessories for softies, too. Buttons are also very useful for creating jointed limbs. I buy most of my buttons at rummage sales. I tend to buy them when I see them, then sort and store them so that they are at the ready when a new project that requires a button presents itself.

Eyes and Noses ● Having just the right eyes for a toy can make all the difference between a cute, appealing expression and one that falls flat. For a very simple and quick set of eyes, sew on a pair of beads. I collect plastic and glass beads in a variety of diameters to use as eyes. Even though I sew the beads on with extra-strong thread, bead eyes may not be the best choice for a toy that will be given to a young child.

If you often make toys for children, check out the variety of safety eyes available through doll and teddy bear supply companies. Once installed correctly, safety eyes are very secure and cannot be pulled off by little hands. Safety eyes are eyes attached to plastic posts and then firmly secured with a plastic washer. Safety eyes come in sizes as small as 4 mm and as large as 36 mm and are available in a huge variety of colors. Also look for cat eyes with elongated pupils, frog eyes, owl eyes, wiggle eyes, and oval eyes.

For toys that are meant for older children or are being made as collectibles, consider eyes with wire backs. These may come as two eyes connected to one another by a wire or as individual eyes with a loop of wire on the back. If the eyes are connected you'll have to cut them apart with wire cutters and then form loops on the back of each one yourself. Wire-backed eyes are secured to the softie with strong thread. You can find wire-backed eyes in plastic and glass from 4 mm to 36 mm and in a huge variety of colors. Also look for corner eyes (with whites), glass googly eyes, alive eyes (with large pupils), carnival eyes (black with white highlights), border eyes (with black borders), and fantasy eyes (with drawn-in lids). Shoe-button eyes are black glass eyes with wire backs that are made to look like old-fashioned shoe buttons.

Although you can always embroider noses on a softie, plastic and leather animal noses are also available through teddy bear supply companies. These come in rubber, flocked plastic, leather, and glass anywhere from 8 mm to 30 mm and work similarly to safety eyes. I've seen them in black, brown, peach, yellow, and red.

Yarn ● A stash of random yarns left over from other projects is a boon to a softie maker. I often find skeins of beautiful yarn at thrift shops. You never know when you might need a particular yarn to make a horse's mane, a fuzzy pompom tail for a bunny, or a fluffy beard for a goat!

Embroidery Floss and Perle Cotton ● I love embroidery floss! It comes in such a wide variety of colors—just looking at it makes me want to get into the studio and embroider! Embroidery floss is a loosely twisted six-strand thread that is somewhat glossy. I often separate out two or three strands from a length of floss to use for embroidering features on toys. I have found that the most useful colors for toy making are white, cream, brown, and black floss, but embroidery floss is not expensive, and it is nice to have a rainbow of colors available for decorative stitching. When I open a new skein of floss I wrap it around a small rectangle of cardboard with a slit cut in the side for tucking in the ends. I punch a hole on the short end of the cardboard and string it on a large key ring. This way my floss doesn't get tangled.

Perle cotton is a shiny, twisted two-ply thread that cannot be divided. It comes in a variety of sizes: sizes 5, 8, and 12 are the most common, with size 5 having the largest diameter. I love perle cotton for embroidering noses and for making whiskers, and I always keep cream, brown, and black perle cotton at the ready in my toy-making workspace. When perle cotton is called for in the projects in this book, use size 12.

DESIGNING STUFFED ANIMALS

A stuffed animal (which I also refer to as soft toy or softie) is a three-dimensional object sewn from fabric and stuffed with soft stuffing. It may be large or small, simple or highly detailed, cute or scary, intended as a child's plaything or as a sculptural object. Creating the sewing pattern for a softie is an art form that requires you to visualize how two-dimensional paper pattern pieces come together to create a three-dimensional object.

Visual Research and Sketching

You do not need to be good at drawing to create a stuffed animal pattern. Softie patterns are based on simple shapes: cubes, spheres, tubes, and cones. To get a sense of how these shapes comes together to form a particular subject, begin by gathering images. Photographs are a good place to start. Try to find two or three profile images that allow you to clearly see the head, body shape, legs, and other relevant details. Examining commercially produced stuffed animals and plastic toys is helpful for envisioning the three-dimensional shape of an animal. I find that cartoons and sculptures are also great source materials. Looking at the ways other artists have distilled, and perhaps exaggerated, a particular animal's features is very useful. Illustrators have already worked to simplify animals in drawings, exaggerating the features to make it easily recognizable, and accentuating cuteness. If you struggle with drawing facial features, the animal illustrations in children's books can be especially helpful. What shape are the eyes, and where are they placed on the head? How is the nose drawn? And the smile? All of these characteristics can be imitated with fabric, embroidery floss, doll eyes, and buttons.

Before you begin sketching, look over the images you have gathered and ask yourself, what are the most evocative features of this creature? What makes a cat a cat? Is it the ears? Whiskers? The little triangular nose? The long, swishy tail? The stance? You may want to exaggerate some of these features, like a caricature, or stylize them in the style of Japanese kawaii, for example.

Think also about whether you are going for a cute, baby-animal look or something more hard edged and strong looking. Big eyes set low on a round face, for example, create a cute face, whereas smaller eyes set farther up on a more chiseled face give the appearance of an older, more powerful animal.

Now begin to sketch. If you are creating a standing four-legged animal, you want to focus on sketching a good profile. If you are making a flat toy that is seen head-on, sketch it as you would see it.

You can either sketch the toy full-size or enlarge (or reduce) it on a copier later. Start with lighter, more feathery lines and then go back over them with a more confident line once you have drawn the shape you like. At that point, I find it helpful to tape my sketch up on a wall and view it from a distance to get a new perspective. Continue to edit your sketch until you have solid, confident lines that you are happy with.

Using Freezer Paper for Creating, Cutting, and Sewing Patterns

I don't like to wing it! Sewing a new softie without a pattern means wasting time and materials on something that most likely won't work. I make a paper pattern for every softie I create. I think it is much easier to think through how the toy will be constructed, and what shape each piece needs to be for it to all fit together three-dimensionally, if I draw out the pattern pieces on paper first. Having a paper pattern means it will be easier to make edits later and to learn from your mistakes. You can always change the shape of paper pattern pieces once you've sewn up a muslin prototype by either trimming the paper pattern pieces down or retracing and altering them as needed. And once you've created a pattern that works, you can easily sew the toy again and again.

I prefer to use freezer paper for all of my patterns. It saves me time and increases my accuracy when sewing softies. Freezer paper has several qualities that make it ideal for softie patterns. One side of the paper is matte and one side is shiny; the matte side is easy to draw on with a regular pencil and eraser. Freezer paper is just translucent enough that you can lay it on top of a sketch and see well enough to trace the lines; I transfer my sketches onto freezer paper by tracing them. Once they are all traced and labeled as to what they are, I use a pair of scissors designated for paper to cut out my pattern pieces. Freezer paper is not expensive, so I don't feel badly if I have to throw failed pattern pieces away.

And now the truly wonderful quality of freezer paper comes into play: the shiny side of freezer paper adheres temporarily to fabric with the heat of an iron. I simply lay the pattern piece on top of the fabric, shiny side down, and press it with a warm iron. No pins are needed. If you cut a sheet of freezer paper to 8 1/2 x 11 inches (21.6 x 27.9 cm), you can run it through your printer. If you scan a pattern, either your own or one from this book, or if you'd like to download a pattern online, you can print it directly onto the matte side of the freezer paper and cut it out. For other pattern pieces I simply cut around the freezer paper, then pull it off.

The freezer paper comes off easily and can be adhered again and again and it doesn't harm the fabric in any way, whether you adhere it to the right or wrong side of the fabric. I've used freezer-paper pattern pieces more than a dozen times before the adhesive wore off of the shiny side. When that happens, simply retrace the pattern piece onto fresh freezer paper. Once the pattern is adhered, I cut the fabric 1/4 inch (6 mm) away from the edge of the pattern pieces to add a seam allowance.

For small or detailed pieces such as claws, beaks, or fins, for example, I stitch directly around the freezer paper while it is still adhered to the fabric, pull it off after the stitching is completed, and trim close to the seam line (figures 1 and 2). A paper pattern that is adhered to the fabric during stitching allows me to get a highly accurate outline of the shape of the pattern piece.

I store each of my freezer paper patterns in a labeled envelope for future use. Another storage idea is to place each pattern in a labeled plastic sheet protector and then put all the sheet protectors into a binder.

Because I love freezer paper, and I think it really improves the ease and accuracy of sewing softies, I call for it in almost every pattern in this book. But if you do not have freezer paper, you can trace the pattern pieces onto tracing paper, cut them out, and pin them to your fabric, or, for more durable pattern pieces or

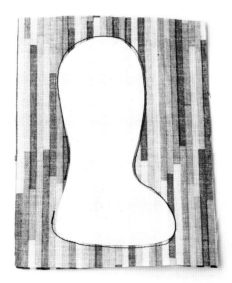

figure 1

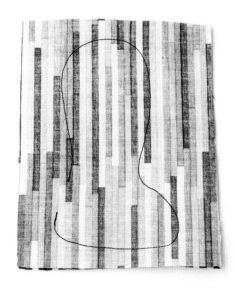

figure 2

when working with synthetic fabrics that cannot be ironed with a hot iron, cut the pattern pieces from regular paper and then trace them onto stiff cardboard. Or you can trace the pattern pieces onto stiff plastic, like an acetate report cover, with a permanent marker. You can even hole-punch these and clip them together with a binder ring for storage. I recommend using either a disappearing fabric marker or chalk (depending on how light or dark your fabric is) to trace around the cardboard or plastic pieces, as opposed to a regular pencil or a permanent marker. The outlines will become your stitching lines, but there is always some chance that the outlines may show on the finished toy if your stitching was slightly inaccurate or if the marker bleeds. Fabric marker or chalk lines can be erased, whereas pencil or permanent marker cannot (figure 3).

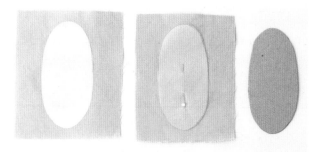

figure 3

Drawing and Editing a Pattern

To turn your sketch into a sewing pattern, spend some time thinking about those basic shapes again. Are the legs tubes? Is the head a sphere? Could the muzzle be a cone? Where could you cut the sketch apart, and where will you need to add more width to fill out the shape? Where should the seams be located?

I start by going over my sketch with pencil to get a solid, dark line. Then I place a piece of freezer paper on top and trace over the outline of the body. This becomes the pattern piece for the side body. From there I keep placing new freezer paper over the sketch and drawing out the remaining pattern pieces: the underbody, the ears, the tail, the gussets, and so on.

Once I have a set of pattern pieces I am ready to sew a prototype. Sewing and stuffing prototypes is a vital part of pattern development. Even the most experienced pattern drafter will find places in a first-draft pattern that are not quite right and need some editing. Patterns that include many pieces, especially those with head gussets, underbody gussets, and darts, are certain to come out misshapen in some way when you first draft a pattern. Edits may be extensive or subtle, but they always improve the final pattern, so don't skip this step!

It is important also to take the time to stuff each prototype carefully. It may seem time-consuming, but you cannot really see where the mistakes are until you have fully stuffed the toy.

After the first prototype is sewn and stuffed, look at it carefully from all directions. Take a marker and draw on it, marking areas that need taking in or bumping out, shortening or lengthening. Hold your pattern pieces up to the finished toy and use a pencil to transfer the markings onto the pattern pieces.

Now try again! Trace your pattern pieces onto fresh freezer paper and redraw the problematic areas. Cut out the fresh pattern pieces and sew a second prototype. I think it is valuable to save all of the prototypes until you are satisfied with the pattern and have sewn the finished toy. This allows you to look back at your work, to see how it changed, to remember the corrections you made. Sometimes you may want to go back to some aspect of a prior version. Once you have the pattern finalized, remove the stuffing from the prototypes. Fluff up the stuffing that has become compacted and put it away to use for future projects.

Making prototypes can sometimes feel very time-consuming, as though you've wasted time sewing something that didn't work. When this happens to me, I try to take a deep breath and remember that this is how design work gets done. That time was not wasted; it was spent learning, experimenting. Even if I am not able at that time to actually figure out how to make the idea in my head a reality in fabric, I may come back to it a year from now and it all becomes clear to me. Design work cannot be rushed. It is a slow process. Setting a piece aside for a few hours or a few days usually brings a fresh perspective and a new solution to a pattern construction problem.

Marking the Fabric

I like to use a disappearing, water-soluble fabric marker to mark light-colored fabrics, and chalk on darker fabrics. To make the marker disappear, fill a spray bottle with water and spritz the area lightly. Some fabric markers may look like they have disappeared, but after machine washing, brownish stains will in fact appear where the lines were drawn, and others will become permanent if the mark is heat-set with an iron, so read the instructions on the marker's packaging carefully. Chalk rubs off easily. If you are using a napped fabric or fabric with a deep pile, you can take a small stitch leaving long thread tails to mark the fabric. These thread marks are called tailor's tacks.

Some plush makers use pencil or mechanical pencil to mark fabric, especially for tracing pattern pieces. A pencil line is very fine and shows up especially well on quilting cottons and helps you sew seams accurately. There is always the risk, though, that the lines may show through on the right side of the toy. This is another reason I prefer to use freezer paper for patterns. I don't recommend using a permanent marker unless you are sewing with a fabric like faux fur that has a very opaque backing and cannot be pressed with a hot iron; the chance that the marker lines will show through is just too great (figure 4). One of the wonderful things about freezer paper is that you can sew around it while it is adhered, eliminating the need to trace your pattern pieces onto the fabric at all.

Considering the Grain Line

It is a good idea to cut your softie pattern pieces on the straight grain because this gives you strong pieces that will sew together neatly, retain their shape, and hold up best under the stress of stuffing. If you cut two matching pattern pieces that are going to be sewn together along their outline, such as two head pieces, and one piece is cut on grain and the other is not, it will be very difficult to line up their edges accurately because the piece that is cut off grain will stretch in a different way than

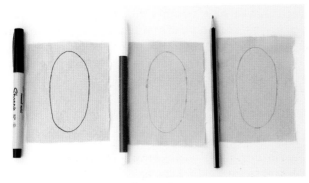

figure 4

the piece that is cut on grain. The seam that connects these two pieces will be wavy, and the edges will end up mismatched, not because you didn't sew accurately, but because you didn't cut the both pieces on grain. And no matter how carefully you stuff the toy, it will still be misshapen.

To understand grain you need to think about how woven fabric is made. Warp yarns are vertical on a loom. These yarns are very strong because they are held in tension during the weaving process. The vertical direction of the warp yarns is referred to as the straight grain. The selvage, or finished edge, of fabric runs parallel to the warp yarns and is an easy way to find the straight grain of the fabric. Weft yarns are then woven in and out horizontally between the warp yarns. Weft yarns run perpendicular to the warp yarns, and are referred to as the cross grain. The 45° angle that goes diagonally across the fabric is called the bias. The bias is stretchier and has more give than either the straight grain or the cross grain. Typically, the side body and legs are cut on the straight grain to take advantage of its strength. The gussets should also be cut on the straight grain because they are stressed once the toy is stuffed. Draw an arrow indicating the grain direction on each pattern piece so that you know how to place the pattern piece on the fabric (figure 5).

If you are anything like me, you are sewing softies with bits of scrap fabric that have long since been separated from their selvage edges, and therefore you don't have a quick reference for finding the straight grain and have to examine the weave closely to find the grain lines. If the fabric is stretchy, like fleece, you can pull it in one direction and then pull it in the other. The direction that has the least give and feels the tightest is the straight grain.

Paying attention to grain direction can mean the difference between a softie with odd bulges and ripples and a softie that is smooth and rounded in all the right places.

Cut One, Reverse One

When you cut the fabric for softie patterns you frequently need to "cut one, reverse one." This means you need to cut each pattern piece one way, then turn the fabric over and cut a second piece as a mirror image. Another way to do this is to fold the fabric in half and cut two layers at the same time; one will be a mirror image of the other (figure 6).

Softies are almost always sewn right sides together. This means placing the mirror-image pattern pieces you have cut out with the "right" sides of the fabric facing each other. You will sew the pattern pieces together on the "wrong" side of the fabric and then turn the softie right side out. This way your stitches are hidden inside the softie's body and will not be seen (figure 7).

Adding a Seam Allowance

A seam allowance is the space between the stitching line and the edge of the fabric. I do not add a seam allowance to my individual pattern pieces when I draw them; instead, I focus on getting the right shape, and then I eyeball the seam allowance as I cut each piece out of fabric. When you design your own patterns, you can adopt my eyeballing method, or draw in a 1/4-inch (6 mm) seam allowance on your paper pattern using a tape measure or sliding gauge, then cut the fabric directly around it (see page 164).

For the patterns in this book, you will need to add a 1/4-inch (6 mm) seam allowance on most of the templates (unless otherwise indicated). To do this, either eyeball it when you are cutting the fabric or use a

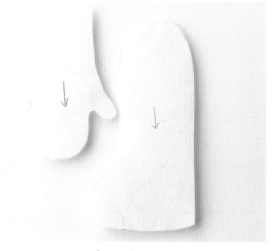

figure 5

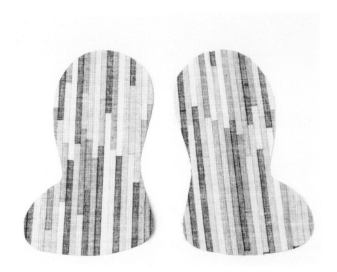
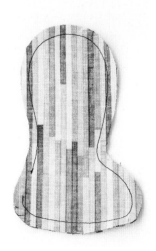

figure 6   figure 7   figure 8

sliding gauge set at $^1/_4$ inch (6 mm). Line the sliding gauge up with the edge of the pattern piece and use a disappearing fabric marker or chalk to make a dot $^1/_4$ inch (6 mm) away. Move the gauge over $^1/_2$ inch (1.3 cm), and make another dot. Continue all the way around the pattern piece, making dots $^1/_4$ inch (6 mm) away from the edge of the pattern piece every $^1/_2$ inch (1.3 cm). Connect the dots to create a $^1/_4$-inch (6 mm) seam allowance, then cut the fabric along this line (figure 8).

Positioning the Needle

Softie pattern pieces are often very small and have narrow seam allowances. When you are sewing two pieces together with a $^1/_4$-inch (6 mm) (or narrower) seam allowance, you should move the needle position on your sewing machine all the way to the right, if possible. This way your fabric is still engaged with both feed dogs even while you are stitching next to the edge of the fabric. (The feed dogs feed the fabric evenly under your machine needle.) If you leave the needle in the center position and try to stitch very close to the edge of the fabric, the fabric is only engaged with one feed dog and is not held securely, leading to messy, uneven stitching.

Choosing Fabric

Softies can be made from almost any kind of fabric. Faux fur, old socks, fleece, leather scraps, wool-blend felt, quilting cotton, felted sweaters—there really is no limit when choosing fabrics for your softie project. That being said, certain materials lend themselves particularly well to softie making.

Consider whether your toy will be cuddled and played with or put on a shelf for display. Soft fabrics like felted wool, velour, and fleece make toys with soft furs that children will love to hug.

I find it difficult to sew softies with either very lightweight or very heavyweight fabrics. Softie bodies go through quite a bit of wear and tear during turning, and their seams are stressed during stuffing. Very lightweight fabrics, such as voile, tear too easily and show every lump of stuffing or every tiny inaccuracy in the stitching. Heavyweight fabrics can be difficult to turn right side out, especially if you are sewing small pieces like arms or horns.

Fabrics like burlap that have a very open weave are challenging, too. The stuffing may show through the weave, and the fabric may pull apart at the seams. I like to stick with tightly woven fabrics when I make softies.

MAKING STUFFED ANIMALS

Cutting out, stitching, stuffing, and detailing stuffed animals takes skill and practice. There is a certain amount of trial and error involved in developing a new pattern, but there is also a set of methods that, once practiced and mastered, helps you develop new patterns and sew additional toys with relative ease, allowing you to experience the thrill of bringing a successful new softie to life.

Pinning

I love pins! They are like tiny fingers that hold things in place when you can't. Just as you should take the time to prewash and iron your fabric before cutting into it, taking the time to pin well always pays off in the end! Softie pattern pieces are often very small and very curvy, and softies are often sewn in relatively thick fabrics such as fleece, wool, and faux fur. To sew two small, curvy, thick pattern pieces together accurately, pinning is essential. I place a pin at least every $1/4$ inch (6 mm), and often as close as every $1/8$ inch (3 mm). Pin perpendicular to the edge of the fabric so that you can easily grasp each pin head and pull the pins out just before your machine needle gets to them.

Sewing Machine Stitch Length

It is vital to use a very short stitch length when sewing stuffed animals. When a soft toy is stuffed, the seams become stressed. If you sew with long stitches, the stuffing will find an easy way out if the stitches are too long. Raw, fraying edges of fabric may also be pushed out. In both instances, the toy is very difficult to repair, and you are better off starting again with a small stitch length.

For general softie sewing I recommend a stitch length of 2 mm (13 stitches per inch [2.5 cm]) or less. For basting (see page 27), a longer stitch length of 4 mm or 5 mm (5 or 6 stitches per inch [2.5 cm]) is recommended to allow for easy removal of basting stitches.

In figure 1 you can see a softie part sewn with a 4 mm stitch length, and the same part sewn with a 1.5 mm stitch length. Notice the stuffing that has escaped between the stitches in the 4 mm example.

Sewing Machine Tension

Tension on a sewing machine refers to the amount of thread let out with each stitch. Tension that is too tight creates puckering and weak stitches that snap when pulled. If the tension is too loose, you will have long, loopy stitches that do not hold the seam together firmly. The tension level is determined by the type of fabric you've selected. Because softies can be sewn from all types of fabrics of many different weights—sometimes within the same project—you may need to adjust the tension on your sewing machine as you go. To perform a quick test to make sure that the tension setting is appropriate, sew a sample with the top thread and bobbin in different colors. On this sample (figure 2) the tension on the line of stitching on the left is too tight; the red bobbin thread is showing through. The tension on the stitching on the right is too loose; each stitch is a loose loop, and the stitches will not hold the layers of fabric together well. The stitching in the center shows the correct tension: taut, even stitches with only the top thread visible.

Backstitching

Whenever you begin stitching pattern pieces together, you should take a few backstitches to reinforce the stitching line. Backstitch at the end of stitching as well. I compare backstitching to tying a knot: it secures the stitches so that they will not come loose when the seam is stressed. It is particularly important to take a few backstitches when you are stitching both the start and the end of the opening through which the softie's body will be turned right side out because this area will be stressed during the turning and stuffing process. Without backstitches to reinforce the seam, the opening will likely widen, making it more difficult to sew it closed neatly.

Checking and Reinforcing Seams

After you have stitched the softie pieces together, take a minute to examine the seams on the front and back. Softie pattern pieces are often very small and may have very narrow seam allowances. Because of this, and because softies are going to be stuffed and all of the imperfections will be pushed outward, accuracy in sewing seams is important. After I sew one softie pattern piece to another I examine both sides carefully to see if there are any areas in which one layer of fabric did not get caught in the seam or the stitches were just too close to the edge and the fabric layers may pull apart when stressed by stuffing. When I find those spots, which I inevitably do in every project, I go back to the machine and stitch them again—this time just inside the first stitching line, to reinforce the seam (figure 3). If you aren't sure that the stitches will hold in a particular area, you can even reinforce them with a third row of stitching. It is much easier to make these repairs now than to find them later when the piece has already been turned and partially stuffed. If the two layers of fabric were really misaligned and your stitches are way off, it means you did an insufficient

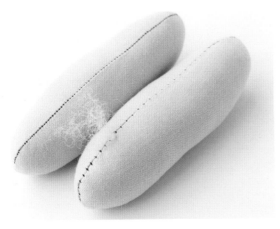

figure 1

figure 2

job pinning the layers together before taking them to the machine. Unpick the stitches and start over; otherwise, the softie part will be misshapen.

Even though I check the seams carefully, occasionally I find a hole while I am stuffing. Sometimes it is possible to take a few ladder stitches by hand to repair the area after stuffing. If the hole is in a conspicuous part, though, you may need to unstuff, turn the toy wrong side out, fix the hole on the machine, and then turn right side out and restuff.

Unpicking Stitches

Mistakes are a big part of the creative process, however much we would like to avoid them! I can't tell you how many times I have cut pattern pieces incorrectly or sewn them together wrong. If you've made a sewing mistake, don't try to unpick the seam with a pair of scissors because you run the risk of accidentally cutting a hole in the fabric. Use a seam ripper! It is the right tool for the job. Softies are sewn using a very small stitch length, so unpicking can be somewhat tedious. Take a deep breath and be patient!

To unpick the seam, turn the fabric over to the wrong side where the bobbin thread is located. The bobbin thread is a bit looser than the top thread and is therefore more easily unpicked. Use a seam ripper to cut through every third or fourth stitch made by the bobbin thread. Then gently pull the fabric apart along the seam. Once you can insert the seam ripper between the two fabric pieces, use it to carefully cut each stitch apart. A lint roller is terrific for quickly pulling out all of the loose bits of thread that remain. Now you are ready to fix the mistake!

Clipping Curves

Softies often have small, detailed parts such as horns, toes, and flippers that are sewn on the wrong side and need to be turned right side out and stuffed. To turn a softie part right side out successfully, you need to take some time and special care to clip the curves of each piece. Use a small pair of sharp scissors for this task. Use pinking shears to quickly and easily clip all of the seam allowances on a piece that just has gentle curves.

A curve can either be an inside curve, like the curve between two fingers, or an outside curve, like the curve of the fingertip. Inside curves are clipped by making a series of small cuts through the seam allowance almost up to the stitching line. When the piece is turned right side out, these cuts pull apart (away from one another) and allow the curve to lie flat without any puckers. Traditionally for outside curves, a series of small triangular notches are cut in the seam allowance so that when the piece is turned, the triangles join together and the piece lies flat. I almost never clip notches in the outside curves when sewing softies, though. Softie parts generally have narrow seam allowances, which means that there is less fabric to bunch up inside once a part is turned right side out. I find simply clipping the outside curves saves time and is usually sufficient.

In figure 4 you can see two identical lizard feet. On one (at right) I didn't clip the curves; although I sewed it carefully, the foot is extremely puckered. On the other (left) I clipped the curves, especially between each toe, and it lies flat and is ready for stuffing.

figure 3

figure 4

Leaving an Opening

When you design a pattern, you need to mark a space through which the softie can be turned right side out and stuffed. Estimate how wide of an opening you think is required to fit the entire piece through. Thin and stretchy fabrics can be pulled through a narrower opening than thicker, stiffer fabrics. No matter how carefully you stitch the opening closed, it will be apparent that the stitching in that area is different. For this reason I like to locate the opening in the most inconspicuous place possible. Between the two underbody pieces is my favorite spot for an opening on a four-legged animal. On other toys I try to leave the opening where it will be covered by a tail that is attached with ladder stitches after the body is stuffed.

Basting

Sewing softies almost always entails working with very small pieces of fabric. When those small pieces need to be held in place accurately, sometimes pins are just too bulky. Basting is a lifesaver and helps you achieve neat, accurate stitching. Machine-basting is useful for holding sewn, turned pieces in place before they are permanently attached to a softie. To baste, set your machine stitch length to 4 mm or 5 mm (5 or 6 stitches per inch [2.5 cm]). Do not backstitch; just take a few stitches across the piece to hold it temporarily (figure 5). Once the softie is turned right side out, these long basting stitches are easily removed with a seam ripper.

Hand-basting is very useful, too. If I have a bird's beak or a puppy's ear all stitched up and turned right side out, I tuck the raw edges under by 1/4 inch (3 mm) and hand-baste them in place with long, straight stitches. Then I can easily and neatly ladder-stitch the appendage to my softie, pulling out the basting stitches once it is securely attached.

Turning

One of the fussiest parts of the softie-making process—and the part that can lead to the most frustration—is turning the sewn pieces right side out, especially if the pieces are very tiny. When turning is difficult, you may strain the seams, tear a hole in the fabric, or—if the opening is not wide enough—tear the opening. It may even seem sometimes like a piece is just impossible to fully turn.

In fact it is possible to turn almost any softie piece right side out if you sew them properly and use a few special techniques for turning.

Successful turning actually begins with one of the very first design choices you make: your choice of fabric. If you choose a fabric that is thick but without stretch, such as a heavy corduroy, and you use it for a pattern that includes small parts that must be turned, you are bound to have trouble. For small pieces, choose a fabric with a lighter weight or some stretch.

The next step for successful turning is trimming the seam allowance, clipping the corners, and clipping the curves. I trim the seam allowances on small pieces to within 1/8 inch (3 mm) of the stitching line before turning to reduce bulk. If there is a sharp corner, I cut across it, close to the stitching line. Then I clip all of the curves (figure 6).

figure 5

figure 6

Now that the piece is prepared, you are ready to turn it right side out. Having the right tool for the job really helps! There are many tools people use for turning, including knitting needles, chopsticks, paintbrushes, long-handled tweezers, and the eraser end of pencils. Although I've used all of these at some point, the absolute best, most effective tool for this job by far is a hemostat.

Pull the extremities into the body cavity first. If you leave the extremities unturned and try to turn them later, once the bulk of the body is right side out, you run a higher risk of accidentally poking a hole in them with the tip of your hemostat. By turning them first, you gently pull them into the body, and when the body is finally turned, the extremities will pop out fully turned (figure 7).

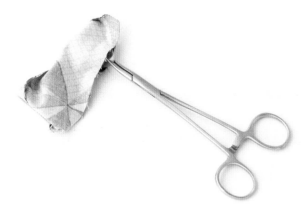

figure 7

figure 8

Once all the extremities are pulled inward, begin by pulling the largest one out through the opening. If you tug too hard with the hemostat there is a good chance you will tear a hole in the fabric, so be gentle and go slowly. Once the largest extremity is through the opening, put your hemostat down and use your fingers to pull it out all the way. Fingers are the most sensitive tool and the least likely to tear or stress the softie's body too much. Twist and gently pull, working the entire body out through the opening. This is why backstitching on either side of the opening is key. You don't want the opening to tear wider during this process.

Once the body is fully turned, use your hemostat to gently push out the details around the softie's body. Because you have preturned the extremities, though, this is not a difficult job.

Stuffing

Stuffing is one of the most important steps in softie making. When the stuffing is done well, the finished toy is firm, smooth, and completely filled out, from its tiniest extremity to its widest part. When it is done poorly, the finished toy is lumpy in some parts and hollow in others, and it may not stand properly. It is easy to ruin a beautifully designed soft toy with a poor stuffing job.

Perhaps the most important thing to remember about stuffing a softie is that it is a slow process. Stuffing can take as long, or longer, as cutting out and sewing the softie together. If you get swept away in the excitement of seeing the finished product quickly you run the risk of messing it up entirely with a hasty stuffing job. My best advice is, if at all possible, cut and sew in one work session, and turn and stuff in another.

When I have selected my stuffing material and am ready to begin, I pull off a small piece of stuffing with the end of my hemostat and push it up into the farthest extremity of the sewn form. If it is a very tiny area, I use a smaller hemostat and a very tiny bit of stuffing. I continue to push small pieces of stuffing into the extremities until they are all full, turning and molding the piece in my hands as I go, checking all the while that the stuffing is even and firm. For stuffing the very smallest digits I recommend using a stuffing fork. (For more information about the stuffing fork, including how to make your own, see lesson 39 on page 126.)

Starting with the extremities is crucial because they will be impossible to access once the body is stuffed.

I generally like my toys stuffed firmly, but in some cases, such as when making a toy for a baby, a squishy, huggable body is better.

If you are making a toy with joints or one that will need to sit or stand on its own, it is important to stuff it so that it is almost rock hard. The stuffing will inevitably shift and condense over time. When you think you have stuffed it completely, stuff it more! You can always get just a bit more stuffing in there! Then close the opening with ladder stitch (see below). When the opening is nearly closed, use the tip of your hemostat to push a few more small wads of stuffing in under the opening to prevent sagging in that area once it is sewn shut.

Try not to stretch or fray the raw edges with your turning or stuffing tools. If need be, temporarily cover each side of the opening with masking tape or zigzag stitch the edges of the opening on the machine to serve as protection during turning and stuffing. This way the fabric at the opening will be intact and easier to stitch together neatly.

Ladder Stitching

When I teach softie-making classes, my students tell me that learning the ladder stitch is a revelation to them. Once they see how the ladder stitch makes an invisible attachment between softie parts and an invisible closure to openings, their eyes open wide, and they suddenly feel confident in their softie-making skills!

Ladder stitch is a much better choice than overcast stitch for closing openings in softies.

Overcast stitches are more visible and more likely to look sloppy. Figure 8 shows two identical softie pieces, one closed with overcast stitches (left) and the other with a ladder stitch (right). Although you can still locate where the opening existed in the ladder-stitched example, the closure is neat, and the stitches are nearly invisible. And thread that is slightly lighter in color than your fabric will stand out less if any of the thread does end up showing.

To close an opening using a ladder stitch, insert your needle from inside the body cavity, coming out through one side of the end of the opening (figure 9). Now take a small running stitch alternately on either side of the opening, passing the needle under the fold on each side so that the thread is hidden (figure 10). After a few stitches you will see how ladder stitch got its name: the stitches between the opening look like the rungs of a ladder (figure 11). Make a few stitches, then pull the thread tight, and the opening will lace up, with the raw edges turning inward (figure 12). I use extra-strong thread when I am ladder-stitching an opening, or when I am using ladder stitch to attach two parts, because standard-weight sewing thread tends to break when pulled too tightly. If the thread does break, you'll need to start over.

figure 9 *figure 10* *figure 11* *figure 12*

figure 13

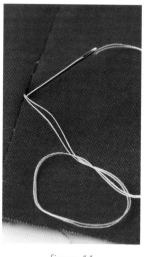

figure 14

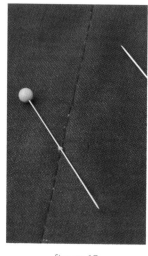

figure 15

figure 16

Finishing

When you have finished ladder-stitching you will need to tie off the end of the thread to secure it. Wrap the thread around itself in a big circle. Pass the needle through the circle to form a big, loose knot (figure 13). Insert the needle back through the fabric where the thread came out (figure 14). Stick a pin through the circle, then pull the thread so that the knot tightens around the pin (figure 15). Remove the pin and give the thread a tug to pull the knot under the seam.

To hide the thread tails, bring the needle back up to the right side of the fabric a few inches away (figure 16). Give the thread tails a tug and, holding them taut, cut them close to the fabric (figure 17). This way the thread ends disappear inside its body.

If you are ladder-stitching an ear, a tail, or another appendage to a softie's body, or if you are embroidering details, you'll need to hide the knot at the beginning of stitching as well as at the end. There are two ways to hide a knot at the beginning of stitching. You can insert the needle in an inconspicuous place, like behind the ear, and bring it out where you will begin sewing. If the thread color matches the fabric and the fabric has a long pile, you can leave the knot on the surface and it won't be seen. Otherwise, you can tug on the thread and pop the knot inside the toy

so that it gets buried in the stuffing. Popping the knot inside, however, leaves a tiny hole in the fabric. To avoid this, insert the needle between the machine stitches along a seam. The knot will pop between the stitches and into the body of the toy without piercing a hole in the fabric itself. If you pull on the thread and the knot is not popping inside, it means you've passed the needle between the threads of the fabric and not between the machine stitches. Cut the thread off the needle and try again.

figure 17

Hand Stitches

There are a few hand stitches that are very useful for sewing stuffed animals. None of them is very fancy or difficult to learn, but neat and even hand-stitching does take patience and practice. Of all of these, the ladder stitch is the most vital for softie making because it allows you to make an invisible attachment and closure. Use the running stitch for basting, too—just don't tie a knot at the end of the thread so you can easily pull out the stitches later.

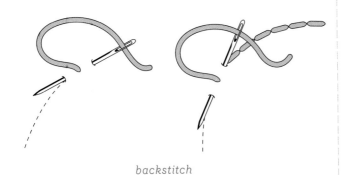

backstitch

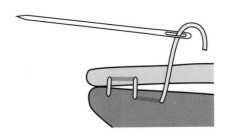

ladder stitch

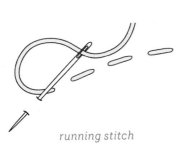

running stitch

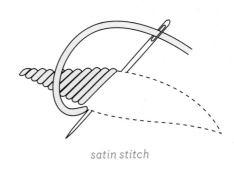

satin stitch

stem stitch

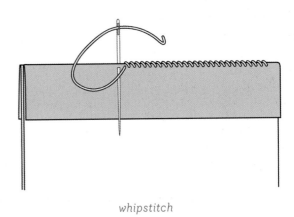

whipstitch

Part 2:
PROJECTS

FISH

The simplest softie pattern you can make is an outline toy. Start with a smooth line drawing like you find in a child's coloring book. With just a little tweaking you can turn this drawing into an original softie pattern. Enlarge the drawing to the size you'd like the finished softie to be, trace each part onto some freezer paper, and you're ready to get started!

Steps

1. Trace the pattern pieces (page 165) onto freezer paper with a pencil. Cut them out, transferring all the markings. Cut the tail apart from the body.

2. Fold each piece of fabric in half, right sides together, so that you can cut two mirror images of each pattern piece at once. Iron on the freezer paper patterns, add ¼-inch (6 mm) seam allowance, and cut two Tail pieces, two Body pieces, and two Head pieces from your selected fabrics. Transfer all markings using a disappearing fabric marker.

3. Place one Tail piece on top of one Body piece, right sides together, and stitch from A to B (figure 1). Repeat for the other Tail and Body pieces.

4. Place the remaining fin fabric right sides together and iron the Top Fin and Side Fin pattern pieces on top. Stitch directly around the freezer paper, without any seam allowance, being sure to leave the openings as marked. Repeat so that you have two mirror-image side fins (figure 2). Pull off the freezer paper.

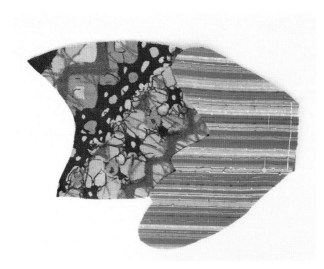

figure 1

figure 2

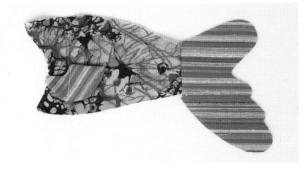

figure 3

5. Clip the curves and turn the top fin and side fins right side out, pushing out the curves with the tip of your hemostat. Press.

6. Place one side fin against one body piece, matching up the raw edges between points F and G. Check to make sure that the straight edges of the side fins are facing the top of the fish (figure 3). Baste in place. Repeat for the second side fin and body piece.

7. Sew one Head piece to one Body piece, matching up the raw edges between points C and D, catching the raw edges of the fin in the seam. The curve of the head should be opposite the curve of the body and requires a bit of easing to fit properly (figure 4). Repeat for the other Head and Body pieces.

8. Place the top fin upside down against the body, matching up the raw edges between points D and E. Baste in place (figure 5).

9. Place the two fish pieces right sides together and pin all the way around. Stitch the fish together beginning at point H and ending at point I, leaving the opening for turning and stuffing as marked.

10. Clip the curves and turn the fish right side out. Stuff the fish firmly, beginning with the tail, using small pieces of stuffing.

11. Close the opening with a ladder stitch.

12. Using the Head pattern piece or a circle template as a guide, cut out two circles of yellow felt for the eyes. Sew the doll buttons to the yellow circles with a single straight stitch with black perle cotton. Whipstitch the yellow circles to the fish with white perle cotton. Alternatively, you can sew on circles of black felt for the pupils. (See lesson 3 on page 40 for more on eyes and eye placement.)

13. Draw the mouth where desired with a disappearing fabric marker. Thread an embroidery needle with a single length of black perle cotton and knot the end. Insert the needle under the chin (at the seam) and come up at the corner of the mouth on one side. Tug on the perle cotton to pull the knot inside the body. Bring the needle around to the other

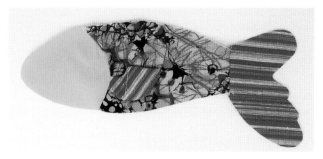

figure 4

figure 5

corner of the mouth, insert it, and come out in the center of the mouth at the seam where the two head pieces are joined. Take a small stitch in the center to tack the mouth in place. Form a small knot on top of the

tack, then insert the needle through the knot, bringing it out as far away from the mouth as possible, and cut the thread end close to the body so that it gets buried inside the stuffing.

Lesson 1: Creating a Simple Outline Toy

The simplest softie to design is an outline toy. Think of it like an embellished pillow. Begin by gathering some images to use as visual research: photos, illustrations, plastic toys, and commercial stuffed animals are all great sources of inspiration. Here I am using a photograph of a long, slender fish with a curvy tail because this is the kind of fish I'd like to create (figure 1). Open your sketchbook and get out a pencil and an eraser. It's time to make a sewing pattern for a new softie!

The goal here is to sketch a coloring-book-style outline of the subject. If the blank paper is intimidating, begin by drawing just the basic shapes. Then go back and re-fine the drawing bit by bit. It doesn't need to be perfect! In fact, all you really need is a good outline. Keep tweaking until you are satisfied (figure 2).

figure 1

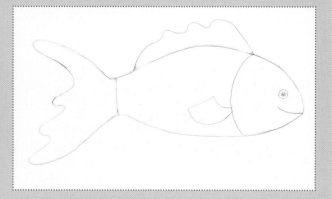

figure 2

Place a sheet of freezer paper, matte side up, over your sketch and trace the outline of the body. This tracing will become the basis for the main pattern piece of your softie. The next step is to add details. Working from your sketchbook, draw in the fins, the eye, and the smile. Place freezer paper on top and trace each of these features; the fins and the eyes are cut as separate pattern pieces.

Now look over your freezer-paper pattern pieces. You may need to make a few modifications to turn them into softie pattern pieces. Any especially skinny parts (think legs, arms, claws, horns, a tail) need to be widened a bit to account for the three-dimensional nature of a toy once it is stuffed. For the Fish, I went back and erased the tail and fins on my original drawing and re-drew them wider.

If you want your toy to be larger or smaller than your sketch, enlarge or reduce your pattern pieces on a photocopier. Either cut a piece of fresh freezer paper to 8½ x 11 inches (21.6 x 27.9 cm) and print your resized pattern directly onto it, or retrace it by hand onto fresh freezer paper. Cut out all of your pattern pieces and label them. You now have the pattern for an outline toy (figure 3).

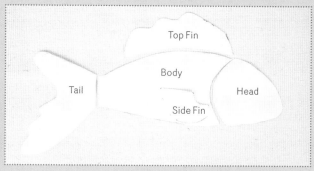

figure 3

Lesson 2: Attaching Details

Now you need to decide how you will attach the "detail pieces" to the softie's body. For the Fish, the detail pieces are the top and side fins.

There are two important factors to consider when selecting the best method of attachment. First, you want the joining seam to be as strong as possible; machine-sewn seams are usually stronger than hand-sewn seams. Second, you want the point of attachment to be as elegant as possible. In most cases, an invisible seam is most desirable. No matter which method you choose, you'll first need to sew the detail pieces together and turn them right side out. Consider the following methods and choose the one that works best for your design.

The easiest way to attach a detail piece is to simply stitch it down right on top of the body. To do this, first fold the raw edges of your detail pieces under or to the wrong side about ¼ inch (6 mm) and press or baste them in place. Then use the sewing machine to top-stitch the pieces to the softie's body before you sew the body pieces together. Although this method creates a strong attachment, the stitches are visible (figure 4). If a row or two of visible machine stitches enhance your design, this would be a good choice.

A second option is to wait until your softie's body is sewn, turned, and stuffed, and then ladder-stitch your pieces to the body. Fold the piece's raw edges under and either press or baste them in place. Then pin and stitch them to the stuffed, turned body. The pieces will be hand-stitched, which means the attachment will probably not be as strong as it would be were it stitched by machine. Ladder-stitching parts in place does make an invisible seam, though, and if you think the toy will be played with somewhat gently, or if you use extra-strong thread and very small hand-stitches, ladder-stitching pieces in place after stuffing may be the right choice (figure 5). With both topstitching and ladder-stitching pieces in place, you are able to add details wherever on the body you'd like them to go. This flexibility is a big advantage of both of these methods.

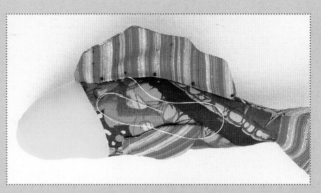

figure 4

figure 5

A third method of attachment is to catch the detail pieces in a seam as you sew the softie's body together. Catching pieces in the seam creates an attachment that is both strong (sewn by machine) and invisible (the stitches are on the inside of the body and therefore are not seen). There is no need to turn in the raw edges on the detail piece for this method. Simply lay the detail piece on the body, right sides together, so that the raw edges of the detail piece are lined up with the raw edges of the body, and pin or baste the detail piece in place. Place the second body piece on top, right sides together, like a sandwich, and sew around the outline. The raw edges of the detail pieces will be caught in the seam. In my fish pattern, the top fin of the fish is attached using this technique.

What if you want an invisible, strong attachment for a detail piece in the middle of the body? You could create a seam in which to insert the pieces. By piecing the mustard-colored head fabric to the blue-green body fabric on the fish, I created a seam between two pieces of fabric. This seam gave me an opportunity to insert a side fin between the head and the body (see figures 3 and 4 on pages 36 and 37). You should view any seam as just that: an opportunity to insert a detail that will be attached in a strong and invisible manner.

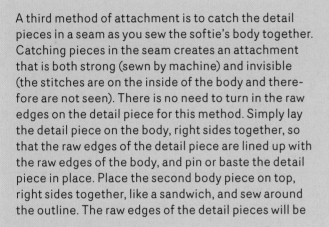

Alternative Types of Stuffing

● **Polyester fiberfill** is the most commonly available stuffing for soft toys, but it is by no means the only one. You may want to explore some other stuffing options, depending on the type of toy you want to create and your feelings about using a man-made stuffing material.

● **Wool stuffing** is not much more expensive than polyester and has some wonderful properties. Wool warms in your hands as you work with it, is lightly scented from the sheep's natural lanolin, and can be packed very firmly. Keep in mind, though, that a toy stuffed with wool is not machine washable. I especially like to use it to stuff toys made from wool fabrics, or art toys that will be displayed but not played with. For my favorite source for wool stuffing, see the Resources section on page 191.

● Vintage soft-toy patterns call for **kapok stuffing**. Kapok fibers come from the seedpods of the tropical ceiba tree. Kapok is not commonly available now, having been largely replaced by polyester fiberfill. Other plant-based stuffing choices, including cotton, bamboo, and hemp, are easier to find, though, and are good non-animal products for natural toys. These can be ordered online through natural fibers websites. Experiment with new types of stuffing to see which works best for your toys. Each one of them behaves differently during stuffing, play, and washing. (Pellet-type stuffing is described on page 119, and excelsior stuffing is discussed on page 132.)

Lesson 3: Button Eyes and Felt Eyes

Determining the placement of the eyes on the face is one of the most important design decisions you'll make when creating a new soft toy. The eyes are the key to the overall expression of the face, and they are the first thing viewers see when they look at your toy.

Before I sew or glue the eyes to the toy, I like to play around with possible placements using pins with relatively large black heads. Moving the pin heads around helps me see what expression the face will have with the eyes in various positions. They are also useful for checking the symmetry of the eyes before sewing (figure 6).

Push the pins into the stuffed face where you think they might look best, then step away and see what you think. Once you have the pins where you want the eyes to go, mark the spot with a disappearing fabric marker

or chalk. Pins are much easier to rearrange than stitched or glued-down eyes!

When you sew a button eye to a soft toy, you want to be sure it is fastened securely. If you watch children play, they often pick up the toy by the button eye and drag it around! The button is likely to get tugged and pulled on quite a bit in the course of a toy's life, so use extra-strong thread and tie it off with a few good knots. But if you are planning to give the toy to a baby, avoid button eyes completely; buttons can be a choking hazard.

Once you have your shapes cut out, use a glue stick to hold them together temporarily, and use the glue stick to temporarily affix them to the toy's body. Then go back and stitch the eye down with thread or perle cotton. If parts of the eye, like the pupil, are too small to stitch, you could glue them permanently with craft glue.

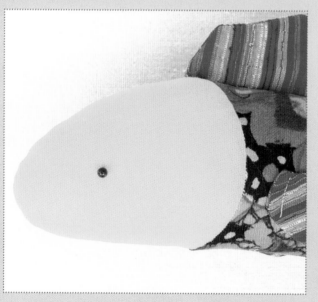

figure 6

Although plain buttons can be just perfect as eyes, there are a few ways to make button eyes look more lively (figure 7). A dark eye looks nice with a white highlight. Use white button thread to sew the button to the toy's face, and the thread can serve as a highlight. Layer a smaller button on top of a larger button to give the appearance of a pupil and the white of the eye. Cut a felt pad a bit larger than a button and use it underneath the button to give more emphasis to the eye. The felt pad could be round or more almond shaped. You could even cut two felt pads—one for the white of the eye and one for the eyeball—and then use a button as the pupil.

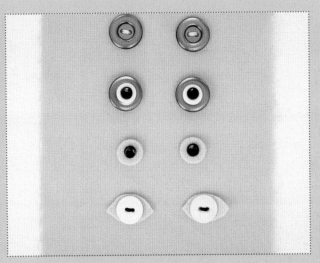

figure 7

Making a Baby Toy with a Bell and Crinkle

You can make a toy appealing to a baby by selecting soft, bright fabrics and creating a cute face, but you can also enhance the toy with sound. If you'd like to insert a bell or squeaker, place it inside a piece of nylon pantyhose so that the stuffing doesn't get inside it and muffle the sound (see the photo below). Place the bell near the side body with only a little bit of stuffing between it and the side of the toy. If you bury the bell too deeply, the sound will be hard to hear.

Babies enjoy the sensation of crinkling toys in their hands. To add crinkle to unstuffed parts of a toy, cut a clean, crinkly chip or cereal bag using the pattern piece, then place it on top of the layers of the fabric pattern pieces. Stitch it together with the other pieces, joining it in the seam. Turn the part right side out so that the crinkly part is on the inside.

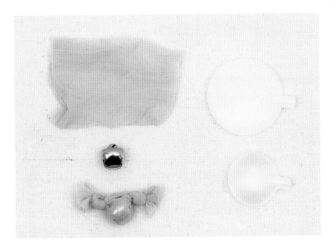

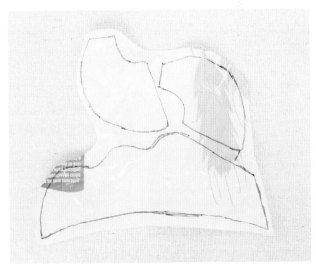

BUMBLEBEE

Circles, squares, rectangles, and triangles can be the beginning of an endless assortment of charming softies. Start doodling features on a circle, and before you know it you have the beginning of a new softie pattern! I came up with this pattern during a morning of playing with basic shapes in my sketchbook: the body and head of this bumblebee are simply two spheres sewn and stuffed separately before being joined together.

Steps

1. Trace the pattern pieces (page 166) onto freezer paper with a pencil. Cut them out, transferring all markings.

2. Cut two 2 x 16-inch (5 x 40.6 cm) strips of yellow felt and two 2 x 16-inch (5 x 40.6 cm) strips of black felt with a rotary cutter on a self-healing cutting mat. Using all-purpose white thread and a ¼-inch (6 mm) seam allowance, stitch the strips together along the 16-inch (40.6 cm) sides, alternating colors to create stripes. Press seam allowances all in one direction.

3. Iron the Body pattern piece onto the striped fabric and cut out five identical body pieces, adding a ¼-inch (6 mm) seam allowance to each. Iron the Head pattern piece onto the yellow felt and cut out five identical head pieces, adding a ¼-inch (6 mm) seam allowance to each (figure 1).

4. Iron the Stinger pattern piece onto a scrap of black felt. Place a second scrap of black felt beneath it and stitch with black thread directly around the freezer paper, leaving the bottom of the stinger open as marked. Cut around the pattern piece, ⅛ inch (3 mm) from the stitching line. Pull off the freezer paper. Use the same technique to stitch two antennae. Use hemostats to turn the stinger and antennae right side out (figure 2).

Basic Sewing Tool Kit (page 11)

¼ yard (23 cm) each of wool-blend felt in yellow, black, and white

All-purpose polyester thread in white and black

Extra-strong thread in white

Rotary cutter and self-healing cutting mat

4 ounces (112 g) of fiberfill stuffing

1 white felted-wool ball, 15 mm in diameter

Hole punch

5-inch (12.7 cm) doll needle

24-inch (61 cm) length of perle cotton in black

16-inch (40.6 cm) length of clear thread

figure 1

figure 2

figure 3

figure 4

figure 5

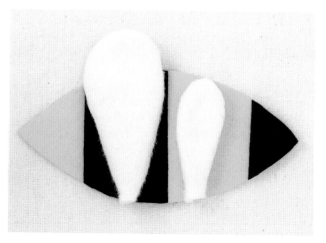

figure 6

5. Iron the Large and Small Wing pattern pieces onto a scrap of white felt. Place a second scrap of white felt beneath it and stitch with white thread directly around the freezer paper, leaving the bottom of each wing open. Cut around the pattern pieces, ⅛ inch (3 mm) from the stitching line. Pull off the freezer paper. Repeat to create a second set of wings. Turn the wings right side out (figure 3).

6. Place the antennae against the first head piece where the marks indicate, lining up the raw edges with the edge of the head piece (figure 4). Pin.

7. Using white thread, sew the first head piece to the second from point A to point B, catching the raw edges of one antenna in the seam (figure 5). Continue to sew the head pieces together one at a time, leaving a 1-inch (2.5 cm) opening between head pieces 3 and 4, as marked, for turning and stuffing. The raw edges of the second antenna will be caught between the seams on head pieces 5 and 1.

8. Turn the head right side out and stuff firmly. Close the opening with a ladder stitch using extra-strong thread. With a disappearing fabric marker and a circle template, trace a circle with a 1-inch (2.5 cm) diameter onto the back of the head. This circle will be used as a stitching guide when the head is sewn to the body.

9. For the eyes, cut the felted-wool ball in half. Punch two circles from black felt with your hole punch. Glue a black circle to each felted-ball half with fabric or craft clue. Glue the felted-ball halves to the front of bee's head. Use pins to hold the eyes in place until the glue dries. Alternatively, whipstitch the pupils to the eyes and the eyes to the face.

10. Draw the mouth with a disappearing fabric marker. Thread a doll needle with a single 24-inch (61 cm) length of black perle cotton and knot the end. Insert the needle into the back of the head in the center of the circular stitching guide, coming out where the mouth begins. Take one long stitch to create the mouth. Take a small stitch in the center to tack the mouth in place to form a smile. Bring the needle out through the back of the head and knot it off. The knots will be hidden when the head is sewn to the body.

11. Place the stinger against one body piece where the mark indicates, lining up the raw edges with the point of the body piece. Pin.

12. Place two wings against one body piece where the marks indicate, lining up the raw edges (figure 6). Pin. Repeat for a second body piece.

13. Using white thread, sew the body pieces together one at a time. The raw edges of the wings will be caught in the seams between body pieces 2 and 3, and 5 and 1. Leave a 1-inch (2.5 cm) opening between body pieces 3 and 4 for turning and stuffing.

14. Turn the body right side out and stuff firmly. Close the opening with a ladder stitch using extra-strong thread. Using a disappearing fabric marker and a circle template, trace a 1-inch (2.5 cm) diameter circle on the front of the body slightly above the point where the body pieces meet. The circle will be used as a stitching guide when the head and body are joined.

15. Ladder-stitch the head to the body with extra-strong white thread, matching and using the circles as a stitching guide (figure 7).

16. Thread fishing wire through the bumblebee's back and tie it in a loop for hanging.

figure 7

Lesson 4: Sewing a Sphere

The Bumblebee is made up of two spheres. To create the spheres I sewed together five wedge-shaped pieces; think of each wedge like the segment of an orange. To draw a wedge pattern piece, start with a straight line. Make sure it curves out on either side, and keep the shape symmetrical both side to side (horizontally) and up and down (vertically).

Wedge-shaped pieces have the potential to create other three-dimensional shapes, too. If you sew just four wedges together you will get a football shape. Four very wide wedges will make a round, squat shape. Wedges that are wider on one end than the other will make a carrot, like the Bunny's carrot on page 66 (figure 1).

Think creatively about what animals these footballs, spheres, and carrots could become. In your sketchbook, draw one of these shapes and start adding features to make it into an animal. Could it be a squid or a sheep or a mouse?

Wedges are only one way to create a fabric sphere. An alternative is to make a sphere that is sewn like a baseball. Cut two pattern pieces from the Baseball Head template (page 166), marking the center as A on one and as B on the other. Place the two pieces perpendicular to one another, matching A to B (figure 2),

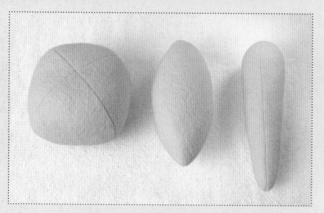

figure 1

figure 2

figure 3

figure 4

figure 5

figure 6

and sew the pieces together, leaving a gap for turning and stuffing. This creates a nice, round sphere with continuous rounded seams (figure 3).

A third way to sew a sphere is to create a pattern piece made up of six pentagons (there is a Pentagon Head template on page 166), one in the center with each of the other five adjoining one of the edges of the center pentagon (figure 4). Cut two and sew the pentagon edges together on each one (figure 5). Then sew the two pieces together around the middle of the sphere, leaving a gap for turning and stuffing. This creates a sphere with many small, dartlike seams (figure 6).

The spheres created with each of these three methods have different seam lines, so keep that in mind when you select the sphere pattern that will work best for your project. Seams are opportunities for inserting pattern pieces. Think about where you could insert fins, spikes, antennae, wings, or legs. Seams are also visible in the finished piece, so consider how the seams will fall if the sphere is to become a face.

If you choose to sew a sphere from a woven fabric instead of felt, take care when cutting the body pieces that all of them are on grain. Otherwise, the ball will be misshapen once it is stuffed.

Lesson 5: Felted-Ball Eyes

The eyes on the Bumblebee are created by cutting a felted-wool ball in half and then attaching a hole-punched circle on top of each half. This is a quick, easy eye to make. You can either felt your own balls from wool roving or buy a bag of wool-felt balls to use. If you would prefer not to use glue, you could neatly stitch the eyeball to the felted ball and then stitch the ball to the bee. Or, using a barbed felting needle, stab the ball to needle-felt it directly to the toy's body. Use either 100 percent wool felt for the bee's body or a wool-blend felt with a high percentage of pure wool for best results. (See Surface Design for Felt on page 48 for more on needle felting.)

Lesson 6: Ladder-Stitching One Shape to Another

The head of the Bumblebee is stitched to the body using a ladder stitch (page 31). To get a neat and firm attachment between these two spheres, draw a stitching guide on each one with a disappearing fabric marker using a circle template (figure 7). Follow the guide with your needle using extra-strong thread and a ladder stitch. Take a few stitches before pulling the thread taut so that you can follow the stitching guide as you go. Once you have stitched around the circular guide you will have a strong, invisible attachment between the two spheres.

figure 7

Surface Design for Felt

Surface design is one way to make your softie truly one of a kind. Some options for enhancing felt before cutting out the pattern pieces include machine-stitching designs such as the straight lines used on the Ram's horns; dyeing or bleaching; sewing pleats, tucks, or other folds in the fabric; and stamping or painting with fabric paint. Once the animal is stuffed, you can add further details with seed beads, fabric paint, or decorative embroidery such as French knots.

You can even needle-felt details right onto the fabric. Needle felting is the process of interlocking wool fibers by stabbing them over and over with a special barbed needle. To needle-felt successfully you need to be attaching wool fibers to a surface that is at least 80 percent wool. You'll need some wool roving, available at many knitting stores and online, as well as a barbed needle and a pad to place underneath your project. Needle felting can be used to add spots to a wool giraffe or Dalmatian, for example, or it can be used as an alternative way to create facial features. To begin, use a disappearing fabric marker or chalk to draw an outline of the shape you'd like to create on the softie's body. Pull off a piece of roving twice as large as the shape and lay it on top. Stab the roving with the barbed needle, focusing especially on the outline of the shape. Continue to stab the roving until it lays flat against the softie's body, all of the fibers are adhered to one another and to the body, and the area is no longer fuzzy. If some fuzz persists, use small embroidery scissors to trim it away.

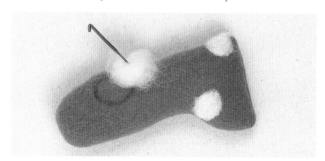

Lesson 7: Other Shapes— Cube, Cylinder, and Triangle

If you have selected one of your square or triangular animal sketches to make into a softie, you can easily sew a soft cube, cylinder, or pyramid. To make a cube, sew six identically sized squares together. To make a cylinder, first cut two same-size circles. Next, you need to find the circumference of the circle: measure its diameter and multiply it by 3.14. (I knew high school geometry would come in handy sometime!) Cut a rectangle with the width equaling the circumference measurement by any length you'd like, depending on how tall you want the cylinder to be. Sew the rectangle, shorter sides together, leaving an opening for turning. Then sew one circle to one end and the other circle to the other, easing the circle to the rectangle as you go (figure 8). To make a pyramid, sew four triangles together, one at a time. These shapes are the building blocks of new softies.

figure 8

Gathered Circle Eyes

To create bulging eyes, try gathering and then stuffing a circle of fabric. Use a disappearing marking pen and circle template to draw a circle on your fabric that is five times as large as the desired eye. Cut out the circle. On the wrong side of the fabric use extra-strong thread to make a running stitch all the way around the perimeter of the circle, leaving a ⅛-inch (3 mm) seam allowance. Place a wad of stuffing in the center of the circle, then slowly pull the stitches tight, adding more stuffing as needed, until you have a firm, gathered circle. Take a few small backstitches and tie off the thread. Add a pupil and an eyeball with felt, paint, buttons, or beads. Press the eyes to the toy, pin, and ladder-stitch them in place so that the stitches are not visible.

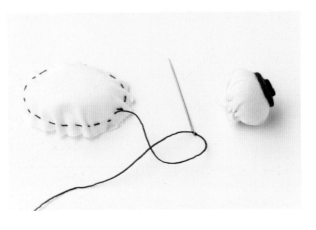

ELEPHANT

By creating this animal (which I made from a soft 100 percent wool sweater that I felted with hot water in the washing machine and then ran through the dryer), you are making a truly three-dimensional stuffed animal that stands on four feet. The key to the construction of this pattern is the underbody gusset, and once you get some practice with this crucial pattern piece, you can begin to design any number of standing animals.

Steps

1. Trace the pattern pieces (page 167) onto freezer paper with a pencil. Cut them out, transferring all of the markings.

2. Adding a ¼-inch (6 mm) seam allowance and remembering to reverse one of each piece, cut two Side Body pieces, two Underbody pieces, two Ear pieces, one Mouth piece, and one Tail piece from the felted wool sweater. For me, the easiest way to do this is to press the freezer paper pattern piece to the fabric, then cut out ¼ inch (6 mm) away from the edges of the pattern piece. Transfer all the markings to the felted fabric.

3. Adding a ¼-inch (6 mm) seam allowance and remembering to reverse half of the pieces, cut two Ears from the patterned quilting cotton, four Tusks from the white quilting cotton, and one Mouth piece from the white quilting cotton. Without adding any seam allowance, cut two Eyelids and 12 Toes from gray felt. Cut two Whites of the Eyes from white felt, two Eyeballs from light brown felt, and two Pupils from black felt, all without additional seam allowances.

4. Use a craft knife or a small pair of sharp scissors to cut the slit in each Side Body where indicated.

5. Place a quilting cotton ear piece and a felted wool sweater ear piece right sides together and stitch around, leaving an opening for turning and stuffing as marked. Repeat for the second ear. Clip the curves and turn the ears right side out and press. Fold the wool side of the ear over the cotton side along the fold line as marked and baste (figure 1). Repeat for the second ear.

TOOLS & MATERIALS

Basic Sewing Tool Kit (page 11)

Felted wool sweater in gray

Piece of patterned quilting cotton or batik, 8 x 12 inches (20.3 x 30.5 cm), for the inner ears

Piece of quilting cotton in white, 6 x 6 inches (15.2 x 15.2 cm), for the tusks and inside the mouth

Scraps of wool-blend felt in gray, white, light brown, and black for the eyes, tail, and toes

Sewing machine needle appropriate for sewing wool and fleece (14/90)

All-purpose polyester thread to match the fabrics

Extra-strong thread to match the fabrics

8 ounces (224 g) of fiberfill stuffing

12-inch (30.5 cm) length of white perle cotton for highlights on the eyes

figure 1

11. Pin the remainder of the elephant's body together and stitch it closed from point A, around the top of the back and along the head and trunk, ending at point B.

12. Clip the curves and turn the elephant right side out. Stuff firmly. Use extra-strong thread to close the opening with a neat ladder stitch.

6. On the right side of one side body, slide the raw edges of one ear through the slit so that the cotton side of the ear is face up and the wool side is against the wool body. Fold the body over the ear along the slit and pin the ear in place. Sew across the slit about ⅛ inch (3 mm) from the edge, closing it up entirely and trapping the raw edges of the ear in the seam. Repeat for the other ear and side body (figure 2 shows how the slit looks from the wrong side of the fabric once it is closed and figure 3 shows how it looks from the right side).

7. Fold the tail along the marked fold line and press. Lay the tail against the right side of one side body with the pointed end aligned with the edge of the side body. Baste in place (figure 4).

8. Fold the top of one underbody down toward the legs on the fold lines, right sides of the fabric together, as marked, and pin in place. Sew along the dotted dart line on each side (figure 5). Repeat for the other underbody piece.

9. Sew the underbodies together across the top, from point A to point B, leaving an opening as marked for turning and stuffing (figure 6).

10. Pin one underbody to one side body, right sides together, beginning at point A and extending downward along each leg and foot and back up to point B. Stitch. Repeat for the other underbody and side body (figure 7).

figure 2

figure 3

13. Stitch the cotton mouth piece to the wool mouth piece, right sides together, along the curved edge from point C to point D, leaving the straight edge open. Clip the curves and turn the mouth right side out. Turn the raw edges under ⅛ inch (3 mm) and press. Stitch the mouth to the body as marked using a ladder stitch.

14. Place two tusk pieces right sides together and stitch the tusk along the curved edge from point E to point F, leaving the straight edge open. Clip the curves and turn the tusks right side out. Turn the raw edges under and press. Stuff the tusk firmly. Place each tusk against the elephant's body as marked and use a few pins to hold the tusks in place. Stitch the tusks to the body using small ladder stitches.

figure 6

figure 4

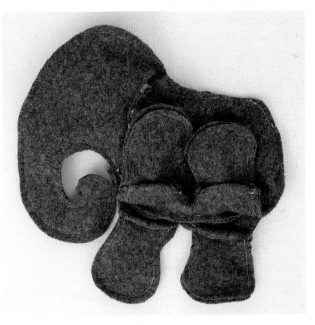

figure 7

figure 5

15. Fold the eyelids in half and press. Layer the black pupil on top of the light brown eyeball, and the eyeball on top of the white of the eye. Use small dabs of craft glue to hold each layer in place. Repeat for the other eye. For the eye highlights, take three small, straight stitches with white perle cotton from the back of the eye through the top right side of the pupil. Repeat with the other pupil. Slide a finished eye between the layers of the eyelid (figure 8). Use a small dab of craft glue to affix the back side of the white of the eye to the bottom portion of the eyelid. Pin the eye to the elephant and whipstitch in place with small, straight stitches. Repeat for the other eye. Alternatively, whipstitch the eye layers in place with coordinating thread.

16. Place three toenails at the base of each leg. Use a glue stick to hold them in place temporarily, then whipstitch in place.

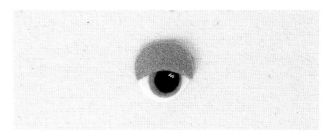

figure 8

Lesson 8: Underbody Gussets

To create a truly three-dimensional toy that can stand up on its own you need to incorporate a gusset into your pattern. A gusset is a piece of fabric that is inserted into a seam to add width or breadth. In soft toy design, gussets are most commonly added at the head and on the underside, or underbody, of the animal. The head gusset gives the animal's head a rounded, more lifelike shape (see page 62 for more about head gussets). The underbody gusset allows the animal to stand up by adding breadth between the legs. In a toy with an underbody gusset the front and back legs are parallel to one another.

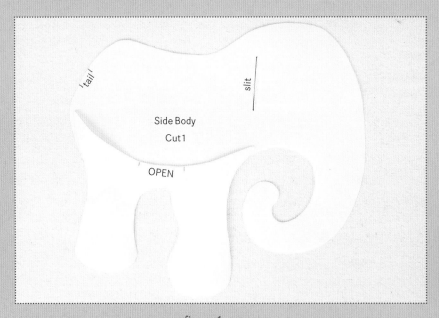

figure 1

It can be difficult at first to imagine the shape of an underbody gusset and how changes in that shape affect the shape of the toy once it is stuffed. As with any aspect of pattern drafting, the more times you draw and sew animals with underbodies, the more intuitive the process becomes. Underbody gussets, along with head gussets, are the parts of softie pattern drafting that are most often in need of edits. Remember to sew a muslin prototype of your softie (see page 20) before cutting and sewing with a more expensive or treasured fabric.

To begin drafting a pattern for the underbody, retrace the side body pattern piece. About one-third of the way up from the bottom of the belly, draw a horizontal line that extends across the body. This line should dip downward in the center and be higher on each side (figure 1). This downward dip pulls the belly of the animal inward so that it doesn't appear distended once the animal is stuffed. Everything below the horizontal line will be the underbody. Mark an opening, about 1 inch (2.5 cm) long, in the middle of the line for turning and stuffing. This is the beginning of an underbody. Now you need to add darts.

Lesson 9: Setting the Legs on Darts

The most crucial aspect of an underbody gusset is to set each leg on a dart. A dart is a fold that is sewn into fabric to provide shaping. In this case the function of the dart is to pull the top of each leg inward, instead of allowing the legs to splay out, which would happen if the underbody were attached without darts. Figure 2 shows an elephant without darts on the underbody gusset (left) and one with darts (right). Darts are not hard to create, so don't skip this step.

Look at the underbody pattern piece. Draw a horizontal line at the top of each leg, where it meets the belly. This will be the fold line. Now draw an oval around this line.

figure 2

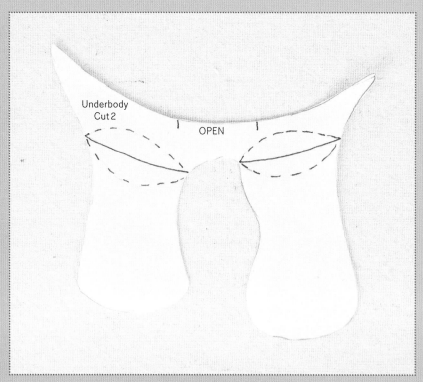

Underbody
Cut 2

OPEN

figure 3

The oval is the dart. I like to use a dotted line for the oval to mark it as a stitching line (figure 3). Although it may seem counterintuitive to sew an oval at the top of each leg, by removing this fabric you are not detracting from the overall length of the outline of the animal's body but are just removing excess fabric from the top of the inner leg, thus pulling the leg thread.

If you are sewing an animal with only two legs, such as a bird, or an insect with many legs, you can easily create an underbody using the methods described above, drawing the appropriate number of legs and making a dart in each.

Simple Strip Gusset

The simplest gusset of all is just a strip of fabric of consistent width sewn between the two body pieces. This gusset adds breadth between the front of the body and the back, like the gusset that makes up the sides of a mattress. The toy will be more full, although somewhat squared off, like a throw cushion.

A strip gusset has an even width all the way around and therefore it does not enhance the contours of the toy. A gusset that narrows and widens as it moves over the body's outline not only adds breadth, but begins to control the toy's overall shape.

Lesson 10: Cutting a Slit to Insert a Detail

The Elephant's ears are attached through a slit cut in the body fabric before the body is sewn together. Inserting a detail piece in a slit creates a strong, invisible attachment and can be used anywhere on the body. Essentially, you are creating a seam where none existed in the pattern.

To attach a detail by cutting a slit, first sew and turn the detail piece (if it is a detail made from a single layer of nonfraying fabric such as felt or synthetic suede, for example, just cut it out). You can stuff the detail piece if you'd like, but be sure to leave enough unstuffed fabric at the raw edges so that you will be able to fit them under the presser foot. You can also fold the piece, as I've done with the Elephant's ear, or gather it with a running stitch pulled tight. Measure the length of the raw edge on your detail piece. This measurement will be the length of the slit. Transfer that measurement to the body where you want to attach the piece and mark it with a disappearing fabric marker or chalk. Note that the slit can be straight or curved. Carefully cut the slit with either a craft knife or a pair of small, sharp scissors. From the right side of the side body, insert the raw edges of the detail piece through the slit to the wrong side. Fold the body over the detail piece so that you can slide just the slit and raw edges under the presser foot. You want to sew both sides of the slit together, with the raw edges of the detail piece in between, similar to creating a tuck. Pin the detail in place and stitch the slit closed, being sure to catch the raw edges of the detail piece in the seam (see figure 2 on page 52). This method is commonly used for attaching ears and tails to an animal, but it could be used for attaching any detail piece where you want a strong, invisible point of attachment.

Lesson 11: Eyelids

To create eyelids, trace the eye pattern piece onto a fresh sheet of freezer paper. Using the eye as a guide, draw a half-moon eyelid slightly larger than the eye. Fold the freezer paper in half so that the top of the eyelid is on the fold. Flip the freezer paper over to the blank side and trace the eyelid. Open up the freezer paper, and you'll have a mirror image of the eyelid, connected at the fold. If your eye is three-dimensional (for safety eyes or felted ball eyes), you will want to draw the eyelid pattern so that the top portion of the eyelid is larger than the portion that will be underneath to account for the space taken up by the raised eye (figure 4). When designing eyelids, keep in mind that the more the eyelid covers the eyeball, the sleepier the expression.

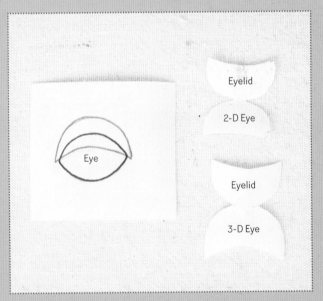

figure 4

RAM

This Ram has a more realistic appearance than the first three softies because it has a rounded head that comes together by creating head gusset pattern pieces. Learning to draft a head gusset opens up new design possibilities and takes your patterns to the next level of sophistication. Make this Ram to get a feel for how head gussets work. It has a wide head gusset, which gives it a more youthful, cute appearance, and the gusset contours on the front end to accentuate the shape of the nose.

To give the Ram's horns a striated appearance I created a surface design on a piece of wool-blend felt by sewing rows of straight stitches 1/2 inch (1.3 cm) apart. I cut the horns from this decorated felt and then sewed them together. Firm stuffing makes the horns naturally curve outward, like the horns on a real ram.

Basic Sewing Tool Kit (page 11)

1/4 yard (23 cm) of white sherpa fleece

1/4 yard (23 cm) of white wool-blend felt

1/4 yard (23 cm) of gray wool-blend felt, plus a 28 x 28-inch (71 x 71 cm) square for the horns

Sewing machine needle appropriate for sewing wool and fleece (14/90)

All-purpose polyester thread in white

Extra-strong thread in white

Ball-point awl or doll needle

2 gray safety eyes, 12 mm in diameter, with washers

11 ounces (308 g) of fiberfill stuffing

18-inch (45.7 cm) length of pink embroidery floss

Embroidery needle

Steps

1. Trace the pattern pieces (page 168) onto freezer paper with a pencil. Cut them out, transferring all of the markings. Cut the Head Gusset pattern piece apart.

2. Iron the following pattern pieces to the fleece, adding a ¼-inch (6 mm) seam allowance all the way around; cut two Side Bodies from fleece (reversing one), two Ears from fleece (reversing one), and half of the Head Gusset from fleece. Transfer all of the markings with a disappearing fabric marker.

3. Iron the following freezer-paper pieces to the white felt, adding a ¼-inch (6 mm) seam allowance all the way around; cut the other half of the Head Gusset, two Face pieces, two Ear pieces, and two Tail pieces. (Remember to reverse one of each duplicate piece cut.) Transfer all of the markings with a disappearing fabric marker.

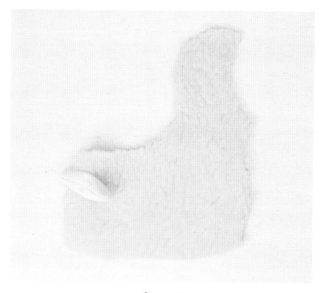

figure 1

figure 2

figure 3

4. With the freezer paper still attached, sew the two tail pieces together, leaving the bottom open for turning and stuffing. Trim around the tail to within ⅛ inch (3 mm) of the stitching line. Pull off the freezer paper and use a hemostat to turn the tail right side out. Squish the tail so that the seam is in the middle, and baste it to the right side of one side body piece so that the raw edges of the tail line up with the edge of the body piece (figure 1).

5. Place one felt ear piece on top of the right side of one fleece ear piece. Pin and stitch around, leaving the bottom open as marked for turning. Trim the seam allowance to within ⅛ inch (3 mm) of the stitching line and use a hemostat to turn the ear right side out. Fold the ear on the fold line, with the felt on the inside, and baste the fold (figure 2). Baste the ear against the fleece of one side body piece (fleece side down) as marked so that the raw edges of the ear line up with the edge of the side body piece (figure 3). Repeat for the second ear, basting it to the other side body piece.

6. Use an awl to poke an eye hole in each felt face as marked. Push the awl all the way through the felt to create a large enough hole for the shank of the safety eye (figure 4); if the hole is still too small, cut a few tiny snips on the edges of the hole with the tip of a small scissors to widen it. Push the shank of a safety eye from the front of the face through the hole to the back and secure it from the back by sliding the plastic washer over the shank until the eye is flush with the fabric (figure 5). Repeat to attach the other eye to the other face piece.

figure 4

7. Place one face piece on top of one side body, right sides together. Match up points E and F. The curves are opposing, so ease them to match one another and pin well. Stitch from point E to point F, catching the raw edges of the ear in the seam. Repeat for the other face and body pieces.

8. Place the fleece half of the head gusset against the felt half, right sides together, and stitch (figure 6). Line up the seam on the head gusset with the seam on one side body where it meets the face. Pin in place. Stitch one side of the head gusset to one side body and face from point A to point B. Repeat for the other side of the head gusset and the other side body and face.

9. Adding a ¼-inch (6 mm) seam allowance, cut two Front Legs, two Back Legs, and two Underbodies from gray felt. Cut two Underbody tips from white fleece and stitch each one to an Underbody piece, right sides together. Sew oval darts on each underbody (see lesson 9 on page 55). Stitch the underbodies together along the top, from point C to point D, leaving an opening for turning and stuffing.

10. Place one back leg and one front leg upside down on top of one side body, right sides together, and stitch in place (figure 7). Repeat for the other front and back legs and the other side body.

11. Open out the underbody and pin one side of it to one side body, right sides together. Stitch, beginning at point C, going down each leg and across the belly and ending at the lower neck at point D. Repeat for the other underbody.

12. Stitch the rest of the animal together from point C up to point B and from point A to point D.

13. Clip the curves and turn the Ram right side out. Stuff firmly. Close the opening with a neat ladder stitch using extra-strong thread. Use an awl (or doll needle, if desired) to gently pull the furry bits of fleece free from the seams.

14. Stitch the nose and mouth with three strands of pink embroidery floss using long straight stitches (see lesson 15 on page 65 for more on embroidering noses and mouths with straight stitches).

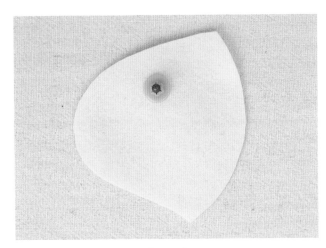

figure 5

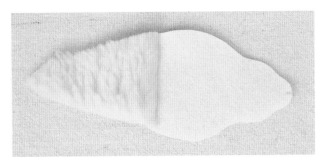

figure 6

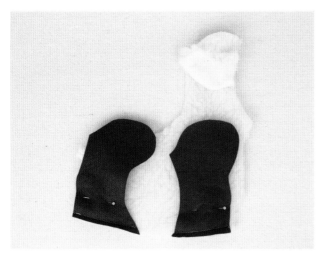

figure 7

figure 8

15. Use a ruler and chalk to mark straight lines every ½ inch (1.3 cm) across the entire piece of the 28 x 28-inch (71 x 71 cm) square of gray felt. Using white thread, stitch across those lines with a stitch length of 3 mm, or 9 stitches per inch (2.5 cm) (figure 8). From this fabric, cut two Horn pattern pieces without the end curve (reversing one), and two with the end curve (reversing one). Place one curved Horn piece on top of one without the curve, right sides together. Stitch, leaving the base open for turning and stuffing. Repeat to create the second horn. Clip the curves and trim the seam allowances at the tip of the horns.

16. Use a hemostat to carefully turn the horns right side out and stuff firmly (see lesson 14 on page 64 for tips on turning narrow pieces). Fold the raw edges inward and baste. Pin each horn to the Ram's head just behind the ears so that the curved portion is lower toward the body and the uncurved portion is higher and toward the ear. Stitch in place with extra-strong thread using a small ladder stitch. Pull the horns outward gently to bend them as desired.

Lesson 12: Head Gussets

A head gusset is a piece of fabric inserted between the two side body pieces at the head to provide breadth and dimension to a softie's head. The simplest kind of head gusset is a pointed oval, or wedge-shaped piece (similar to the wedge shape used in lesson 4 on page 46 to make a sphere). For your first softie with a head gusset, try using this very simple gusset shape. Begin by considering where you would like the head gusset seam to

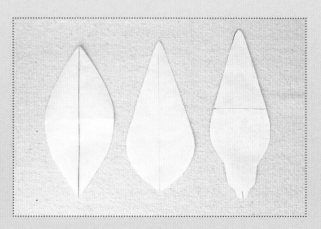

figure 1

begin and end. I like the head gusset to begin where the nose will be on the softie's face, because the V-shaped seam that is created at the start of the gusset resembles a nose. You could have the gusset begin under the chin, however, or at the crown of the head. The gusset widens from that point to create the round fullness of the head and then narrows again. I usually have the gusset end at the nape of the neck. Make pencil marks on your side body pattern piece indicating where you'd like the gusset to begin and end. Use a flexible tape measure to measure this distance. Transfer that measurement to a piece of freezer paper by drawing a straight line of the same distance. This is the length of your head gusset. Now draw a pointed oval around the line. Think about how wide you would like the oval to be: a narrow gusset may give the head a more adult, muscular look, while a wider gusset may give the softie a cuter, more babyish feel. If the gusset is very wide, the head will lose its round shape and look more like the base of a pyramid.

To make a more nuanced head shape, the gusset can be manipulated to give the head more definition. The gusset could be wider on one end, perhaps up front near the forehead, and narrower on the other. The front end of a head gusset can also be drawn in a way that defines the shape of a snout or nose. To make this more nuanced gusset, look back at your visual research images and sketch the shape of the animal's nose in more detail in your sketchbook. Now redraw the end of the gusset as though you were looking down on the animal from above. Bring the gusset in and out where the nose contours inward and outward (figure 1). Make sure the gusset is symmetrical from side to side.

As with drawing the pattern for the underbody, the head gusset pattern piece is likely to need edits before it creates a toy that looks just right. Be sure to make a muslin prototype for your softie before sewing it up with more expensive or treasured fabrics (see page 20 for how to make a muslin prototype).

Lesson 13: Safety Eyes

A quick, easy way to create a compelling set of eyes on a softie is to use safety eyes. So called because they are securely fastened to the softie's body with a plastic washer, safety eyes are readily available at most fabric stores and online through doll- and teddy bear–making suppliers. Many people choose to use safety eyes when sewing toys for children, although an embroidered eye is the absolute safest solution if choking is a concern. Safety eyes come in a large variety of sizes, anywhere from 4 mm to 21 mm, and in a wide variety of colors, including brown, green, blue, gray, clear, yellow, and orange. Cat eyes with narrow pointed pupils as well as rounded frog eyes are also available. (An assortment of safety eyes is shown on page 13.) Safety eyes are made from plastic. The back of the eye is a shank, and each eye comes with a plastic washer that fits securely over the shank.

Safety eyes must be inserted before the animal is stuffed. Mark the spot where you would like the eye to be, then insert an awl between the woven fibers of your fabric, pushing in the awl to slowly stretch the weave and widen the hole. If the hole needs to be widened still, remove the awl and use the tip of your hemostat to widen it further. If you are working with a nonwoven fabric, like the felt used on the Ram, you'll have to poke a hole in the fabric to insert the eye. Otherwise, though, try not to actually cut a hole in the fabric. A hole can stretch over time and weaken the structure of the toy. From the right side of the fabric, slide the eye's shank through the hole until the eye is resting flush with the fabric. From the wrong side, slide the washer over the shank until it is flush with the fabric and the eye is securely attached (see figure 5 on page 61). Once the washer is slid over the shank it is nearly impossible to remove it. If you do need to remove the eye you may need to use wire cutters to cut the shank, thus ruining the eye. A hole will be left in your fabric as well, so that pattern piece will either need to be repaired or, more likely, replaced. So think carefully about the placement of the eyes before you use safety eyes!

Lesson 14: Increasing Your Success with Long, Narrow Parts

Ram horns, long tentacles, bird beaks, monster claws, and the like can lead to frustration when you reach inside, even with the correct tool such as a pair of hemostats, only to end up pulling and tugging and sometimes accidentally tearing a hole in the fabric and never succeeding in turning the piece to the right side. When you go to turn a toy right side out, always pull these small, skinny parts and any extremity into the body first before pulling the body itself out through the opening.

There are a few ways to increase your success at turning. First, when designing patterns be sure to widen those areas that are very long or very skinny. You don't want to widen them so much that the overall look is compromised, but consider widening very narrow areas a bit more than you might think necessary.

When selecting fabrics that will be used to make long skinny parts, choose material that is not too thick or stiff. An upholstery-weight fabric or thick faux fur, for example, may make a narrow area impossible to turn.

When you draw sharply pointed pattern pieces, round or square them off a bit on the end. That way, when you sew them you'll take a few stitches across the point. Although you may worry this will lead to a squared-off or dull point, in fact it will allow you to turn the piece completely right side out instead of having fabric stuck unturned inside the point. When the rounded or squared-off piece is stuffed, it will still be quite pointy like the horn on the Ram.

If turning a point is still giving you trouble, even when you have selected an appropriate weight fabric, widened the pattern piece a bit, and stitched across the point, it may be that you just need a little help getting the turn started. In this case, a clean drinking straw is a great tool to have on hand. I like to use a stronger straw, like those commonly found in coffee shops or take-out restaurants. Push the straw into the piece as far as it will go. Then use your hemostat to push the tip gently down into the straw as far as you can. Pull the straw out and put your hemostat inside the piece where the straw was. Open the tip of your hemostat and grasp the tip of the piece, pulling it out through the opening. For very tiny pieces you can purchase turning tubes from specialty doll-making supply companies. These very narrow brass tubes function in a similar way to the drinking straw, but on a much smaller scale (for more information on turning an especially long piece, see lesson 39 on page 126).

How Much Stuffing Is Enough?

When I teach softie making, one question my students ask most often is, "How much stuffing is enough?" My answer? More than you think! Here is the Ram next to the 11 ounces (308 g) of stuffing it took to fill him. It's a lot! Keep in mind that stuffing naturally settles and compresses over time. So stuff, stuff, and then stuff some more. When you think you've stuffed the toy fully, set it aside and come back later. Then push in a little bit more stuffing. (Read more on stuffing softies on page 28.)

Lesson 15: Embroidering a Nose and Mouth with Long Straight Stitches

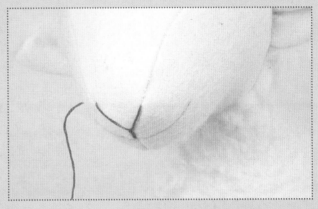

figure 3

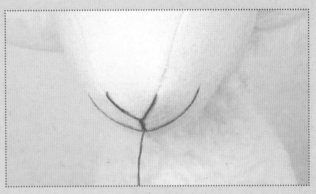

figure 4

Perhaps the most compelling part of a softie is its face. No matter how well constructed the body may be, the facial expression can make or break the look of the finished toy. Although the eyes are an important feature on the face, the nose and mouth enhance the charm of the face as well. The Fish (page 34) and the Bumblebee (page 42) both have mouths made from one long straight stitch. The Ram has a V-shaped nose and a smile, also made from long straight stitches. You do not need to be especially skillful at embroidery to make this kind of nose and mouth, and it can be done quickly after the toy is turned and stuffed.

To make a nose and mouth like those on the Ram, use a disappearing fabric marker or chalk to draw a V-shaped nose, the line below it, and a smiling mouth below that on the stuffed head or face. Take an 18-inch (45.7 cm) strand of six-ply embroidery floss and pull off three strands (save the other three strands for another use). Thread the three strands through an embroidery needle and knot the end. Insert the needle 1 or 2 inches (2.5 or 5 cm) away from one nostril through the stitches

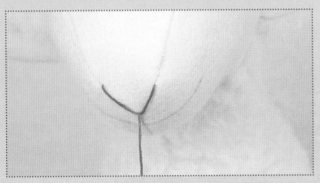

figure 2

of a seam and come out at the nostril. Give the thread a tug, and the knot will pop into the body and be buried in the stuffing inside. Insert the needle through the other nostril and out at the bottom of the V. Catch the loop with the needle, pull the thread taut, and you have a V-shaped nose (figure 2). Now insert the needle into the bottom of the line that extends down from the V and come out at the end of one side of the smile (figure 3). Insert the needle into the end of the other side of the smile and come out at the bottom of the line. Catch the loop with the needle, pull the thread taut, and you have a smiling mouth (figure 4). Insert the needle through the center of the smile and bring the needle out in an inconspicuous spot, such as under the chin or behind one ear. Knot the end of the thread and insert it back into the same spot. Insert the needle through the center of the smile and bring the needle out again, an inch (2.5 cm) or so away, and give the thread a tug to make the knot pop into the softie's body.

BUNNY

For this softie I took the basic body form of a doll and added an animal's head. Any number of animal dolls can be created this way; just change the shape of the ears and add different facial features and the appropriate tail. The great thing about a doll-like animal is that you can dress it! Making a wardrobe of little clothes and accessories for your softie is wonderful fun. You can easily turn scraps of treasured fabric, tiny buttons, and bits of trim into dresses, trousers, vests, and shoes—playthings any child would find irresistible.

Steps

FOR ONE BUNNY

1. Trace the pattern pieces (page 170) onto freezer paper with a pencil. Cut them out, transferring all of the markings onto the paper pattern pieces. Make sure to add ¼-inch (6 mm) seam allowance when cutting the fabric, unless otherwise specified.

2. Cut two Body pieces, two Head pieces, two Footpads, and one Head Gusset from the peach felt. Transfer all of the markings onto the cut-out fabric pieces using a disappearing fabric marker.

3. Iron the Leg pattern piece to a double layer of peach felt. Pin the layers together. Stitch around the Leg pattern with the freezer-paper pattern still adhered, leaving the openings at the top, side, and where the footpad will go, as marked. Trim around the pattern piece ⅛ inch (3 mm) from the stitching line, then pull off the pattern piece. Repeat for the other leg.

4. Place one footpad against the bottom of one leg and sew half way around the foot, from point C to point D (figure 1). Sew the other half of the footpad to the remainder of the foot. Clip the curves and turn the leg right side out. Squish the top of the leg so that the seam is in the middle and press (figure 2). Repeat for the other leg.

5. Iron the Arm pattern piece to a double layer of peach felt. Pin the layers together. Stitch around the Arm pattern with the freezer-paper pattern still adhered, leaving the openings at the top and side, as marked. Pull off the pattern piece and trim the seam allowance to ⅛ inch (3 mm) from the stitching line. Clip the curves, especially between the thumb and hand, and turn the arm right side out (figure 3). Press. Repeat for the other arm.

TOOLS & MATERIALS

Basic Sewing Tool Kit (page 11)

FOR ONE BUNNY

¼ yard (23 cm) of peach wool-blend felt

⅛ yard (11.5 cm) of lavender wool-blend felt for the inner ears, nose, and eyes

Scraps of white and gray wool-blend felt for the eyes

All-purpose polyester thread in white, lavender, and gray

Extra-strong thread in white

6½ ounces (182 g) of fiberfill stuffing

36-inch (91 cm) length of white perle cotton

18-inch (45.7 cm) length of light gray embroidery floss

Embroidery needle

Beeswax

1-inch (2.5 cm) diameter white pompom or white yarn and a pompom maker

FOR THE CARROT

Scraps of wool-blend felt in orange and two different greens

All-purpose polyester thread in orange

1 ounce (28 g) of fiberfill stuffing

continued on next page

FOR THE DRESS, HAIR BOW,
AND SHOES

2 fat quarters of quilting cotton
for the dress

17 inches (43.2 cm) of decorative
trim for the dress

Scrap of green wool-blend felt
for the bow

Scrap of gray-green wool-blend
felt for the shoes

All-purpose polyester thread
to coordinate with the dress
and shoes

2 metal snap sets for the dress,
size 1/0

4 small buttons to match
the dress fabric

2 small green buttons
for the shoes

FOR THE VEST AND PANTS

Scrap of green wool-blend felt
for the vest

1 fat quarter of quilting cotton
for the pants

All-purpose polyester thread
to match the pants fabric

1 metal snap set for the vest,
size 1/0

1 small decorative button
for the vest

7 inches (17.8 cm) of elastic,
1/4 inch (6 mm) wide,
for the pants

Small safety pin

6. Lay the body pieces on top of one another and stitch around from point F to point I, point J to point K, and point L to point H, leaving openings to insert the arms and legs and at the top for turning and stuffing.

7. Insert one turned arm into the body, thumb down, aligning the raw edges with the edge of the body from point E to point F. Pin and stitch across the body from point E to point F, catching the raw edges of the arm in the seam. Repeat for the other arm, attaching it from point G to point H.

8. To keep the arms out the way while you attach the legs, pull both arms up so that the hands extend out of the neck hole (figure 4). Insert one turned leg into the body, toe down, aligning the raw edges with the edge of the body from point I to point J. Pin and stitch across the body from point I to point J, catching the raw edges of the leg in the seam. Repeat for the other leg, attaching it from point K to point L.

9. Clip the curves. Pull the arms and legs out through the neck opening and then pull the entire body right side out. Stuff the legs and arms through the openings in their side seams. Use extra-strong thread to close the openings with a ladder stitch.

10. Stuff the body firmly through the neck opening. Use extra-strong thread to take a running stitch along the top edges of the neck. Pull the stitches tightly to gather the neck and tie a knot to hold the neck closed.

11. Iron the Ear pattern piece to one piece of lavender felt. Place the lavender felt on top of a piece of peach felt. With the freezer-paper pattern still attached, stitch around the ear shape, leaving the straight bottom edge open for turning and stuffing. Pull off the pattern piece and trim the seam allowance to 1/8 inch (3 mm). Clip the seam allowance at the tip of the ear to get rid of some bulk. Turn the ear right side out. Repeat for the other ear.

12. Fold the ear in half along the fold line as marked on the pattern piece so that the lavender felt is on the inside. Press. Lay the ear against one head piece as marked, aligning the raw edges of the ear with the edge of the head piece. Baste in place (figure 5). Repeat for the other ear, basting it to the other head piece.

13. Stitch the head gusset to one head piece from point A to point B, catching the raw edges of the ear in the seam. Repeat for the second head piece and ear. Remove the basting stitches from the ear. Stitch the remainder of the head from point B to the nape of the neck and from point A to the base of the neck, leaving the bottom of the neck open.

14. Clip the curves. Pull the ears out through the neck, then pull the rest of the head out through the neck. Stuff the head firmly all the way down to the neck opening. Turn the raw edges of the neck opening under and baste by hand. Center the head on the body and pin in place. Using extra-strong

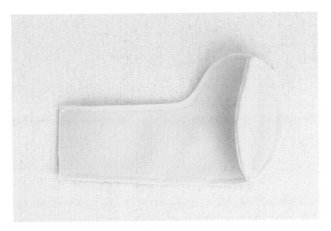

figure 1

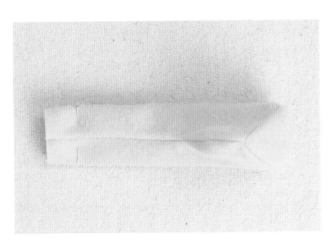

figure 2

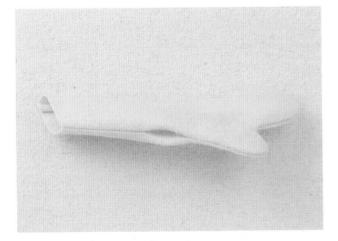

figure 3

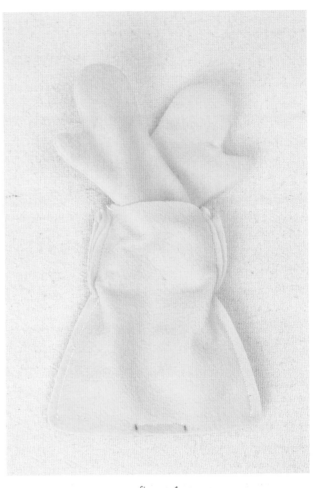

figure 4

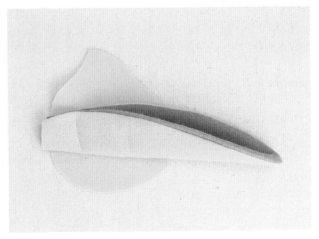

figure 5

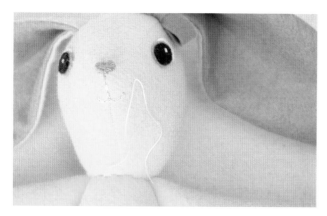

figure 6

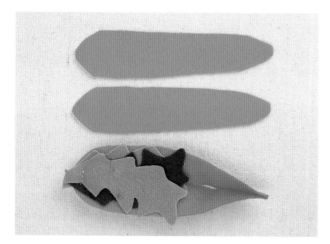

figure 7

figure 8

thread, ladder-stitch the neck opening to the body, covering the gathering stitches at the top of the body. Push a little extra stuffing into the neck as you stitch, filling it out so that the neck is firm.

15. For the nose, cut a small heart shape from lavender felt and whipstitch it in place. For each eye, use a circle template to draw and cut two same-size circles from felt, one lavender and one white, and one smaller circle from gray. Layer the felt circles, offsetting them from each other, with the gray on top, then the lavender, and then the white, and use a glue stick to hold the layers in place temporarily. Sew three small stitches with perle cotton through all three layers to create a highlight on the gray part of the eye. Whipstitch the gray layer to the lavender layer and the lavender layer to the white layer using thread that matches each layer. Use craft glue to attach the eyes to the head. Use an overcast stitch to sew the white eye layer to the head with white thread.

16. With a disappearing fabric marker, draw the line extending down from the nose and draw the smile. Use a stem stitch to embroider the line and the smile using two strands of light gray floss and the embroidery needle (see page 31 for the stem stitch).

17. For the whiskers, run perle cotton across beeswax to add stiffness. Take a tiny stitch to the right of the nose with a length of white perle cotton threaded on an embroidery needle. Tie off with a double knot. Repeat twice more close to the first whisker until you have a total of three whiskers to the right of the nose (figure 6). Make three whiskers to the left of the nose in the same manner.

18. For the tail, sew either a store-bought white pom-pom or a pompom made with white yarn in place with extra-strong thread.

FOR THE CARROT

19. Cut four Carrot pieces from the orange felt, adding a ¼-inch (6 mm) seam allowance around each piece. Iron the Carrot Leaf pattern piece to the green felt and cut around the pattern piece, adding no seam allowance. Repeat until you have three leaves. Stitch the first carrot piece to the second from top to bottom, leaving an opening as marked. Stack up the carrot leaves and place them upside down on top of the carrot pieces that have been stitched so that the ends of the leaf stems extend to the top edge of the carrot. Baste in place (figure 7). Stitch the first two carrot pieces to the third, and then to the fourth, without leaving any further openings. The stem end of the leaves will be caught in the seam. Clip the curves and turn the carrot right side out through the opening. Stuff firmly and use orange thread to close the opening with a ladder stitch.

FOR THE DRESS, HAIR BOW, AND SHOES

20. For the dress: Fold one piece of quilting cotton in half and place the dress pattern on the fold. Iron the pattern piece in place and cut it out, adding a ¼-inch (6 mm) seam allowance (less near the straps where there is less room). Repeat for the other piece of quilting cotton. To add trim, place the trim upside down against the bottom edge of one dress piece. Use steam from the iron to shape the trim to the curve of the bottom of the dress. Baste along the edge of the trim to hold it in place. Place the dress pieces right sides together and stitch all the way around, catching the edge of the trim in the seam and leaving an opening on one side as marked. Clip the curves and turn the dress right side out through the opening. Press. Close the opening with a ladder stitch. Remove the basting stitches on the trim. Sew one side of the snap to one side of the dress, and the other snap to the other side, as marked. Try the dress on the Bunny. Bring the straps around to the front and pin in place. Remove the dress from the Bunny and sew the straps in place by stitching a small button on each side of each strap; the dress is reversible, so you want a button on both sides of each strap (figure 8).

21. For the hair bow: Iron the Shoe Strap / Hair Bow pattern piece to the strip of green felt and cut it out. Fold the strip into a long loop and use a dab of craft glue to hold the ends together. Wrap the shorter Middle of Hair Bow strip around the center, gathering it slightly, and use a dab of craft glue to hold the ends in place. When the glue is dry, add another dab of craft glue to the back of the bow, place it on the Bunny's head at the base of the ear (see figure 9), and use a pin to hold it in place while the glue dries. Alternatively, stitch the bow to the Bunny with a few small stitches.

22. For the shoes: Cut out the Shoe pattern piece from freezer paper. Fold the piece of gray-green felt in half and iron the toe of the Shoe pattern piece on the fold as indicated. Cut out, adding a ¼-inch (6 mm) seam allowance. Stitch the heel together. Repeat for the other shoe. Iron the Footpad pattern piece to the doubled gray-green felt and cut it out, adding slightly more than a ¼-inch (6 mm) seam allowance. Pin a footpad to the bottom of a shoe and stitch all the way around. Turn the shoe right side out. Repeat for the other shoe. Iron the Shoe Strap / Hair Bow pattern piece to the doubled gray-green felt and cut out. Put a shoe on the Bunny and mark where you think the shoe strap should be placed. Stitch a shoe strap to the inner part of the shoe by creating an X with green thread. Stitch it to the outer part of the shoe by sewing on a small green button (figure 9). Repeat for the other shoe.

figure 9

23. For the vest: Fold the green felt in half and iron the Vest pattern piece on the fold as indicated. Cut out exactly around the pattern piece, adding no seam allowance. Trace the armhole using a disappearing fabric marker or chalk and mark the fold line. Remove the pattern piece. Cut out the armhole using small, sharp scissors and press the collar down on the fold line. Sew one side of the snap to the inside of the vest on one side, below where the button will go. Sew the button on top to hide the stitches that hold the snap. Sew the other side of the snap to the outside of the vest on the other side (figure 10).

24. For the pants: Fold the quilting cotton right sides together and place the pattern piece on the fold as marked. Cut out, adding a ¼-inch (6 mm) seam allowance. Repeat so that you have two matching pants pieces. Fold the bottom of each Pants piece up ⅛ inch (3 mm) and press, then fold up another ⅛ inch (3 mm) and press again, as marked. Stitch along the folded edge to create a hem. Fold the curved crotch seam inward ⅛ inch (3 mm) as marked and press. Stitch along the folded edge to create a hem. To create a casing for the elastic, fold the top of the pants down ⅛ inch (3 mm) and press, then fold down ¼ inch (6 mm) and press again, as marked by the dotted line. Stitch along the very bottom of the fold to create a casing (figure 11). Repeat for the other pants piece. Fold one pants piece in half, right sides together, and stitch up the leg seam (stopping at the crotch). Repeat for the other pants piece. Now place the two pants pieces right sides together and stitch the crotch seam up to but not through the waist, leaving an opening on one crotch seam for the pompom tail, as marked. Turn the pants right side out. Attach one end of the elastic to a small safety pin and thread the elastic through the casing at the waist. Lap the elastic ends over one another and take a few stitches with extra-strong thread to hold the elastic ends together.

figure 10

figure 11

Lesson 16: Inserting Big Parts in a Seam

The strongest, neatest method to attach arms and legs to a softie is to sew them to the body by machine. The usual method would be to lay the stuffed arms and legs across the body and then sew the body pieces together, catching the raw edges of the appendages in the body seam. But the stuffed arms and legs of this softie are too bulky to fit inside the body. The solution is to stitch them to the body, turned but unstuffed, leaving an extra opening in one side seam of each arm and each leg as described in steps 7 to 9 on page 68. Close the openings with a ladder stitch. Stuff the appendages after turning the toy right side out.

When you design a pattern that has big parts like this that you'd like to attach by catching them in a seam, place the extra opening in those parts strategically so the closures will not be noticeable on the finished toy. Even if your ladder stitch is very tiny and neat, a hand-sewn seam will never look identical to a machine-sewn one.

Lesson 17: Footpads and Shoes

To give the feet on this Bunny a more three-dimensional feel, I added oval-shaped footpads to the bottom of each foot. Draft the footpad pattern piece by marking the bottom of the leg pattern where you'd like the footpad to begin and end. Measure the distance between these two spaces and transfer this measurement to a piece of freezer paper. Draw an oval of the same length (figure 1). You can make the foot taper toward the ankle and widen at the toe if you'd like, or keep the oval symmetrical, as I've done on the Bunny.

Stitching the footpad to the bottom of the leg can be fiddly. The stitches are made in a small space and need to be accurate. Before you stitch, pin the footpad to the edges of the foot every ⅛ inch (3 mm). Taking the time to pin well will mean more accurate stitching! When I stitch a footpad, I move the needle position on the machine all the way to the right. That way the fabric is still in contact with both feed dogs, but I am able to stitch right up next to the edge of the fabric. Alternatively, use the zipper foot, which will similarly allow you to stitch very close to the edge of the fabric. You may want to make small clips in the seam allowance at the bottom of the leg to allow it to spread out and better hug the curves of the footpad.

Stitch with the leg fabric facing up and the footpad underneath. Lower the machine needle into the last stitch you took on the leg at the toe, then lower the presser foot and stitch from the toe to the heel. With the needle in the down position, raise the presser foot, swivel the footpad around, and lower the presser foot. Stitch from the heel to the toe (see figure 1 on page 69). If you find machine-stitching the footpad too difficult, stitch by hand using a short backstitch.

With footpads, the feet of your softie have soles, making it easy to create shoes for your softie to wear. Felt and synthetic suede are good materials for shoes because they do not fray and therefore the shoe can be cut from a single layer without any hemming. To create the sole pattern, use the footpad pattern piece, adding

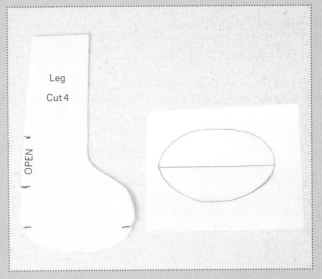

figure 1

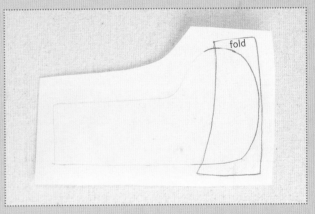

figure 2

an extra ⅛ inch (3 mm) to the seam allowance when you cut it out to account for the width of the stuffed foot. For the side of the shoe, trace the bottom part of the leg pattern onto a fresh piece of freezer paper. Draw a curved line both down from the heel and straight toward the toe, then widen the pattern piece on each side to account for the width of the stuffed foot (figure 2). Cut the side of the shoe with the toe on the fold to get a symmetrical shoe. Bows, ribbon laces, and buttons make good embellishments for shoes. If you are giving the doll to a small child it might be best to sew the shoes to the feet so that they aren't immediately pulled off and lost.

Lesson 18: Whiskers

I've added whiskers to the Bunny to give the face another endearing note. Whiskers can be made from standard sewing thread, extra-strong buttonhole thread, perle cotton, embroidery floss, waxed upholstery thread, monofilament, fishing wire, or even dental floss. If you are using thread or floss, consider running them through beeswax for added stiffness.

If you'd like to be sure to get evenly spaced whiskers, first mark three or more dots with a disappearing fabric marker on either side of your softie's nose. Then thread a 24-inch (61 cm) length of floss or whatever you've chosen through an embroidery needle, but don't knot the end. Insert the needle into the first dot, coming out right next to it—just a few threads of fabric away. Leave a 2-inch (5 cm) tail and cut the thread from the needle 2 inches (5 cm) away from the fabric. Tie the tail and the thread together twice, making a sturdy double knot. With the remainder of the 24-inch (61 cm) length re-thread the embroidery needle and continue taking a small stitch at each dot and tying the thread tail to the thread in a double knot until you have created all of the whiskers.

Once the whiskers are attached, you can trim them and then tame them a bit with a burst of steam from a hot iron.

Adding a Tag to Your Softie

A tag can give your handmade softie a professional finish. Like a signature on a painting, the tag tells the toy's recipients who the artist is and reminds them that this toy was indeed created by a person and not mass-produced. If you plan to sell your softies, a tag can add a professional finish to your toy and will remind buyers where to find more toys from the same maker.

You can order woven tags with your name or business name, or you could use a fabric-ink stamp pad to stamp twill tape or other ribbon. Then, either pin the label to the finished toy and securely stitch it in place, or fold the ribbon in half, wrong sides together, and insert it in a seam as you make your softie. For a less permanent option, print, write, or stamp your name on white shrink plastic. Punch holes with a hole punch on either edge, then shrink it according to the package instructions. Stitch or tie the shrink plastic tag to your softie.

Lesson 19: Dressing and Accessorizing Your Softie

Small scraps of quilting cotton and felt and a few buttons and leftover trim are all you need to make an array of clothing and accessories for your softies. The very simplest outfit can be made by cutting a neck slit in a long rectangle of felt and sliding it over the softie's head. Tie a ribbon around the waist and you have a little tunic.

More intricate clothing comes together with pattern pieces made from tracing the softie's body. Add some length on each side, to accommodate the stuffing, and then draw in the details such as a neckline or collar, straps, a waist, or pant legs. Hemming a pair of tiny pants or a dress can be done by hand, or you can double fold and stitch the raw edges before sewing up the garment, as I have done on the Bunny's pants. The dress is reversible, giving the girl Bunny two different looks.

If sewing doll clothes is new to you, the clothes for these Bunnies are a good way to begin. Get a feel for some basic clothing construction techniques, then build a wardrobe from there. Try making overalls, a skirt, or an apron. If your softie will go to a young child, choose closures that are easy to use. Elastic requires no fastening at all, and nothing is easier than hook-and-loop tape. For an older child, snaps, buttons, zippers, and laces make getting the softie doll dressed even more fun.

Creating a Lovey, Hobbyhorse, or Faux Taxidermy

Once you have a good pattern for a gusseted head, not only can you create a standing animal, like the Ram (page 58), or a doll-like animal like the Bunny, but you can also use the head pattern to create a "lovey" blanket, a hobbyhorse, and even faux taxidermy.

For the lovey, sew two squares of soft, fleecy fabric right sides together, leaving an opening on one corner. Clip the corners and turn the square right side out through the opening. Attach the stuffed gusseted head with a ladder stitch.

For the hobbyhorse, cover the end of a thick dowel or cut-off broomstick with a wad of fiberfill stuffing and wrap it a few times with a rag to cushion the end. Sew and stuff an enlarged version of the gusseted head, leaving an empty cavity in the stuffing, and insert the end of the dowel. Push more stuffing around the dowel to hold it in firmly, then wrap twine around the base of the fabric where it meets the dowel and hot glue the underside of the fabric to the dowel to hold it in place.

For the faux taxidermy, purchase a wooden plaque for a few dollars at the craft store and stain or seal it. Sew an enlarged version of the gusseted head, adding a few inches of neck to the pattern. Leave the opening for turning and stuffing at the nape of the neck. Turn and stuff the head and affix it to the plaque at the nape of the neck with epoxy or hot glue.

PUPPY

This soft, furry Puppy is reminiscent of my favorite childhood stuffed animal, Barnard, to whom I was very attached. A cuddly and cute dog with an endearing expression and cocked head, this guy is sure to become a child's treasured softie. His rounded face, achieved by cutting and sewing darts in the cheeks, gives him a babyish appearance. Gathering within each dart makes the cheeks even more full. Gathering is also used on the ears and tail as an easy way to close an opening and add fullness and dimension.

Steps

1. Photocopy the pattern pieces (page 172), glue the copies onto cardboard with a glue stick, and cut them out. Cut the tail apart along the line.

2. On the wrong side of both the white and the brown faux fur, use a permanent marker to draw an arrow indicating the direction of the nap. When cutting, follow the nap direction indicated on the pattern pieces and add a ¼-inch (6 mm) seam allowance. From brown fur, using either a permanent marker, a disappearing fabric marker, or chalk, trace and cut out two Side Body pieces (reversing one), four Footpads, two Tail base pieces (reversing one), two Ears (reversing one), and two Head pieces (reversing one). Transfer all of the markings. From white fur, use a disappearing fabric marker to trace and cut out one Head Gusset, two Muzzles (reversing one), two Underbodies (reversing one), and two Tail tips (reversing one). Transfer all of the markings to the fabric. Trace the Ear pattern onto a doubled piece of white cotton with a disappearing fabric marker and cut out.

3. Place one muzzle piece on the side of one head piece, right sides together, as indicated. Line up the curves and pin well; some easing will be required. Stitch the muzzle to the head side as marked (figure 1). Repeat for the other muzzle and head piece.

4. Using extra-strong thread, hand-stitch a series of running stitches up the long side of the dart on one head piece (figure 2). Pull the stitches so both sides of the dart are the same size and evenly distribute the gathers. Pin the dart right sides together and machine-stitch it closed (figure 3). Repeat for the other head piece.

TOOLS & MATERIALS

Basic Sewing Tool Kit (page 11)

½ yard (45.7 cm) each of faux fur fabric in brown and white

Scraps of quilting cotton in white and black for the inner ears and the nose

All-purpose polyester thread in white and black

Sewing machine needle appropriate for sewing faux fur (14/90 is recommended)

Extra-strong thread in white and black

Cardboard

Black permanent marker

15 ounces (420 g) of fiberfill stuffing

2 black animal eyes, 14 mm in diameter, with wire-loop backings

36-inch (91.4 cm) length of waxed upholstery thread

Ball-point awl

5-inch (12.7 cm) doll needle

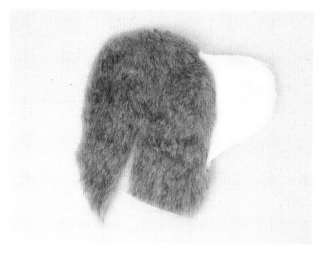

figure 1

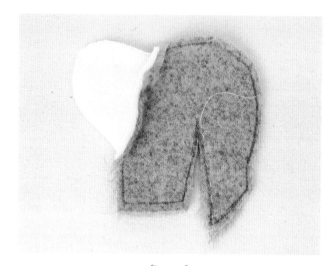

figure 2

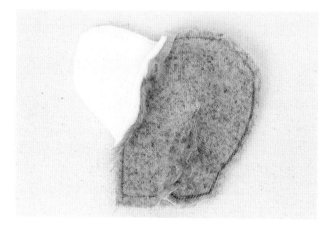

figure 3

5. Pin the head gusset to one head piece, right sides together, from point E to point F, and stitch. Repeat, stitching the other side to the other head piece.

6. Stitch the remainder of the head together, from point F to the nape of the neck, and from point E down the remainder of the muzzle and the front of the neck. Clip the curves and turn the head right side out.

7. On one underbody piece, fold the legs upward along the fold line as marked, right sides together, and stitch the oval darts. Repeat for the other underbody piece. Place the underbodies right sides together and stitch along the top from point C to point D, leaving the opening as marked (figure 4).

8. Place one side of the underbody against one side body piece, right sides together, matching up the legs, and pin in place. Stitch from point C, down the back leg, stopping at the mark where the footpad will be attached. Begin again at the second mark for the footpad and continue to stitch up the space between the legs and down again to the front leg. Stop and start again, leaving space for attaching the footpad, as marked, and ending at point D. Repeat to attach the underbody to the other side body (figure 5).

9. Place all four footpads on your worktable and make sure the nap is all going in the same direction. When sewn, the nap should go toward the back of the animal. Pin one footpad to the bottom of one leg, right sides together, and stitch around. Sewing footpads is fiddly; if you find it difficult to do by machine, hand-stitch

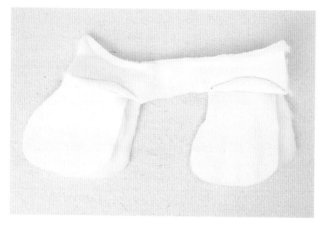

figure 4

figure 5

figure 6

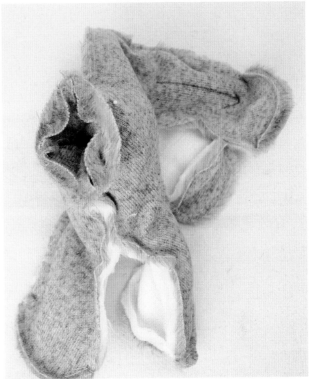

figure 7

each footpad using extra-strong thread and small back-stitches (see page 73 for how to sew footpads). Repeat for the other three footpads (figure 6).

10. Finish stitching the remainder of the Puppy's body from point C to point A and from point B to point D, leaving the neck open.

11. Insert the right-side-out head into the inside-out body (figure 7). To create a Puppy with a turned head, rotate the head inside the body as much as you'd like. Align the raw edges of the neck, pin, and stitch in place either by machine or, if it is too fiddly to fit under the presser foot, by hand with extra-strong thread using small backstitches (figure 8).

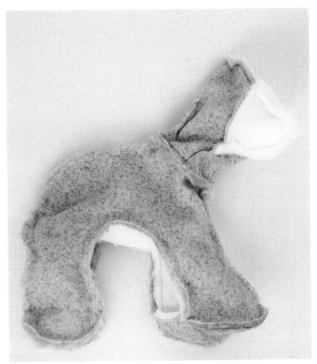

figure 8

figure 9

figure 10

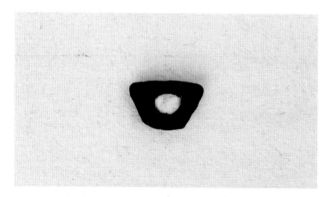

figure 11

12. Clip the curves and turn the Puppy right side out. Stuff firmly. Close the opening with extra-strong thread using a ladder stitch.

13. Place one tail tip on top of one tail base, right sides together, and stitch. Repeat for the other tail tip and base. Place the tail pieces right sides together and stitch around, leaving the opening as marked. Clip the curves and turn the tail right side out. Stuff firmly. Take a running stitch by hand using extra-strong thread all the way around the tail opening. Pull the thread tight to gather the opening closed, pushing the raw edges of the fabric into the tail (figure 9). Tie off. Pin the tail to the body as marked and ladder-stitch it in place using extra-strong thread.

14. Place a white cotton ear on top of a faux fur ear, right sides together. Pin, then stitch around the ear, leaving an opening as marked. Clip the curves and turn the ear right side out. Take a running stitch by hand using extra-strong thread all the way around the ear opening. Pull the thread tight to gather the opening closed, pushing the raw edges of the fabric into the ear (figure 10). Tie off. Repeat for the other ear. Place the ears on the body as marked. Pin and then ladder-stitch them in place using extra-strong thread.

15. Use a pencil to trace the Nose onto freezer paper and cut out the pattern piece. Iron the Nose pattern piece to the doubled black cotton. Use black thread to stitch directly around the Nose pattern piece, with no seam allowance, while it is still adhered to the fabric. Pull off the pattern piece and cut out the sewn nose ⅛ inch (3 mm) from the stitching line. Clip the curves. Pinch one layer of the nose fabric and make a small snip in the center. Pull the nose right side out through the snip. Use a hemostat to lightly stuff the nose (figure 11), and close up the X with a few overcast stitches using extra-strong black thread. Place the nose on the muzzle just above point E (with the stitched side facing the fur). Pin and then ladder-stitch it in place using extra-strong black thread.

16. Attach the wire-loop eyes with a 36-inch (91.4 cm) strand of waxed upholstery thread following the instructions in lesson 23 on page 84.

17. Use an awl to gently pull the pile out of the seams (to create a seamless look).

Lesson 20: Fabrics with Nap or Pile

Fabrics with nap or pile have a raised, directional surface texture. Mohair, synthetic fur, velvet, velveteen, corduroy, brushed denim, terry, and chenille are all fabrics that have nap or pile. On more subtle napped fabrics, like velveteen, the nap is noticeable only when light is reflected on them. Fabrics with more pronounced nap, and fabrics with deep pile like some faux furs, have a more obvious directionality.

In traditional toy making, and traditional sewing in general, pattern pieces are always cut so that the nap goes in the same direction, usually downward. (That said, a toy with the nap of pattern pieces intentionally cut in different directions could be really fun.) When you "pet" the fabric one way, it lies flat, and when you pet it the opposite way, it stands up on end. This is the direction of the nap. Use a permanent marker to draw an arrow on the wrong side of the fabric to mark the nap direction (figure 1). This arrow reminds you of the direction of the nap as you place your pattern pieces so that you can ensure that the nap is going in a consistent direction. If you design a toy made from faux fur, keep in mind that you may need to purchase extra fabric to have enough space to cut out all of the pattern pieces with the nap going in the same direction.

Napped and piled fabrics need special care when pressing because the pile can be crushed or, in the case of synthetic furs, the backing can melt under a hot iron. Always press napped fabrics from the wrong side, testing a small area first. Use a cool iron when pressing synthetic fur. When I sew with faux fur I shy away from using freezer paper because I want to avoid using a hot iron that might melt the fur's backing.

Take special care when cutting fabrics with deep pile so that you don't cut away too much of the pile and, when possible, cut in the direction of the nap. Use small, sharp scissors and cut one fabric layer at a time to retain as much control as possible, keeping the blade as close to the backing of the fur as possible so as to only cut the backing and not the long strands of fur. A craft knife blade works well, too. With some deeply piled faux furs it can be hard to pin the layers together; try using bobby pins or alligator clips instead of pins (figure 2). And if you are struggling to get a deep-pile fabric under your presser foot, trim away some of the pile in the seam allowances of your pattern pieces (figure 3).

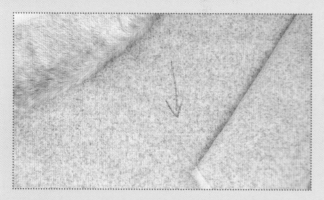
figure 1

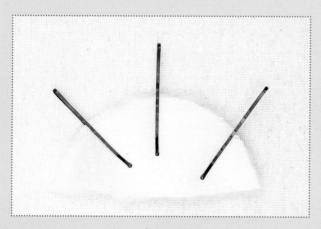
figure 2

figure 3

Markings for eyes, ears, and tails can be difficult to transfer onto napped fabrics, especially those with a long pile. Instead of using a disappearing fabric marker or chalk, try taking a few tailor's tacks (page 21). Using contrasting thread, take a small stitch from the fur side of the fabric and leave a long thread tail. Cut the thread from the needle and tie the thread ends together. Later you can cut the stitch and pull out the tack.

In toys that are made with piled fabrics, some of the pile will get caught in the seams. Once the toy is stuffed, use a ball-point awl to gently free the fur from each seam so that the toy has a fluffy, seamless look (figure 4).

When you get ready to sew two pieces of fabric with nap right sides together it is very important to place a pin at least every ½ inch (1.3 cm), if not closer (I like to pin every ¼ inch [6 mm]!). Napped fabrics placed right sides together tend to shift under the machine needle. If you pin like crazy, though, you'll have an easier time keeping the two pieces of fabric aligned with each other. To prevent slippage, hold the fabric taut both behind and in front of the presser foot as you sew, and try changing the settings on your machine to reduce the pressure on the presser foot.

figure 4

Lesson 21:
Creating a Softie
with a Turned Head

To create a pattern for a softie with a turned head, cut the head off of the body pattern at the neck (figure 5). Sew the body and the head separately. Turn the head right side out and insert it into the body, lining up the raw edges at the base of the head with the raw edges at the top of the neck. (This is similar to setting a sleeve in the armhole of a blouse.) At this point you can rotate the head inside the body as much or as little as you'd like. Once you have it turned as desired, pin and stitch around the neck to attach it to the body (see figure 7 on page 83). Then turn the softie right side out and stuff it as usual. Some uses for this technique might be creating an owl that is looking backward, a family of animals looking at one another, or a tiger with a cocked head as though listening to a sound in the forest.

figure 5

Lesson 22: Darted Cheeks and Gathered Cheeks

Baby animals have large heads with full, rounded cheeks. To give the face this added dimension, cut darts extending from the neck up to the cheeks. The amount of space removed at the dart needs to be added back to the pattern on the side of neck for the circumference of the neck at the base of the head to still match the circumference of the neck at the top of the body. To add this space back in, simply widen the head pattern the same amount you narrowed it by taking the dart (figure 6).

Although just a dart makes a noticeably more rounded cheek, to get an even more significant round shape you can extend the bottom of one side of the dart downward (figure 7). Before stitching the dart closed, take a series of running stitches up the longer side of the dart. Pulling the thread creates gathers and shortens that side of the dart so that it matches the other side. Evenly distribute the gathers along the dart, then sew the dart closed (see figures 2 and 3 on page 82). This technique creates a really rounded cheek that works well not only for a baby-faced softie but also for a rodent like a chipmunk or squirrel or for any big-cheeked animal design.

Using a running stitch pulled tight to gather the openings on the tail and ears on this Puppy is quick and effective. The raw edges are pulled inside and, in the case of the ears, some fullness is added. Be sure to use extra-strong thread so that it won't break while you are pulling the stitches taut.

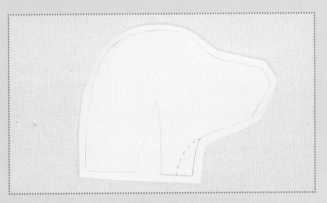

figure 6

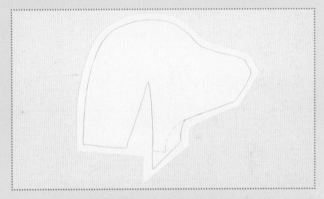

figure 7

Tips on Sewing with Thick Fabrics or Many Layers

Fitting an especially thick piece of fabric, or a fabric "sandwich" consisting of many layers, under the presser foot can be a struggle. To give yourself a bit more room to maneuver, with the presser foot raised, push up on the presser foot bar. This raises the presser foot a bit more, allowing you more room to slide the thick fabric underneath it. Make sure you are using a heavier machine needle meant for thicker fabrics.

Once your thick fabric is positioned and the needle is lowered, it can be hard to get the fabric moving. To do so, grasp both the upper and the bobbin threads with your left hand and give them a tug as you begin to sew. This helps you move the fabric through the first few stitches, and then you can let the machine take over.

Lesson 23: Eyes with Looped Backs

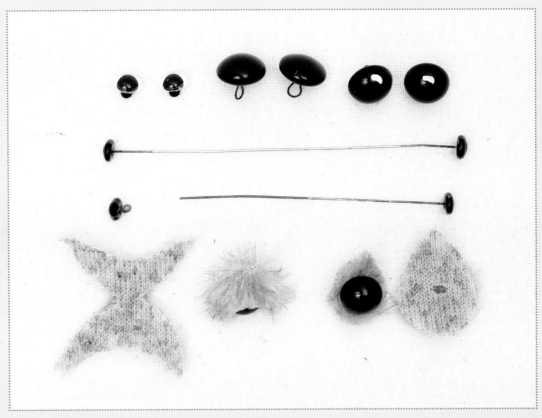

figure 8

Historically, the eyes on stuffed toys were made with shoe or boot buttons, which are now rare. Glass eyes with wire-loop shanks are commonly used on finely made toys now, and they are the eyes I chose for this Puppy. Unlike safety eyes (see page 63), looped shank eyes are inserted after the toy is stuffed. Looped shank eyes come in a variety of sizes (anywhere from 4 mm to 36 mm), colors, and pupil shapes, and they can be made from glass or plastic. Use white enamel paint to add a highlight to plain black glass eyes if you'd like.

Some glass eyes come connected with a length of wire. To create the loop shank, cut the wire apart about ½ inch (1.3 cm) from each eye. Use needle-nose pliers to twist the end of the wire into a loop close to the eye.

Make an eyelid for a looped shank eye by cutting a half-moon shape on the fold (similar to the eyelid shape on the Elephant on page 50). Toward the bottom middle of the half-moon shape, use an awl to poke a small hole to insert the loop shank of the eye. Fold the lid over the

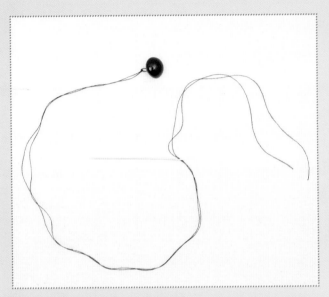

figure 9

figure 10

eye and stitch around to hold it, then attach the eye to the face. A loop-shank eye can also be backed by a small tuft of fur. Cut a shape from fur fabric and cut a small hole in it. Insert the loop shank of the eye, then attach the eye to the face. See figure 8 for examples of looped shank eyes.

To insert looped-shank eyes, cut a long length of extra-strong thread or, ideally, waxed upholstery thread. Thread both ends through the eye of a 5-inch (12.7 cm) doll needle. Thread the tip of the needle through the looped shank of an eye and then through the loop end of the thread. Pull the eye down to form a slipknot around the wire shank (figure 9).

Use an awl or the closed tip of a small pair of scissors to make a hole where the eye should be (for more about eye placement, see Making Your Own Set of Trial Eyes on page 134), moving the awl back and forth to spread the fibers and create a large enough hole to accommodate the shank. Pull the awl out and put the needle into the hole, coming out at the center back of the head. (If the back of the head is not a convenient spot for securing the thread ends, pick another area on the body that will be inconspicuous.) Pull the thread taut to sink the

shank into the hole, then take the needle off (leaving the thread end long). Repeat for the other eye, bringing the needle out at the back of the head right next to the thread ends from the first eye. Pull both sets of thread ends very taut, then knot them together three times to secure (figure 10). Rethread the needle with the knotted thread ends and insert it back into the head at the knot, coming out a few inches away. Trim the thread ends very close to the head to sink them into the body.

LION

This Lion is on the prowl, walking through the forest stalking his prey, and the design demonstrates how to make a softie in motion. When a lion is midstride, the front and back leg on one side are forward while those on the other side are behind. To translate this into a softie pattern, the left side body and underbody pattern pieces need to be different from the right side. Drawing both a left-hand set and a right-hand set is not much more work, and the resulting animal can be very expressive. Adding pointed, alert ears and an upright, curled tail helps create a feeling of movement.

Steps

1. Photocopy the pattern pieces (page 174) and cut them out. Piece together the Right and Left Side Body pieces with a bit of tape. Trace separate pattern pieces for both the Right and the Left Underbodies. Use a glue stick to adhere the pattern pieces to cardboard and cut them out.

2. On the wrong side of the yellow fur use a permanent marker to draw arrows indicating the direction of the nap (see figure 1 of lesson 20, page 81). Cut the pattern pieces on grain, following the nap direction indicated on the pattern pieces and adding a ¼-inch (6 mm) seam allowance. Using a permanent marker, a disappearing fabric marker, or chalk, trace and cut one Right Side Body and one Left Side Body on the wrong side of the yellow fur. Flip the pattern pieces for the underbodies over, then trace and cut one Right Underbody and one Left Underbody. It is really important to flip the underbody pattern pieces over before you trace and cut them because they need to be a mirror image of the side body they go with. Trace and cut four Footpads.

TOOLS & MATERIALS

Basic Sewing Tool Kit (page 11)

½ yard (45.7 cm) of yellow faux fur for the body

Scrap of brown linen for the nose and inner ears

Scrap of white faux fur for the muzzle

Scrap of white muslin for the back of the muzzle

All-purpose polyester thread in white

Extra-strong thread in white

Clear tape

Cardboard

Black permanent marker

Sewing machine needle appropriate for sewing faux fur (14/90 is recommended)

15 ounces (420 g) of fiberfill stuffing

Ball-point awl

5-inch (12.7 cm) doll needle

2 green cat eyes, 14 mm in diameter, with wire-loop backings

36-inch (91.4 cm) length of waxed upholstery thread

Many scraps of yarn in four different colors and/or textures for the mane

4-inch (10.2 cm) curved upholstery needle

3. On the right underbody piece, fold the legs upward along the fold line, as marked, and stitch the oval darts. Repeat for the left underbody piece (figure 1). Place the underbodies right sides together and stitch along the top from point C to point D, leaving the opening as marked.

4. Place the right underbody against the right side body piece, right sides together and matching up the legs, and pin in place. Stitch from point D, down the back leg, stopping at the circle mark where the footpad will be attached. Begin again at the triangle mark on the other side of the back leg and continue to stitch up the space between the legs and down again to the front leg. Stop at the circle and start again at the triangle, leaving space as marked for attaching the footpad, and ending at point C. Repeat to attach the left underbody to the left side body.

5. Stitching on the footpads by machine can be fiddly (see lesson 17 for more on sewing footpads, page 73). If it's easier, stitch the footpads by hand using extra-strong thread and a small backstitch. Place all four footpads on your worktable with the triangle markings on each one facing in the same direction. Pin one footpad to the bottom of one leg, matching up the markings, and stitch

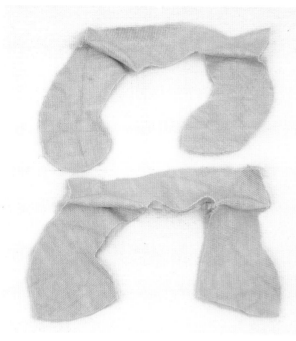

figure 1

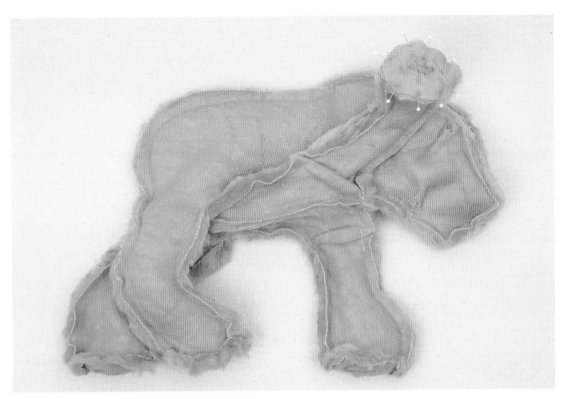

figure 2

halfway around from the triangle to the circle. Start again at the triangle and stitch around the other side of the footpad to the circle. Repeat for the other three footpads (figure 2).

6. Sew the two darts on the side body pieces. Pin the head gusset to one side body, right sides together, from point A to point B, and stitch. Repeat, stitching the head gusset to the other side body piece.

7. Finish stitching the remainder of the body from point A to point C and from point B to point D.

8. Clip the curves and turn the Lion right side out. Stuff firmly. Close the opening with extra-strong thread using a ladder stitch.

9. Trace the Ear pattern piece twice onto freezer paper, once as is and once reversed, and cut out. Iron the Ear pattern pieces onto the scrap of brown linen and pin it to a scrap of yellow fur, right sides together, making sure the nap of the fur is going downward. Stitch around the ears with the pattern pieces still adhered, leaving the bottoms open (figure 3). Pull the pattern pieces off. Trim around the ears to ⅛ inch (3 mm) from the stitching.

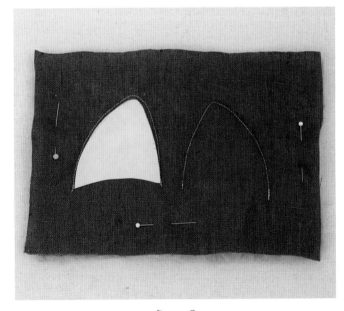

figure 3

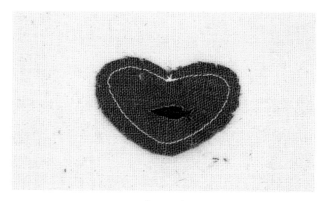

figure 4

figure 5

10. Clip the curves and turn the ears right side out. Use an awl to free the fur from the seams. Pin the ears to the Lion so that they are cupped (see lesson 26 on page 93) and ladder-stitch them in place with extra-strong thread. Remove the basting stitches.

11. Use a permanent marker to trace the Tail pattern onto yellow fur, add a ¼-inch (6 mm) seam allowance, and cut out. Flip the Tail pattern over. Trace and cut out a second tail piece. Pin the tail pieces right sides together and stitch, leaving an opening at the bottom as marked. Trim the seam allowance to ⅛ inch (3 mm). Clip the curves and use hemostats to turn th tail right side out and stuff it firmly. (For tips on turning and stuffing a long, skinny part, see lesson 39 on page 126.) Baste the raw edges of the tail under, then pin it to the Lion and ladder-stitch it in place with extra-strong thread. Remove the basting stitches.

12. Use a pencil to trace the Nose onto freezer paper and cut out the pattern piece. Iron the Nose pattern piece to a doubled piece of brown linen. Stitch directly around the Nose pattern piece, with no seam allowance, while it is still adhered to the fabric. Pull off the pattern

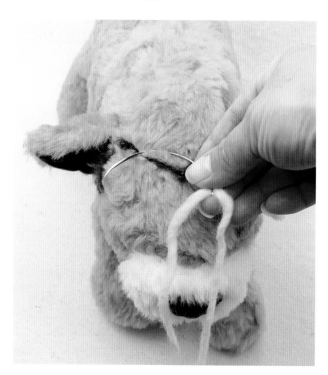

figure 6

figure 7

piece and cut out the sewn nose ⅛ inch (3 mm) from the stitching line. Clip the curves. Pinch one layer of the nose fabric and make a small snip in the center (figure 4). Pull the nose right side out through the snip. Use hemostats to lightly stuff the nose, then whipstitch the hole closed and set it aside.

13. Use a disappearing fabric marker to trace the Muzzle pattern piece onto the backing of the white fur scrap. Place the fur scrap on the white muslin scrap, right sides together, pin, and stitch around the muzzle outline. Trim the seam allowance to ⅛ inch (3 mm) and clip the curves. Pinch the muslin layer and make a small snip in the center (like you did for the nose in the previous step). Pull the muzzle right side out through the snip. Use an awl to free the fur from the seams.

14. Place the linen nose on top of the furry side of the muzzle. Ladder-stitch in place using white extra-strong thread (figure 5).

15. Pin the muzzle in place on the Lion. Ladder-stitch the edge of the white fur to the Lion's yellow fur body using white extra-strong thread.

16. Follow the instructions in lesson 23 on page 84 to attach the wire-loop eyes with a 36-inch (91.4 cm) strand of waxed upholstery thread. Outline the mane with yarn (see lesson 27 on page 94).

17. To make the first strand of the mane, thread a single length of yarn through the eye of the upholstery needle. Use a very long length of yarn; this way you can make many strands of the mane before you have to rethread the needle. Insert the needle into the Lion's head, coming out ⅛ inch (3 mm) away and creating a single straight stitch (figure 6). Leave a 3-inch (7.6 cm) tail and cut the yarn off 3 inches (7.6 cm) from the body. Tie the two yarn ends into a double knot (figure 7). Take a second stitch about ¼ inch (6 mm) from the first one and repeat the process of leaving a 3-inch (7.6 cm) tail, cutting the yarn 3 inches (7.6 cm) from the body, and tying a double knot. Continue taking small, straight stitches ¼ inch (6 mm) from one another and tying off the yarn until you have created a mane that covers the entire neck.

18. Use an awl to free the fur from all of the seams.

Lesson 24: Making an Animal in Motion

Once you've made a four-legged animal with a darted underbody (like the Elephant, page 50, or the Puppy, page 76), it is not difficult to design a pattern for a softie in motion. Start by sketching from photos of the animal moving, focusing on its leg position. The legs on the right- and left-hand sides of the animal will not be parallel because when an animal is in motion, one back leg and one front leg are forward while the other back leg and front leg are behind. On the profile drawing, differentiate the legs on the right side of the body from the legs on the left side by using a different-colored pencil (figure 1). The pattern for an animal in motion therefore needs to have two different side bodies and two different underbodies to reflect the asymmetry of the legs.

figure 2

To create side body pattern pieces from your drawing, use freezer paper to trace the profile including only the right legs. Draw a mirror image of the profile onto freezer paper including only the left legs (figure 2). Be sure to label the side bodies to differentiate between the right and the left.

Trace the bottom half of each side body to create the two underbodies. To mark the top of each underbody, draw a horizontal line across the body and one-third of the way up from the belly (see lesson 8 on page 54). Draw in the oval-shaped darts at the top of each leg (see lesson 9 on page 55). Be sure to label the underbodies to differentiate between the right and the left. Make the pattern piece for each underbody in reverse of its coordinating side body so that they can be sewn right sides together.

Start thinking of creative scenes to set with your moving animal softies. Predator animals stalking their prey, herds running across a prairie, show-jumping horses, and a dog chasing a ball are just a few ideas to get you started.

figure 1

Lesson 25: Turned Appliqué

Sometimes you may want to apply a different color to an animal's skin. If you are sewing a giraffe or a Dalmatian, for example, you may want to add spots or a contrasting muzzle, as I did when I designed this Lion. You could piece the spots to the fabric before cutting out the animal, but there are times when piecing is impractical: there may be so many spots that piecing would be very time-consuming, or you may want to see how the animal looks stuffed before you decide where the muzzle should be located.

In these situations it makes the most sense to appliqué the contrasting fabric to the animal. Turned-edge appliqué is certainly an option, but it can be a bit fussy and time-consuming. To me, the easiest and neatest way to create appliqué pieces for a softie is to sew them to a lightweight background, right sides together, and then turn them right side out and hand stitch them in place.

To create an appliqué piece, such as the nose and muzzle on this Lion, stitch the shape to a piece of muslin right sides together, or, if you are using very lightweight fabrics for your animal and a muslin backing for your appliqué would add too much bulk, sew it to lightweight interfacing instead. Do not leave an opening; just stitch

figure 3

all the way around. Trim the seam allowance to ⅛ inch (3 mm) and clip the curves. Then pinch the muslin layer and make a small snip using the tip of a sharp embroidery scissors (figure 3). Use your hemostats to turn the shape right side out through the snip, being careful not to stretch the snip too wide or tear the backing, especially if you are using interfacing. There is no need to close up the snipped opening neatly; just ladder-stitch the appliqué to the animal. The opening is in the backing and will be hidden.

Appliqué the muzzle to the face along the stitching line between the right and wrong sides of the appliqué. This way the appliqué's backing will be completely hidden! If you'd like to get a trapunto effect, which produces a puffy, raised surface, you can lightly stuff the appliqué before stitching it down, as I did with the Lion's nose.

Lesson 26: Cupped Ears

The ears on this Lion are ladder-stitched to the head after the body is stuffed. When I attach animal ears I always cup them so that the middle section is further back than the edges. Ears on real animals are cupped this way, and doing so gives your softie a more realistic touch (figure 4).

figure 4

Lesson 27:
Outlining the Mane

On an adult male lion there are areas on the head and neck that have long fur, but the fur on the face and forehead is very short and wiry. Before I applied the mane to the Lion, I marked an outline of the areas that would be covered in yarn. This way I knew where to start the mane and where to stop, and I could ensure that the mane would be neat and symmetrical. I trimmed the mane a bit shorter around the face and left longer strands of yarn toward the back of the head and around the neck.

To easily mark an outline for a mane, cut a length of yarn about one and half times the measurement of the head's circumference. Fold it in half to find its center and place it on the center of the forehead where you'd like the mane to begin. Place a pin there and wrap the yarn once around the pin before pushing the pin flush with the head. This will hold the yarn in place. Use the remaining yarn to outline where you'd like the mane to be, wrapping the yarn around pins to hold it in place. Move the pins around until you have the look you desire. Tie the yarn off under the neck. Cut a second length of yarn, 12 inches (30.5 cm) long, and use this to outline the back edge of the mane, tying the yarn off at the nape of the neck (figure 5).

Now you can begin applying the mane, confident in its placement. After you finish, pull off the outlining yarn.

figure 5

Mane Options

To make the mane for this Lion I chose four different wool yarns, each with a different color and texture. I like the interplay between these yarns, and I think using a variety adds depth and interest to the finished Lion. Create a different sort of yarn mane by wrapping yarn around a ruler or a length of cardboard. Slide the yarn off of the cardboard and machine-sew the loops down the center to a thin strip of fabric or bias tape. Then sew the rows of loops to the animal. Either keep the loops intact or cut them apart for a shaggier look. The yarn of a horse's mane could be braided and tied with ribbons.

There are many other creative methods for making a mane on a softie. Keep an open mind when looking through your stash! Unraveled braid, fringe, and other trims could be sewn in rows to make a mane. Tear quilting cotton into strips and wrap them around a ruler or length of cardboard, then slide them off and machine-

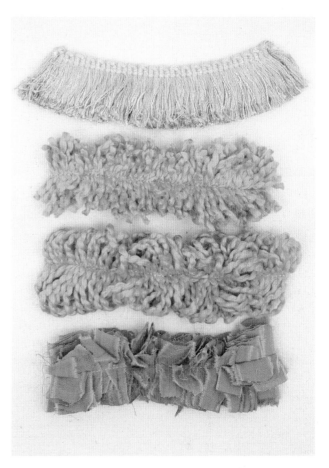

stitch them down the center. Stitch them down in rows to form a mane. Loops of ribbon or lace would also work. A very deep-piled faux fur or felted roving could be appliquéd to the Lion as a mane, as could strips of wool-blend felt that have been fringed along one edge. Almost any kind of textured fabric or trim could be a mane!

For this Cat pattern I wanted to create an animal that was sitting on its hind legs. This is an iconic pose for a cat, but the basic form of a seated animal could be used to create an obedient dog, an alert fox, or a watchful polar bear. In this pattern, imagine that the hind legs are tucked up under the hindquarters so that the back half of the body is all one piece. The front legs extend forward, supporting the body. When creating a seated animal, the profile of the back needs to be convincingly rendered. Study photos of the animal at rest to accurately capture its body contours.

Steps

1. Photocopy the pattern pieces (page 176) and cut them out. Using clear tape, attach the top half of the Side Body pattern piece to the bottom half. Cut the White Fur portion of the Tail pattern piece from the Brown Fur portion. Cut the White Fur portion of the Front Leg pattern piece from both the upper portion on the Side Body and on the Underbody Gusset pattern pieces. Glue the pattern pieces onto cardboard with a glue stick, and cut the out.

2. Before pinning and cutting the pattern pieces, mark the wrong side of the faux fur fabrics with an arrow, using a permanent marker, to indicate the nap direction (see figure 1 of lesson 20, page 81). Cut out all pattern pieces according to the arrows and on grain. Use a permanent marker, a disappearing fabric marker, or chalk to trace the Side Body pattern piece to the wrong side of the brown fur. Add a ¼-inch (6 mm) seam allowance and cut out the side body pattern. Turn the pattern piece over and trace and cut it again so that you have two side body pieces that are mirror images of each other.

3. Trace the lower White Fur portion of the Side Body pattern piece, which you cut apart in step 1, to the wrong side of a scrap of white fur. Add a ¼-inch (6 mm) seam allowance, and cut it out. Flip the pattern piece over and trace and cut it out again.

4. Stitch one white fur foot to one brown side body piece, right sides together (figure 1). Repeat for the other foot and body piece.

5. Trace the Underbody Gusset pattern piece to the wrong side of the brown fur. Add a ¼-inch (6 mm) seam allowance and cut it out. Turn the pattern piece over, trace, and cut it out again so that you have two mirror-image underbody gussets. Transfer the markings for the dart.

TOOLS & MATERIALS

Basic Sewing Tool Kit (page 11)

½ yard (45.7 cm) of brown deep-pile faux fur

Scrap of white faux fur

Scrap of pink fleece

Scrap of light pink felt for the nose pad

All-purpose polyester thread in white

Extra-strong thread in white and brown

Clear tape

Cardboard

Permanent marker

Sewing machine needle appropriate for sewing faux fur (14/90 is recommended)

12 ounces (336 g) of fiberfill stuffing

Ball-point awl

5-inch (12.7 cm) doll needle

2 cat eyes, 14 mm in diameter, with wire-loop backings

36-inch (91.4 cm) length of waxed upholstery thread

Embroidery needle

36-inch (91.4 cm) length of light pink embroidery floss

18-inch (45.7 cm) length of dark pink embroidery floss

¾ yard (68.6 cm) of dark brown ⅜-inch (1 cm) velvet ribbon

figure 1

figure 2

figure 3

figure 4

figure 5

figure 6

6. Trace the lower White Fur portion of the Underbody Gusset pattern piece, which you cut apart in step 1, to the wrong side of a scrap of white fur. Add a ¼-inch (6 mm) seam allowance, and cut it out. Flip the pattern piece over and trace and cut it out again.

7. Stitch one white fur foot to one brown underbody gusset piece, right sides together. Repeat for the other foot and underbody piece.

8. Fold the front leg on one underbody, right sides together, and stitch the narrow oval dart as marked (figure 2). Repeat for the other underbody piece.

9. Stitch the underbody gusset pieces together, right sides facing, along the outer edge from point C to point D (figure 3).

10. Trace the Head Gusset to the wrong side of the brown fur fabric. Add a ¼-inch (6 mm) seam allowance and cut it out. Pin the head gusset to one side body piece, right sides together, matching up points A and B, and stitch (figure 4). Repeat for the other side body piece so that the head gusset is joined to both body pieces.

11. Place one side of the underbody on top of one side body, right sides together, and stitch from point C, around the leg, and down to point D. Repeat, stitching the other side of the underbody to the other side body.

12. Pin and stitch the remainder of the Cat's body together from point A down to the bottom of the back, leaving an opening as indicated for turning and stuffing. Stitch from point C up to point B, leaving the bottom of the body open to insert the base (figure 5).

13. Trace the Base pattern piece onto the wrong side of the brown fur. Add a ¼-inch (6 mm) seam allowance and cut it out. Align the front of the base with the front of the Cat. Pin the base to the bottom of the Cat; some easing will be required. Stitch the base to the Cat (figure 6).

14. Clip the curves and turn the Cat right side out. Stuff firmly. Close the opening with a neat ladder stitch using brown extra-strong thread. Use an awl to gently pull the fur free from the seams (see page 133 for more on working with fur).

15. Trace the tip of the Tail pattern piece onto the wrong side of a scrap of white fur. Add a ¼-inch (6 mm) seam allowance and cut it out. Flip the pattern piece over and repeat so that you have two mirror-image tail tips. Trace the remainder of the Tail pattern onto the wrong side of the brown fur. Add a ¼-inch (6 mm) seam allowance and cut it out. Flip the pattern piece over and repeat so that you have two mirror-image tails. Pin one tail tip on top of one tail, right sides together, and stitch. Repeat for the other tail tip. Pin the two tail pieces together and stitch around the tail, leaving the bottom open for turning and stuffing. Clip the curves and turn the tail right side out. Stuff the tail firmly. Use an awl to free the fur from the seams. Fold the raw edges of the tail under and baste. Pin the tail to the Cat at the bottom of the back and stitch it in place using brown extra-strong thread and a neat ladder stitch. Remove the basting stitches.

16. Trace the Ear pattern piece onto the wrong side of a scrap of pink fleece. Place the fleece on top of a scrap of brown fur and pin the two layers together. Stitch around the Ear, leaving the bottom open for turning and stuffing. Trim the seam allowance to ⅛ inch (3 mm). Clip the curves and turn the ear right side out. Use an awl to free the fur from the seam. Turn the raw edges of the ear under and baste. Repeat to create a second ear. Pin the ears to the Cat's head cupping them slightly

(see lesson 42 on page 135 for more information on ear placement) and stitch in place using brown extra-strong thread and a neat ladder stitch. Remove the basting stitches.

17. Fold a scrap of white fur fabric in half, right sides together, and place the Muzzle pattern piece on the wrong side of the fur, aligning the edge of the pattern piece with the fold as marked. Trace around the pattern piece. Add a ¼-inch (6 mm) seam allowance and cut it out. Fold the muzzle, matching up point E with point E on each side. Stitch one side of the muzzle from point E to point F. Repeat on the other side (figure 7). Turn the muzzle right side out. Fold the raw edges of the muzzle inward ⅛ inch (3 mm) and baste. Lightly stuff the muzzle. Pin the muzzle to the Cat and stitch it on using white extra-strong thread and a neat ladder stitch. When there is about 1 inch (2.5 cm) of stitching left to do, pause to finish stuffing the muzzle by grasping small pieces of stuffing at a time with your hemostat and pushing it inside the muzzle until it is firmly stuffed. Finish stitching the muzzle to the Cat.

18. Follow the instructions in lesson 23 on page 84 to attach the wire-loop eyes with a 36-inch (91.4 cm) strand of waxed upholstery thread.

figure 7

19. Trace the Nose pattern piece onto a small scrap of light pink felt and cut it out directly around the pattern piece with no seam allowance. Trim the fur on the muzzle where the nose and mouth will be with embroidery scissors and use a dab of craft glue to affix the felt nose to the muzzle. Using an embroidery needle, satin-stitch the nose with light pink embroidery floss and create the mouth with dark pink embroidery floss. (For more information on embroidering the nose and mouth, see lesson 30 on page 102.)

20. Use an awl to free the fur from the seams. Tie a bow around the Cat's neck with a length of velvet ribbon. Whipstitch the bow in place if desired.

Lesson 28: Making a Sitting Animal

To create a seated animal with imagined hind legs, begin as you would with most softie patterns by drawing a sketch of the animal in profile. Pay special attention to the curve of the animal's back, neck, and chest to get an accurate drawing. Soften any sharp angles that could protrude awkwardly when stuffed, and widen the legs and feet to account for the stuffing.

I made a flat face for this Cat because I wanted to create a separate muzzle from white fur to be stitched on after the Cat was stuffed. To do this, I drew the front of

the head as a simple rounded shape and made a simple, pointed oval head gusset. The muzzle will give the Cat's face its distinctive shape.

The underbody gusset for a seated animal is similar to that of a standing animal (see lesson 8 on page 54). Draw a line from the neck to the middle of the bottom of the hindquarters. Create a narrow oval dart at the top of the front leg where it meets the body. This will pull the legs inward, allowing the weight of the Cat's forequarters to rest on the front legs.

At the bottom of the hindquarters is an oval-shaped base made from fur (figure 1). The length of the base equals the length of the bottom of the side body pattern piece. I generally wait to draw this pattern piece until after I've sewn the side body completely. Then

I open out the bottom of the side body and sketch around it onto a piece of freezer paper. This way I know I am getting an accurate width for the base.

The chest and underbody of a sitting animal are very exposed. Instead of leaving the opening in the center of the underbody where it would be obvious, locate the opening at the bottom back of the side bodies, where it will be hidden once the tail is attached.

If the space between the front legs and the hindquarters is very narrow in your original profile drawing, exaggerate it when you draw your side body pattern pieces to give you more room for a seam allowance and for stitching (figure 2).

figure 1

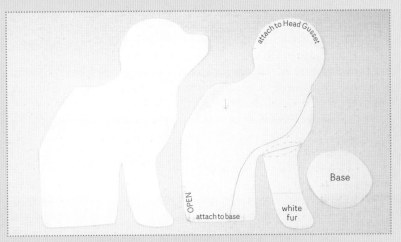

figure 2

Lesson 29: Muzzles, Snouts, and Beaks

Drafting the pattern pieces for a muzzle forces you to think about how to create a small, three-dimensional, stuffed shape. It takes experimentation, and there is some trial and error involved. The best way to learn to create a muzzle is to play with the curves and shapes of the pattern pieces. Get out a fresh sheet of freezer paper and a piece of muslin and start drawing and cutting, sewing and stuffing. Experimentation is a great way to learn, and you just might create a great muzzle that suggests an animal for you to make!

Begin by sketching the profile of the muzzle you'd like to create. For a jowly look, like the muzzle of an adult male animal, curve the bottom of the muzzle profile downward. For a pointed muzzle, like for a mole, draw the bottom of the muzzle pointed upward at a sharp angle.

Consider where you would like to add breadth to the muzzle, if at all. For a thin, pointy muzzle, simply add a seam allowance and cut the two profile pieces from muslin, then sew around them, leaving the back open for turning and stuffing. For a wider muzzle, add a gusset. The gusset can be added to the top edges of the profile pieces, making the muzzle wide at the nose, or to the bottom edges of the profile pieces, making the muzzle wider at the chin. To create a softer transition at the nose, fold the muslin in half and cut the muzzle profile with the tip of the nose on the fold; when you sew the muzzle together there won't be a seam at the nose, and it will have a softer curve when it is stuffed. For an even smoother muzzle, include the gusset in the profile pattern piece, as I have done on the Cat. This eliminates any points in the center of the muzzle.

Sew a muzzle prototype, turn it, and stuff it, then pin it to the animal's face. Do you have the profile drawn right? Could there be more or less breadth on top at the nose—or below at the chin? Should the muzzle be shorter or longer overall?

Instead of a muzzle you may need to make a beak, a snout, or some other kind of nose to ladder-stitch to the animal after it is turned and stuffed. See figure 3 for examples of muzzle snout, and beak types and their corresponding pattern pieces.

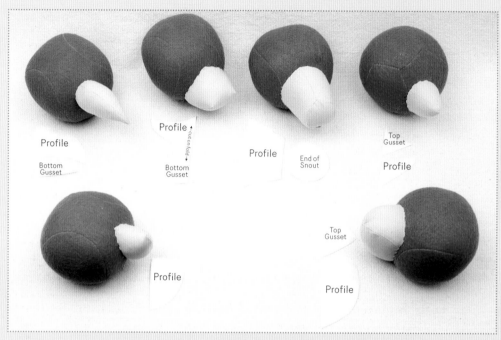

Profile

Bottom Gusset

Profile

cut on fold

Bottom Gusset

Profile

End of Snout

Top Gusset

Profile

Profile

Top Gusset

Profile

figure 3

Lesson 30: Making a Satin-Stitched Nose with a Felt Pad Underlay and a Smiling Mouth

serves as a guide so that you can create neat, even stitches; it also adds a bit of bulk to the nose, helping it stand out from the muzzle.

Trim away the fur from the muzzle where the nose and mouth will be so that the embroidered stitches don't get lost in the fur (see lesson 41 on page 133 for more information on fur). I like to embroider the nose first and then the mouth so that I can position the mouth exactly underneath the nose and judge how long I want to make the line coming down from the nose to the smile.

Use a dab of craft glue to affix the nose pad to the muzzle where you'd like the nose to be. Thread an embroidery needle with three strands of embroidery floss about 18 inches (45.7 cm) long, or with a single 18-inch (45.7 cm) strand of perle cotton, and knot

An easy way to create a neat, satin-stitched nose is to begin with a felt pad of the same color as the nose you'd like to create, but slightly smaller. You won't embroider directly on the felt pad, but over it. The pad

figure 4

figure 5

figure 6

the end. Insert the needle under the felt pad, coming up at the top center of the nose. Insert the needle back down through the bottom center of the nose, coming up just to the right of the top center. Go back down through the bottom center (you enter through the bottom center each time), coming up just to the left of the top center and back down. With the next stitch, come up just to the right of the top center, then go back down and up again just to the left of the top center (figure 4). Keep going, first left and then right, until the entire nose is covered in satin stitch. To finish, take a few invisible stitches under the nose, bringing the needle out through the muzzle. Then cut the thread ends close to the nose so that they get buried inside the muzzle.

To make the mouth, thread an embroidery needle with four strands of embroidery floss 18 inches (45.7 cm) long and knot the end. Insert the needle under the muzzle and come out at the bottom center of the nose, pulling the knot so that it gets buried inside the muzzle. Insert the needle back down where you would like the left side of the smile to end (figure 5). Come back out

where you would like the right side of the smile to end. Before pulling the thread taut, slide your needle under the looped thread (figure 6). Gently pull the thread more taut, and while you do so, you can play with how deep or shallow you would like the sides of the smile to be. Once you have a satisfactory smile, insert the needle into the base of the smile to tack it in place. Then take a stitch or two under the nose and cut the thread ends close to the nose so that they get buried inside the muzzle (figure 7).

figure 7

Adapting a Pattern to Make a Different Animal

When you sit down to draft a pattern for a new animal, don't feel like you need to start from scratch. To adapt an existing pattern, begin by lightly tracing the side body pattern piece onto a fresh sheet of freezer paper. Using the photos and illustrations you have gathered as part of your visual research, begin to sketch a new outline on top of it. Erase the old lines as needed. Sometimes just a few small tweaks can turn a cat into a dog, a horse into a llama, or a fish into a dolphin. Having somewhere to begin helps make the pattern-drafting process less daunting.

CAMEL

I love jointed toys because they can move, which sparks the imagination. A jointed toy invites you to pick it up and play with it, to move it and make it walk. This Camel might want to trek through an arid desert in search of an oasis or lie down on the cool sand in the evening for a rest. Simple joints can be made with thread if you are creating a small toy, or with thread and buttons for a larger toy where the joints need to withstand more weight, like this Camel.

Steps

1. Trace the pattern pieces (page 178) onto freezer paper with a pencil. Cut them out, transferring all of the markings.

2. Fold the light brown felted wool in half with right sides together. Follow the grain direction indicated on all of the pattern pieces when cutting. Iron the Front and Back Leg pattern pieces to the doubled wool. Use a few pins to hold the two layers of wool together. Add a ¼-inch (6 mm) seam allowance and cut out the front and back legs. Use a disappearing fabric marker to transfer the markings to the fabric. Repeat so that you have two sets of front legs and two sets of back legs cut out. Use the same method to cut out the Face, Body, and two sets of Hoofs. Set them aside for now.

3. Pin the dart on the foot of one front leg piece and stitch (figure 1). Repeat for the other front leg piece, creating a mirror image. Pin those two front leg pieces right sides together and stitch around, leaving an opening at the bottom for attaching the hoof and at the top for turning and stuffing (figure 2). Repeat for the second front leg. Sew the darts for both back legs and stitch around in the same manner.

4. Align point E on one hoof with point E on the base of one leg. Stitch from point E to point F1 on the hoof (figure 3). Beginning at point E again, stitch from point E to point F2 on the hoof (figure 4). Stitch the rest of the hoof to the base of the leg. Some easing is required, so go slowly! Repeat for the other three legs.

Basic Sewing Tool Kit (page 11)

1/2 yard (45.7 cm) of light brown felted wool (I used a felted wool scarf)

1/4 yard (23 cm) of dark brown sherpa fleece

Scrap of black wool-blend felt

All-purpose polyester sewing thread in dark brown

Extra-strong thread in white and dark brown

Sewing machine needle appropriate for sewing wool and fleece (14/90)

12 ounces (336 g) of fiberfill stuffing

4 half-ball cover buttons, size 45 (1 1/8 inches [2.8 cm]), or other large-shank buttons

Waxed upholstery thread for the joints

5-inch (12.7 cm) doll needle

1 white felted-wool ball, 10 mm in diameter

Hole punch

18-inch (45.7 cm) lengths of perle cotton in white and black

figure 1

figure 2

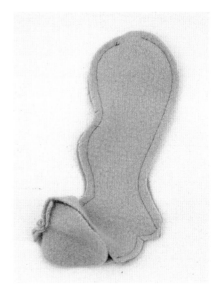

figure 3

5. Seam together a 3 x 8-inch (7.6 x 20.3 cm) piece of light brown felted wool with a 2 x 8-inch (5 x 20.3 cm) piece of dark brown sherpa fleece. Fold this in half along the 8-inch (20.3 cm) length, right sides together, aligning the seam between the light and dark brown fabrics. Iron the Tail pattern on top, aligning the line between the Tail and the Tail Tip with the seam. Use a few pins to hold the two layers together. Stitch directly around the freezer paper, leaving the bottom open. Trim to within ⅛ inch (3 mm) of the stitching line. Use hemostats to turn the tail right side out. Turn the raw edges under and baste.

6. Place a scrap of dark brown fleece on top of a scrap of light brown wool, right sides together. Iron the Ear pattern piece on top. Use a few pins to hold the two layers together. Stitch directly around the freezer paper (figure 5). Trim to within ⅛ inch (3 mm) of the stitching line. Use hemostats to turn the ear right side out. Turn the raw edges under by ⅛ inch (3 mm) and baste. Repeat for the second ear. Set both aside.

7. Fold the dark brown fleece in half, right sides together. Iron the Hump pattern piece to the double layer of fleece. Use a few pins to hold the layers together. Add a ¼-inch (6 mm) seam allowance and cut

out the hump pieces. Use the same method to cut out the Neck. Set aside.

8. Place one hump piece on top of one body piece, right sides together, aligning points C and D. Stitch from point C to point D (figure 6). Repeat for the other hump and body pieces.

9. Iron the Hump Gusset pattern piece and the Head Gusset pattern piece to the wrong side of a single layer of dark brown fleece. Add a ¼-inch (6 mm) seam allowance and cut out the hump and head gussets. Set the head gusset aside for now. To attach the hump gusset, align points C and D and stitch the hump gusset to one hump piece (figure 7). Repeat with the other hump piece so that the gusset is completely sewn.

10. Place one face piece against one neck piece, right sides together, aligning points G and H. Stitch from point G to point H (figure 8). Some easing is required, so go slowly! Repeat for the other face and neck pieces.

11. To sew the head gusset, place it right sides together on top of one face/neck piece, aligning points A and B. Stitch from point A to point B (figure 9). Repeat, attaching the head gusset to the other face/neck piece.

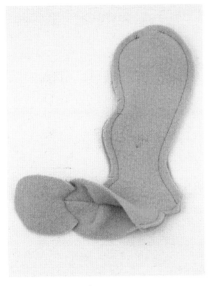

figure 4

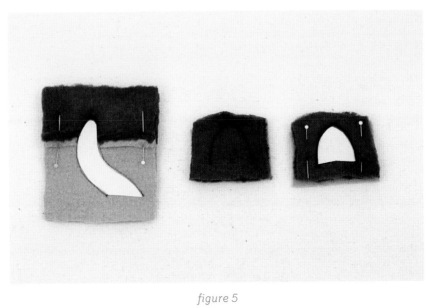

figure 5

figure 6

figure 7

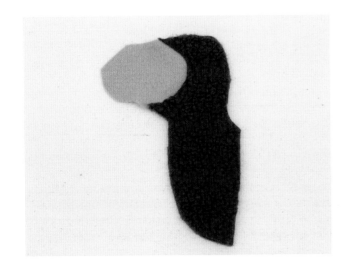

figure 8

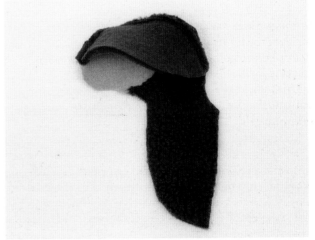

figure 9

16. Pin the tail where the base of the hump meets the body and stitch in place with a neat ladder stitch using extra-strong thread in dark brown. The tail points upwards and is not stuffed.

17. Stuff the feet firmly, pushing small wads of stuffing into each toe of the cleft hoof. Stuff the legs firmly, using less stuffing as you get to the top of the legs.

18. If you are using half-ball cover buttons, snap the button fronts to the button backs per the package directions. See lesson 33 on page 111 for instructions on preparing the legs and attaching them to the body with waxed upholstery thread, a 5-inch (12.7 cm) doll needle, and buttons.

19. Cut the felted-wool ball in half for the eyes. For pupils, punch out two circles from black felt with the hole punch. Use a dab of craft glue to attach each pupil to each wool ball half (or whipstitch the pupils in place with black thread). With white perle cotton, take two small, straights stitches coming up from the back of the wool ball, through the pupil, and back down again to create a highlight on each pupil.

20. Iron the Eyelid pattern to a piece of light brown wool and cut it out with no seam allowance. Repeat to create another eyelid. Glue lashes made from extra-strong brown thread to the back of each eyelid and let the glue dry completely, then trim (see Eyelashes on page 113). Pin each eyelid to the top of each eye. To attach the eyes to the Camel, ladder-stitch the base of each eye and lid to the Camel's face with extra-strong thread.

12. Place one neck/face piece on top of one body piece, right sides together, aligning points I and J. Stitch from point I to point J. Repeat, attaching the other neck/face piece to the other body piece.

13. Stitch around the remainder of the Camel's body from point B to point C, and from point D to point A, aligning the seams between the two colors of fabric as you go, and leaving an opening as marked for turning and stuffing.

14. Clip the curves on the Camel's body and on all four legs. Turn the body and the legs right side out. Stuff the body firmly and close the opening with a neat ladder stitch using extra-strong thread in dark brown.

15. Pin the ears to the side of the head and stitch in place with a neat ladder stitch using extra-strong thread in dark brown.

21. To make the mouth, thread the 5-inch (12.7 cm) doll needle with a single 18-inch (45.7 cm) strand of black perle cotton, tying a knot at the end. Insert the needle behind the ear and come out at the tip of the head gusset where it meets the face, pulling the knot so that it is buried in the stuffing. Insert the needle where you would like the right side of the smile to end, coming out where you would like the left side of the smile to end. Before pulling the thread taut, slide your needle under the looped thread. Gently pull the thread more taut as you form the smile, then insert the needle into the base of the smile to tack it in place. Bring the needle back out behind one ear. Take a small stitch, forming a knot by catching the loop of the thread through the needle before pulling it taut. Insert the needle back down where it came out, and exit a few inches away. Pull the thread taut and cut it off, burying the thread ends inside the Camel's body.

Lesson 31: How to Design a Jointed Animal

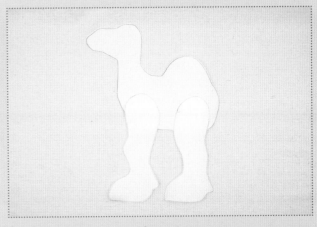

figure 1

Designing a jointed four-legged animal is easier than designing a stable one because you don't need to worry about getting the underbody shaped just right. Instead, the body and the limbs are sewn separately and then attached with one of several jointing methods.

Begin with a sketch on freezer paper of the animal in profile. Where the legs meet the body you'll need to extend them upward, creating an upper thigh and a top for each leg. Fill in the line of the body to extend underneath where each leg will rest. Place a piece of freezer paper on top of your sketch, and then trace the front and back legs and cut them out. Cut out the body from your original sketch. These three pieces make up your basic pattern: a body shape, a front leg, and a back leg (figure 1).

Lesson 32: Thread Joints and Exposed Button Joints

One of the first jointing techniques used on teddy bears in the early 1900s was the thread joint: thread is passed through the body and limbs of the animal and then pulled taut and tied off. Thread joints are most appropriate for a very small toy or a toy that will not be handled much. Over time, thread joints become stressed and snap or tear through the fabric if the toy is heavy or played with a lot. Adding a button on the outside of the limb increases the strength of the joint. (For more complex and stronger jointing methods see the Teddy Bear on page 128.)

When creating a thread or button joint, use an extra-strong thread, such as upholstery thread or button twist, which can withstand being twisted, turned, and pulled very hard. I especially like waxed upholstery thread for making joints because it is extremely strong, and when you pull it tightly, the wax helps it stay taut. Use a long doll needle that can extend through the animal's body from one side to the other. If your needle is too short you run the risk of losing it inside the stuffing when you are attempting to attach the limbs! You'll also need 2 hole, 4 hole, or shank buttons (figure 2).

Before jointing with any method, sew, turn, and stuff the body and each limb separately, then close the openings with a neat ladder stitch.

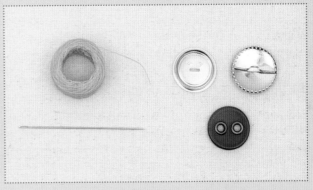

figure 2

To create the joint for one set of legs, thread a doll nee-dle with a doubled strand of extra-strong or waxed up-holstery thread. Make sure the strands are very long, at least four times longer than the width of the toy's body. Do not tie a knot at the end of the thread!

Insert the needle into the body right where the leg will be attached, cross through the body, and come out on the other side, exactly opposite where you entered (figure 3). Leave a 6-inch (15.2 cm) thread tail. Go through one leg from the inside to the outside. Now you want to go back through the same hole you came out of

on the outside of the leg. To make sure you are entering the same exact hole on the outside of the leg, separate the two threads a bit and pass the needle between them (figure 4). When you go through the inside of the leg, go through an inch or so away from where you came up. Take the needle through the body, coming out on the opposite side (figure 5). Go through the second leg from the inside to the outside, then reenter the leg through the same hole you came out of and bring the needle out on the inside of the leg (figure 6). Cut the needle off and pull both sets of threads tight, squeezing the body as you pull and wrapping the thread around

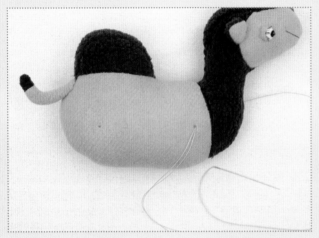

figure 3

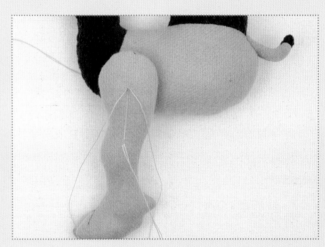

figure 4

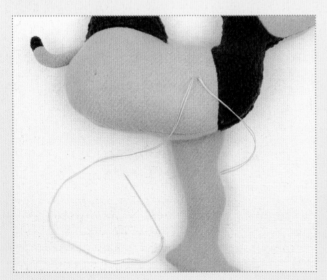

figure 5

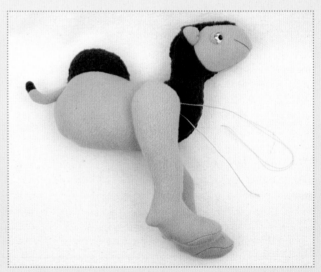

figure 6

figure 7

your fingers to get leverage. Check that the legs are in the desired position. Tie the threads together twice under the leg to form a secure knot. Rethread the needle with the thread tails and pass them under the leg, coming out a little ways away. Pull the thread ends taut and cut them off so that they are buried inside the body.

To strengthen the joint and add a decorative touch to your toy, attach a button to the outside of each leg. Pass the thread through the button when your needle comes out on the outside of each leg. The button adds some strength to the joint, allowing you to pull the legs tighter against the body (figure 7). Alternatively, use elastic thread to give the thread joints some added give.

Lesson 33: Invisible Button Joints

If you'd like a joint that is stronger than a simple thread joint but does not have an exposed button, create an invisible button joint. This technique was originally developed by doll maker Judi Ward and is being shared here with her permission. It is especially useful if you are going to give the toy to a young child who may be somewhat rough with the toy, but could choke on the buttons.

Any kind of large shank buttons will work for this jointing method, and they don't all have to match, but they should be equal in size. I like the shank buttons used to make fabric-covered buttons, called "half-ball cover buttons," because they are large, lightweight, and sturdy. Snap the backing to the button according to package directions (with no fabric covering the button), and they are ready to use.

Stuff the legs, leaving the area at the top unstuffed. Insert the button into the top of each leg with the loop of the shank toward the inner thigh. Center the button so that it is positioned where you would like the leg to be attached to the body of the animal. The shank remains under the fabric. Use a safety pin to temporarily hold the loop of the shank in place from the outside (figure 8). Finish stuffing the leg and close the top of the leg with a neat ladder stitch. Repeat for the other legs.

Thread a doll needle with a double strand of extra-strong thread or waxed upholstery thread. Make sure the thread is very long, at least four times the width of the animal.

Insert the needle through the shank of one button. Cut the thread off the needle and even up the four ends of the thread. Thread all four ends through the eye of the doll needle and insert the needle through the body where you want the leg to be attached, coming out exactly opposite on the other side of the body.

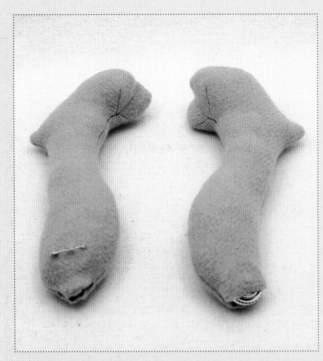

figure 8

Take two threads off the needle. Pass the needle with the two remaining threads through the shank of the second leg (figure 9).

Take those two threads off the needle and rethread it with the other two threads. Pass the needle through the shank again, this time in the opposite direction. Take the thread off the needle (figure 10).

Pull both sets of threads to tighten the joint. You will need to squish the body as you pull, wrapping the thread around your fingers to get leverage. Keep pulling until you have a tight joint. The joint will naturally loosen a bit over time, so make it tight now!

To finish, wrap two threads around the joint in one direction, and the other two threads around the joint in the other direction. Tie the threads together in a knot, then tie again to create a tight double knot. Hide the thread ends by rethreading the needle with all four threads and inserting it back into the body right under the joint. Come out a little ways away, pull the thread taut, and cut it off, burying the thread ends in the stuffing.

figure 9

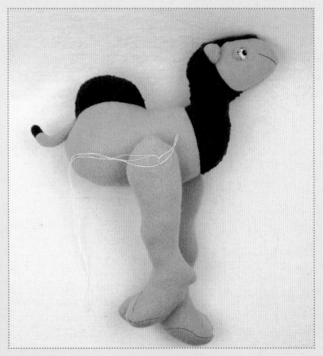

figure 10

Lesson 34: Cleft Hoofs

The cleft hoof is a detail that adds a realistic note to this Camel. To draft a pattern for a cleft hoof, draw the front leg and foot as usual. Then draw an extension to the foot at the toe and cut out a triangular dart on the top of the extension (figure 11). The triangular dart creates a protrusion at the end of the foot that becomes one convex side of the hoof. Repeat for the back leg. Together you will have the two protruding parts of the hoof.

To make the inward-pointing middle part of the hoof, draw a triangular cutout on the hoof pattern piece. The deeper and wider the triangle cut out of the hoof, the more accentuated the inward part of the toe will become (figure 12).

Although it can be fiddly to sew darts on toes and to line up triangular hoof cutouts, a cloven hoof is a neat detail to master and can be used to create a more realistic foot on many different animal designs besides the Camel, including pigs, deer, cows, goats, and sheep.

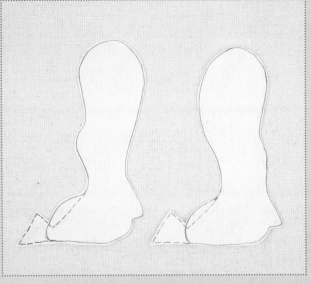

figure 11

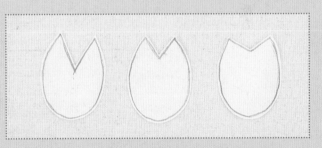

figure 12

Eyelashes

Eyelashes add a charming detail to a softie's face. Some animals, like camels, giraffes, and horses, are known for their eyelashes. An easy way to create eyelashes is to wrap thread or several strands of embroidery floss around your finger about a dozen times. Trim through the loops to create a dozen short, equal lengths of thread. Cover the back of the eyelid with a thin coating of craft glue, then lay the thread on top, extending over both sides of the eyelid. Allow the glue to dry completely, then trim the threads flush with the top portion of the eyelid, leaving them to extend only on the outer portion as lashes. You can trim the lashes, making them shorter or more even as needed, then sew or glue the eyelid to the eye.

MONSTER

Although a plush Monster is not technically a stuffed animal, I couldn't resist including these mythic beasts. Children are at once frightened and fascinated by monsters, and they are fantastic subjects for softie making. I used reverse appliqué to make the eye shapes on this Monster and raw-edge appliqué to attach his hair. These are great techniques to have in your repertoire and use on your own softie designs. And when I just want to let go and have fun with fabrics and color, I make a Monster!

Steps

1. Trace the pattern pieces (page 179) with pencil onto freezer paper and cut them out. Cut out the eyeholes on the Face. Turn the purple faux fur over to the wrong side and use a permanent marker to draw an arrow indicating the direction of the nap (see lesson 20 on page 81 for more on nap).

2. Unless otherwise indicated, add a ¼-inch (6 mm) seam allowance to all of the pattern pieces when you cut them out. For the Monster's face, pin the Face pattern piece to the purple fleece following the direction of the grain as indicated on the pattern piece and cut out. Trace the eyeholes with a disappearing fabric marker or chalk and cut them out with sharp embroidery scissors; do not add a seam allowance to the eyeholes (figure 1). Pin the Hair and Back of Head pattern pieces to the purple faux fur and cut them out; you do not need to add a seam allowance to the hair. Transfer the markings for the ears onto both the face and the back of the head.

3. Cut a 6 x 3-inch (15.2 x 7.6 cm) strip of white felt and lay it across the back of the purple fleece face behind the eyes. Pin in place from the front. From the front, stitch the two together around each eye, ⅛ inch (3 mm) from the cutout. On the wrong side, trim the felt to ⅛ inch (3 mm) from the outer stitching lines of the eyes, keeping the felt in one piece (figure 2).

4. Place the purple faux fur hair right side up on top of the face, lining up the outside edges, and pin it in place. Stitch the hair to the face, ⅛ inch (3 mm) from the edge of the hair from point A to the center of the forehead and then to point B. Use an awl to free the fur from the stitching line.

Basic Sewing Tool Kit (page 11)

Scrap of purple faux fur for the hair and ears

Scrap of purple fleece for the face

Scraps of wool-blend felt in white and black for the eyes, teeth, and pupils

Scrap of wool plaid for the body and legs

Scrap of pink quilting cotton for the mouth

Scrap of brownish printed quilting cotton for the inner ears

Scrap of patterned quilting cotton for the arms

All-purpose polyester thread in white

Extra-strong thread in white

Permanent marker

Sewing machine needle appropriate for sewing faux fur (14/90 is recommended)

Ball-point awl

10 ounces (280 g) of fiberfill stuffing or plastic pellets (see Using Heavier Stuffing on page 119)

Funnel (optional)

Hole punch

figure 1

figure 2

figure 3

5. Fold the wool plaid in half, right sides together. Iron the Body pattern piece on top of the doubled plaid and use a few pins to hold the two layers together. Add a ¼- inch (6 mm) seam allowance and cut out the body pieces. Use chalk to transfer the markings for the legs, the arms, and the opening to the wrong side of both pieces.

6. Fold the pink quilting cotton in half. Iron the Mouth pattern piece on the fold. Add a ¼-inch (6 mm) seam allowance and cut it out. Pull off the pattern piece. Iron the Teeth pattern piece to a scrap of white felt; do not add a seam allowance. Cut out the teeth. Pull off the pattern piece.

7. For the ears, place a scrap of purple faux fur on the brownish printed quilting cotton, right sides together. Trace the Ear pattern onto the back of the fur. Use a few pins to hold the two layers together, and then stitch around the traced ear, leaving the straight side open as marked for turning. Flip the Ear pattern over and repeat to create a second ear that is a mirror image of the first. Trim both to within ⅛ inch (3 mm) of the stitching line, clip the curves, and turn the ears right side out. Use an awl or doll needle to free the fur from the seams.

8. To assemble the front of the body, place the ears on the face where marked, with the brownish print fabric face down on top of the purple fleece, aligning the raw edges of the ears with the edge of the face. Baste the ears in place. Next, make a fabric sandwich. First, lay one body piece right side up on your worktable. Place the teeth along the top, lining up points C and D. Then place the mouth on top, lining up points C and D so that the raw edges are aligned with the top of the teeth and the top of the body. Finally, place the face on top, right sides together with the body, lining up points C and D. Pin the layers together very well

figure 4

figure 5

or baste them. Stitch from point C to point D (figure 3). Press the mouth and teeth downward so that they overlap the top of the wool plaid body and baste them in this position (figure 4).

9. To assemble the back of the body, place the back of the head on top of the other body piece, right sides together, lining up points C and D. Stitch from point C to point D.

10. Fold the patterned quilting cotton in half, right sides together. Iron the Arm pattern piece on top of the doubled fabric. Stitch around the Arm pattern piece, leaving the top open as indicated for turning and stuffing, then pull the pattern piece off and trim to within ¼ inch (6 mm) of the stitching line. Repeat to create a second arm. Clip the curves and turn the arms right side out. Stuff the hands firmly, leaving the top part of the arms unstuffed. Alternatively, use a funnel to fill the ends of the hands with pellets, then fill the remainder of the hands with stuffing but leave the arms unstuffed.

11. Fold a piece of wool plaid in half, right sides together. Iron the Leg pattern piece on top of the doubled fabric. Stitch around the Leg pattern piece, leaving the top of the leg open as indicated for turning and stuffing, then pull the pattern piece off and trim to within ¼ inch (6 mm) of the stitching line. Repeat to create a second leg. Clip the curves and turn the legs right side out.

Stuff the feet firmly, leaving the top parts of the legs unstuffed, or partially fill the feet with pellets like the arms.

12. Place the arms, legs, and ears on top of the front of the body as indicated on the Body pattern, lining up their raw edges with the edges of the body. Note that the feet point outward, the hands point inward, and the cotton side of the ears is face down. Baste across the edges of the legs and arms (figure 5).

13. Place the back of the body on top of the front of the body, right sides together, and pin together, placing a pin every ⅛ inch (3 mm) around to hold all of the parts of the Monster together. Stitch around the outline of the Monster's body, beginning and ending between the legs as indicated on the pattern piece.

14. Remove all of the basting stitches. Clip the curves and carefully turn the Monster right side out through the opening between the legs by pulling the limbs out first and then the head and the rest of the body.

15. Stuff the Monster firmly and close the opening with a neat ladder stitch using extra-strong thread.

16. Use the hole punch to punch two circles from black felt. Attach the circles to the Monster's eyes with a dab of craft glue (or whipstitch them in place with black thread). Use an awl to free the fur from the seams.

Lesson 35: Putting in a Growler, Music Box, or Music Button

A Monster toy excites the imagination. It is a fantasy creature made from fabrics that are bright and colorful in a variety of textures and patterns. A noisemaker can add another layer of sensory interaction. When selecting a noisemaker you can choose from a growler, a music box, or a music button. (For other ideas, see Making a Baby Toy with a Bell and Crinkle on page 41.)

A growler is a small canister containing a noisemaker (figure 1). When the growler is upturned, it growls! Growlers are traditionally used in teddy bear making but could be inserted in any softie during stuffing. To keep the growler from migrating around the softie's body, and to keep the growler's noise from being muffled by stuffing that may get into the holes, put the growler inside a piece of nylon stocking. Knot each end of the stocking. Attach the nylon to the softie with a few hand stitches after the body has been turned right side out.

A music button is a disk that plays a song when pressed. If you are inserting a music button in the hand, or other relatively small part, you may need to leave an extra opening that will accommodate the size of the button. Keep in mind that the music button needs to be placed right up against the "skin" of the softie—in the palm of the hand, in a foot, or under a belly button, for example—so that it can be depressed easily (figure 2). You can cushion the back and sides of the button with stuffing, leaving the front pressed up against the skin. If you want to anchor the button, put it in a piece of nylon stocking using the same method as anchoring the growler.

A music box with a windup key is a classic addition to a toy. The key extends through a seam, allowing the music box to be wound. To insert a music box, sew the body, leaving a small opening along a seam. Turn the body right side out. Place the music box in a piece of nylon stocking knotted on each end and insert the music box, pushing the key out through the small opening. Make sure the raw edges of the opening are turned under. Anchor the stocking with a few stitches to keep the music box from rotating when you turn the key. Stuff the body as usual, taking extra care to stuff all the way around the music box so that it is sufficiently padded and cannot be felt from the outside. Ladder-stitch the opening around the key closed using extra-strong thread in a color that matches the softie's body.

Music boxes, music buttons, and growlers can all be found through teddy bear–making supply sites.

figure 1

figure 2

Making a Muslin Lining When Working with Tricky Fabrics

Fabrics that are very thin, fray easily, or stretch in both directions can prove frustrating for a softie project because toys have to be handled quite a bit while they are being made, and the fabrics are then stressed when the toy is stuffed. If you have your heart set on using such a fabric, sew in a muslin lining to add strength and reduce stretch. To make a lining, cut out each pattern piece twice—once in your chosen fabric and again in muslin. Layer the muslin pieces under each piece, wrong sides facing, and sew the toy together as usual. When you turn the toy right side out, the muslin lining will be hidden inside.

Lesson 36: Using Heavier Stuffing

Sometimes you may want parts—or all of your toy—to be filled with something heavier than soft stuffing. Perhaps you want the limbs to flop or the body to have a weightier heft. I don't recommend using rice or lentils to stuff toys because, if the toy ever comes into contact with water, those stuffing materials will soften and may mold and ruin the toy. Instead, use pellets as filling or a combination of pellets and stuffing. Sometimes called "beads," pellets are tiny, rounded disks made from plastic, ceramic, or glass (figures 3 and 4). They are available by the pound through doll- and teddy bear–making supply companies in either 2 mm, 1.5 mm, or smaller than 1 mm sizes, and they come in clear, white, black, and gray.

When you are ready to fill a softie part with pellets, first pour the bag of pellets out into a wide container. Hold the softie part over the container, then insert the narrow end of a funnel into the part's opening. Use a small

figure 3

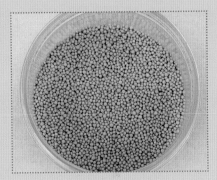

figure 4

figure 5

Making a Toy from a Child's Drawing

Children's imaginations run free of the constraints we tend to self-impose as adults. Their drawings can be a rich source of inspiration and ideas for softie making. Transforming a child's drawing into a real toy that can hugged and squeezed and tucked into bed is fun and satisfying for both you as the maker and the child as the designer.

To make a sewing pattern from a child's drawing, first resize the drawing to make it the size of the toy you'd like to create. Then trace the drawing and cut it apart into separate pieces that will become parts of the sewing pattern. You may need to widen skinny parts like limbs or fingers to make them easier to turn and to compensate for the three-dimensionality of stuffed parts (see lesson 1 on page 37).

To transfer the details of the drawing, tape it to a sunny window, then tape your fabric on top. Use a disappearing fabric marker to draw the lines on the fabric, then embroider or appliqué them either before or after stitching and stuffing the softie.

scoop to spoon the pellets into the wide end of the funnel (figure 5). To avoid pellet lumps that can be seen
and felt through the fabric, first pad the cavity with
bits of fiberfill. Another bit of fiberfill pushed into the
opening just before it is closed acts as a plug, keeping
the pellets from pouring out as you try to ladder-stitch
the opening closed. And be careful to push the pellets
all the way down into the softie and away from any
seams that will be machine sewn. Pellets will break your
machine needle!

Softies for babies will most likely be machine washed
and go through heavy wear and tear. To keep the pellets
from migrating inside the softie's body and to prevent
them from possibly leaking through a weak seam, sew a
muslin bag, fill it with pellets, and then machine-sew it
closed (figure 6). Either sew the bag into a seam when
you sew the softie together or anchor it with a few
stitches to hold it in place. Then stuff the rest of the
softie with fiberfill.

Glass pellets are used for weight. If you make very small
softies, try filling them with tiny glass pellets for a more
substantial toy. Glass pellets are also useful for stuffing

the feet of a toy that you want to stand up or sit up on
its own. The pellets are tiny and relatively heavy, allowing you to mold the feet and help the toy balance. Many
toy makers use a variety of stuffing materials in the
same toy. Don't be afraid to experiment!

figure 6

Choosing Colors

Choosing fabric is a big part of the art of making softies.
Sometimes the choices can seem overwhelming. Even if
you know what kind of fabric you'll be using, how do you
know which colors to choose? When I am in this situa-
tion, I limit my choices by thinking about complementary
colors. Complementary colors are opposite each other
on the color wheel: red and green, blue and orange, and
yellow and violet are complementary colors. When these
pairs of colors are next to one another, they make each
other appear brighter and more vibrant. And these color
combinations are pleasing to the eye. Keeping complementary colors in mind can help you narrow down your
fabric choices.

Neutrals or a monochromatic color scheme can make
a softie appear more sophisticated. A toy sewn up all in
white linen can look very modern and sleek, more like

a home décor object than something for a child. That
same toy sewn in bright green novelty fur and pink polka
dots will have a goofy personality.

Lesson 37: Raw-Edge Appliqué and Reverse Appliqué

The Monster pattern includes two different appliqué techniques, both of which can be used in any number of softie patterns. The hair on the Monster is applied to the body by machine-stitching along the hairline, very close to the edge of the hair, leaving the raw edges of the hair fabric exposed (figure 7). The knit-back faux fur used for the hair does not unravel, so it is suitable for this kind of raw-edge appliqué. Felt is also commonly used to apply features to a softie without having to turn under the edges. For a more finished look, use a zigzag stitch around the edges.

The eyes on the Monster are cut out using reverse appliqué. In reverse appliqué fabrics are layered together and stitched. The top fabric is cut away, revealing the layer beneath. I think reverse appliqué adds a layer of creepiness to the Monster, as though some of his furry skin has been pulled away, exposing his eyes beneath (figure 8). Again, if you don't want to have the raw edges of the fleece exposed, use a zigzag stitch around the eyes instead of a straight stitch. Reverse appliqué could also be used effectively when making insect wings, fish fins, or spots on a toad, or any time you want to show a second layer beneath the skin of the toy.

figure 7

figure 8

Small-Scale Prints

Scale is something to keep in mind when you are selecting a printed fabric to use in softie making. In traditional doll making, the scale of the print on the fabrics matches the scale of the doll. Although you don't have to follow this rule, if the printed design is small you will be able to see more of it in the finished toy. If it is a large-scale print, only a portion of it may show. If you were cutting a set of arms out of fabric with a large-scale print, the arms may appear not to match. To avoid this problem you can "fussy cut" the arms by selecting portions of the large-scale design to cut the arms from.

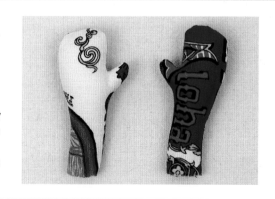

CRAB

This project appeals to the quilter in me. I love piecing together a handful of favorite fabric scraps to create a small piece of patchwork without the expectation of making a whole quilt! That bit of patchwork becomes a unique top shell for this softie crab. You can make any style of patchwork piecing you'd like, or use a few blocks left over from your latest quilt project.

The legs on this crab are long and skinny, but I'll show you a few tricks to help you turn and stuff them with ease. The front claws move back and forth with tab joints, an ideal jointing method for adding movement between segments of a limb.

Steps

1. Trace the pattern pieces (page 180) with pencil onto freezer paper and cut them out, transferring the markings.

2. To create the top of the body, sew a piece of patchwork in any style you'd like to measure 12 x 12 inches (30.5 x 30.5 cm). Place the Body pattern piece on the wrong side of the patchwork and press. Add a ¼-inch (6 mm) seam allowance and cut out the body, transferring the markings for the opening, claws, and eyes with a disappearing fabric marker (figure 1). Do the same thing with the red linen to create the underside of the body. Cut two slits in the red linen as marked for inserting the legs (figure 2). Transfer the marking for the apron.

3. To create the legs, fold the red quilting cotton in half, right sides together. Press the Leg pattern piece on top. Use a few pins to hold the layers together. With the freezer paper still adhered, stitch around the Leg, leaving two openings as marked. Pull off the freezer paper. Repeat until you have eight legs. Trim the legs to within ⅛ inch (3 mm) of the stitching line. Clip the curves and trim away some of the seam allowance at the tip of each leg. To turn each leg right side out, pull the tip through the mid-leg opening first, then use the other opening to pull the leg entirely right side out (see lesson 39 on page 126). Stuff most of each leg, using a stuffing fork, if desired, and leaving 1 inch (2.5 cm) at the top of each leg unstuffed. Ladder-stitch the mid-leg opening closed using red thread.

4. Line up four legs on either side of the red linen body so that the three back legs face the rear of the crab and the fourth one faces the front of the crab on each side of the body (the front of the crab is where the eyes and claws are positioned) (figure 3). Slip the ends of four legs through one slit from the right side and pin in place (figure 4). Fold the body over the slit and stitch over the ends of the four legs to close the slit. Repeat for the other four legs and the other slit (figure 5).

TOOLS & MATERIALS

Basic Sewing Tool Kit (page 11)

Various scraps of patterned quilting cotton to make the 12 x 12-inch (30.5 x 30.5 cm) patchwork piece for the body and claws

¼ yard (23 cm) of red linen for the back of the body and underside of the lower claws

¼ yard (23 cm) of red quilting cotton for the legs and apron (belly)

Scrap of navy blue quilting cotton for the eyestalks

All-purpose polyester thread in red, white, and navy

Extra-strong thread in red, white, and navy

8 ounces (224 g) of fiberfill stuffing

Stuffing fork (optional; see lesson 39 to make your own stuffing fork)

6 doll buttons in light brown

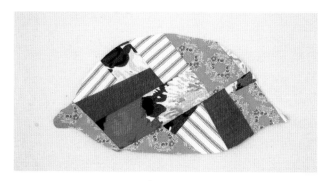

figure 1

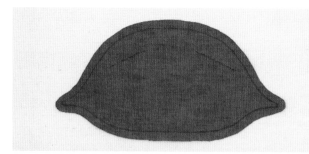

figure 2

figure 3

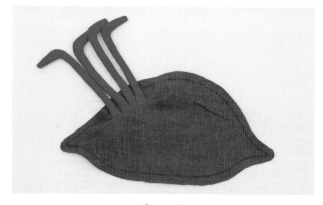

figure 4

5. Pin the top and the underside of the body right sides together, tucking the legs inside. Stitch around the body, beginning and ending at the opening. Clip the curves, trimming away some of the seam allowance on the pointy tips of the crab's body. Turn the body right side out by pulling the legs through the opening one at a time and then turning the remainder of the body. Stuff the body firmly and use extra-strong red thread to ladder-stitch the opening closed.

6. To create the upper claws, fold a scrap of one of the prints used in the patchwork in half, right sides together. Press the Upper Claw pattern piece onto the fabric. With the freezer paper still adhered, stitch around the Upper Claw, leaving an opening as marked. Pull off the pattern piece. Trim to within ⅛ inch (3 mm) of the stitching line. Clip the curves and turn the upper claws right side out. Stuff firmly and ladder-stitch the openings closed with extra-strong thread. Repeat to create a second claw.

7. To create the lower claws, place a piece of the remaining patchwork on top of a piece of red linen, right sides together. Press the Lower Claw pattern piece on top. With the freezer paper still adhered, stitch around the curved edge from point A down around the tips of the claws to point B, leaving the portion above the dotted line open. Trim the lower claw (including the upper unstitched portion) to within ¼ inch (6 mm) of the pattern piece, then pull the pattern piece off. Repeat to create a second lower claw.

8. To create the gusset for the joint, fold the red linen in half, right sides together. Place the Lower Claw Gusset pattern piece on the fold. Add a ⅛-inch (3 mm) seam allowance and cut out the gusset. Repeat for a second gusset. Unfold the gussets and press them flat. Refold each one, wrong sides together, and press to crease them (figure 6).

9. To attach the gusset to the lower claws, spread the unstitched end of the lower claw open. Place a gusset inside, right sides together, matching up points A and B. Stitch one side of the gusset to one side of the lower claw from point A, around the end of the claw, to point B. Flip the lower claw over and stitch the other side of the gusset to the other side of the lower claw from point A, around the end, to point B, leaving an opening as marked. Repeat to stitch the remaining gusset to the other lower claw. Clip the curves and turn the lower claws right side out. Stuff the tips of the claws firmly, leaving the gusset unstuffed. Ladder-stitch the openings closed using extra-strong thread (figure 7).

10. To assemble each claw, slide one end of one upper claw between the sides of the gusset of one lower claw and place a pin on each tab to hold the lower claw in place (figure 8). (See lesson 38 on page 126 for more on tab joints.) Repeat for the other upper and lower claws.

11. To attach the claw parts together with button joints, first thread a needle with a single 36-inch (91 cm) strand of extra-strong thread in white and knot the end. Working on one claw at a time, slide the needle under one tab and come up through the center of the tab. Go up through one hole in a button and back down through the second hole in the button. Pass the needle through the tab, the upper claw, and out through the other tab on the opposite side, attaching a second button in the same way. Go back and forth a few times until both buttons are secure and the upper claw is firmly in place between the tabs of the lower claw. Bring the needle out between one button and the claw, wrap the thread around the needle a few times, and then tie a double knot to secure. Cut the thread. Repeat to assemble the other claw.

12. To attach the claws to the crab's body, pin one upper claw to the underside of the body as marked. Thread a needle with a single 24-inch (61 cm) strand of extra-strong thread in white, tying a knot at the end. Insert the needle through the underside of the upper claw, coming out on the outside of the upper claw and passing through one hole of a button. Go through the other hole of the button and through the claw. Take a stitch through the underside of the crab's body, then go back through the upper claw and the button. Go back and forth a few times so that the claw is firmly attached to the body. End by wrapping the thread a few times around the button where the claw and the body meet and then tying a double knot under the button to secure.

13. To make the apron, fold a scrap of red quilting cotton in half, right sides together, and press the Apron pattern piece on top. With the freezer paper still adhered, stitch around the Apron, beginning and ending at the opening, as marked (figure 9). Pull off the freezer paper and cut out the apron, trimming to within ⅛ inch (3 mm) of the stitching line. Clip the curves and turn the apron right side out. Press. Ladder-stitch the opening closed with extra-strong red thread.

figure 5

figure 6

figure 7

figure 8

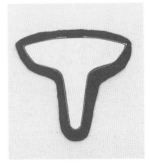

figure 9

14. Place the apron on the underside of the crab as marked. Pin in place and ladder-stitch the apron to the crab using red thread.

figure 10

15. To make the eyestalks, fold the navy blue fabric in half. Press the Eyestalk pattern piece on top. With the freezer paper still adhered, use navy blue thread to stitch around the Eyestalk, leaving the bottom open as marked (figure 10). Repeat for the second Eyestalk. Pull off the freezer paper and trim to within ⅛ inch (3 mm) of the stitching line. Clip the curves and turn the eyestalks right side out. Turn the raw edges under by ⅛ inch (3 mm) and baste. Stuff the eye stalks firmly. Use extra-strong navy thread to ladder-stitch the eyestalks to the body as marked. Remove the basting stitches.

Lesson 38: Tab Joints

The lower front claws on the Crab are hinged to the upper claws with a tab joint. This kind of joint consists of tabs that wrap around a section of the limb, creating a kind of socket (like the Crab's lower claw gussets). The thread holding the joint together acts as a tendon. Tab joints are often used in doll making to create knee or elbow joints, but they can be used in softie making anywhere you'd like to have a hinge-type movement. The jointed parts can be posed.

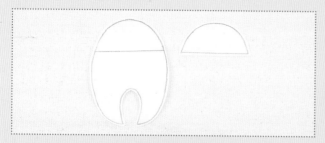

figure 1

To create a pattern for the tabbed portion of the joint, mark the spot on the limb where you would like the tab to begin and draw a line across. Trace the top part of the limb above the line onto a separate piece of freezer paper (figure 1). Placed on the fold of the fabric; this will become the pattern piece for the gusset.

To stitch the gusset in place, sew around the non-gusseted end of the limb, starting and stopping at the straight line. Spread the unstitched ends of the limb apart and fit the gusset between the layers. Stitch the gusset first to one layer of the limb end and then to the other. Once the limb is turned, stuff the tabbed portion only lightly, or leave it unstuffed, because you want to leave plenty of space between the tabs. Fit the tabs around the portion of the limb to be attached. Secure by sewing a button on the outside of each tab with the thread going through the limb to be attached. You now have a portion of a limb that is hinged in a socket and can swing back and forth! You can use several tab joints on a single limb for a toy with a lot of "poseability." If you would prefer not to use a button and your toy is not intended for heavy play, used waxed upholstery thread for a more subtle attachment.

Lesson 39: Turning and Stuffing a Long, Skinny Part

Don't feel limited in your design process by the difficulty of turning and stuffing a long, skinny part. Go

ahead and design that praying mantis, add those butterfly antennae, and create that mouse's tail! Long, skinny parts are no more challenging to turn and stuff than any other part of a softie—once you know a few tricks.

First, if the part is very long and you know you'll have a hard time reaching your hemostat all the way inside, leave a second opening about halfway down the side. To turn the part right side out, reach your hemostat into this side opening and pull the tip of the piece inward.

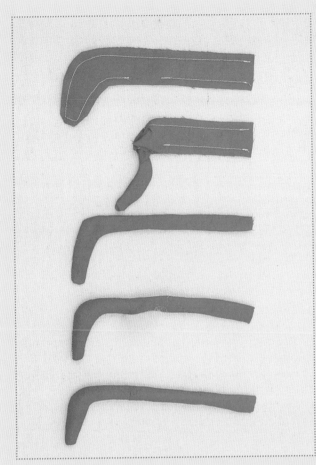

figure 2

Take your hemostat out and then reach into the regular opening at the end of the part, grasping the tip and pulling the part right side out all the way. You can also stuff the tip of the piece through the second opening, then close it up and stuff the remainder of the piece through the top opening (figure 2).

Another trick is to place a length of extra-strong thread with a knot at one end between the layers of the piece so that the knot extends past the seam allowance (figure 3). Stitch the layers together, stitching over the thread as you go. To turn the part right side out, tug on the thread. Once the part is fully turned, remove the thread.

A turning tube is a handy tool for turning long, skinny parts, too. (Learn to use a turning tube in lesson 14 on page 64.)

When it comes time to stuff very narrow sections of a softie, the best tool to use is a stuffing fork. A stuffing fork is a rod with a two-pronged tip. Stuffing forks are commercially available from doll-making supply stores, but it is easy to make your own from a long doll needle. First, push the sharp end of the needle into a cork so that you don't accidentally pierce yourself or the fabric. Then transform the eye of the needle into a two-pronged fork by snipping off the end of the eye with wire cutters (figure 4).

To use a stuffing fork, cup a small wad of stuffing in the palm of your hand. Holding the fork with the other hand, put the prongs into the stuffing and twirl the fork around and around. The stuffing will begin to wad up on the end of the fork, making it look like a cotton swab. Continue twirling until the wad is tight (figure 5). Insert the end of the fork into your long, skinny part, pushing it down all the way to the tip in one smooth motion. Pinch the fabric and pull out the fork. The wad of stuffing will remain inside the narrow area. You will be surprised at how tiny an area can be stuffed with this specialized tool. If you've ever admired the stuffed fingers on an art doll and wondered how they were done, now you know!

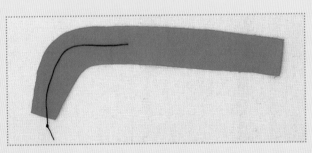

figure 3

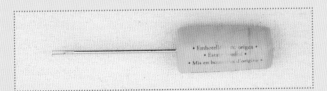

figure 4

figure 5

TEDDY BEAR

The most classic stuffed animal of all time is the teddy bear, and it's a great toy to have in your repertoire. Traditional teddy bears are designed with hard joints that allow the head, arms, and legs to move and be posed. They are typically made from natural fabrics that hold up very well to years of play, and they have an appealing appearance that seems to beg for a hug and kiss goodnight.

This pattern for a classic teddy shows you how to use some of the specialized teddy bear–making materials, and how to achieve that classic teddy look. But don't feel like these methods can only be used in making teddy bears! Hard joints can be used in other softie patterns, and fine fabrics, like the mohair used here, make a luxurious softie, no matter what kind of toy it is. And if you are designing a teddy bear, don't feel limited by the classic teddy design. Bears can be made in wild colors and creepy or fantastical forms. Let this Teddy Bear be a jumping-off point for your own toy designs!

Steps

1. Trace the pattern pieces (page 181) onto freezer paper with a pencil. Cut them out, transferring all of the markings.

2. Before pinning and cutting the pattern pieces, use a disappearing fabric marker or chalk to mark the wrong side of the mohair with an arrow indicating the nap direction (see lesson 20 on page 81 for more on nap). Use the arrows on each pattern piece as a guide to cutting the fabric with the nap in the correct direction and on grain.

3. Because mohair is expensive, I cut it one layer at a time to make sure I am cutting accurately. Place all of the pattern pieces except the Footpad on the mohair and pin them in place. Add a ¼-inch (6 mm) seam allowance and cut out all of the pieces. Flip the Head, Leg, and Arm pattern pieces over and cut a second set. Cut a total of four Ear pieces and four Leg pieces. Use a disappearing fabric marker to transfer the markings onto the backing of the fabric.

4. Cut the Arm pattern piece along the line where the Paw Pad will be attached, as marked, to make the inner arm. Cut one inner arm from mohair, then flip the pattern piece over and cut a second one, adding a ¼-inch (6 mm) seam allowance all the way around the inner arm, including along the straight edge where the Paw Pad will be attached.

Basic Sewing Tool Kit (page 11)

¼ yard (23 cm) of bronze medium-sparse 1-inch (2.5 cm) curly mohair

Scrap of light brown faux suede for the paws and footpads

Scrap of dark brown wool felt for the nose pad

All-purpose polyester sewing thread in brown

Extra-strong thread in brown

Sewing machine needle appropriate for sewing mohair and faux suede (14/90)

Ball-point awl

5 pairs of 30 mm plastic disk joints

12 ounces (336 g) of fiberfill stuffing or excelsior (see page 132)

12-inch (30.5 cm) length of thread or yarn for outlining the muzzle

36-inch (91.4 cm) length of dark brown embroidery floss for the nose

Embroidery needle

2 black animal eyes, 10 mm in diameter, with wire-loop backings

36-inch (91.4 cm) length of waxed upholstery thread

5-inch (12.7 cm) doll needle

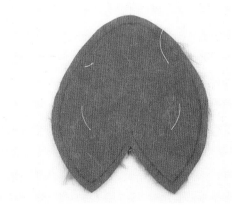

figure 1

figure 2

figure 3

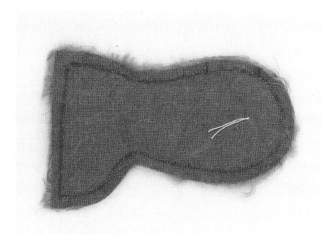

figure 4

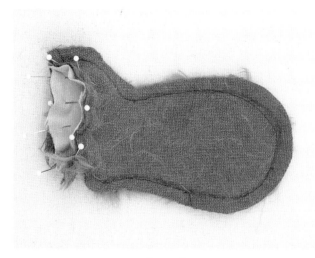

figure 5

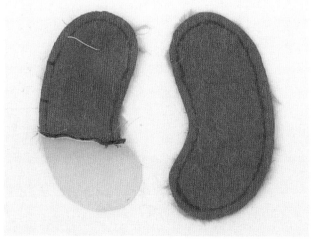

figure 6

5. Pin the Paw Pad and Footpad pattern pieces to the wrong side of the faux suede. Add a ¼-inch (6 mm) seam allowance and cut them out. Cut a second Footpad. Flip the Paw Pad over and cut a second one.

6. For the body, first make tailor's tacks (see page 21) at each mark on the back to indicate the placement of the joints (figure 1). Then pin and close the darts on the front and the back (figure 2). Pin the front to the back, right sides together, and stitch, beginning and ending at the marked opening and skipping stitches at the neck as marked. Clip the curves and turn the body right side out. Use an awl to free the fur from the seams.

7. To make the head, pin the head gusset to one head piece from point A to point B and stitch (figure 3). Pin the gusset to the other head piece and stitch. Stitch around the remainder of the head, leaving the opening as marked and skipping stitches at the neck joint as marked. Clip the curves and turn the head right side out. Use an awl to free the fur from the seams.

8. For the legs, first make tailor's tacks on the inner legs where the joints will be (figure 4). Next, pin two mirror-image leg pieces right sides together and stitch from point C, around the top of the leg, to point D, leaving the opening as marked and leaving the bottom of the leg open to attach the footpad. Repeat for the other leg. Match one footpad to the bottom of one leg, right sides together, from point C to point D, and pin in place (figure 5). Stitch around the footpad either by machine or by hand using extra-strong thread and a small back-stitch. (For more on stitching footpads see lesson 17 on page 73.) Clip the curves on each leg and foot and turn the legs right side out. Use an awl to free the fur from the seams.

9. For the arms, first make a tailor's tack on the inner arms where the joints will be. Then, place one paw pad on top of one inner arm, right sides together, lining up the straight edge, and stitch across. Repeat for the other paw pad and the other inner arm (figure 6). Place one inner arm on top of one outer arm and pin. Stitch around the arm, beginning and ending at the opening as marked. Repeat for the other arm. Clip the curves and turn the arms right side out. Use an awl to free the fur from the seams.

10. For the ears, place one ear piece on top of another, right sides together, and stitch around, leaving the bottom open. Repeat for the other ear. Clip the curves and turn the ears right side out. Use an awl to free the fur from the seams. Turn the raw edges of each ear under by ⅛ inch (3 mm) and baste.

11. To assemble the Teddy Bear, begin by jointing the head to the body. (See lesson 40 on page 133.) Slip the post of a joint in through the opening in the head. Push the end of the post out through the hole created by the skipped stitches at the neck, making sure the raw edges of the fabric at the opening are tucked under (figure 7). Slip a washer through the opening in the body and slide it over the post. Slip a locking washer into the body and push it down over the post so that it clicks and is pushed down as far as it can go. Joint the arms and legs in the same way (figure 8).

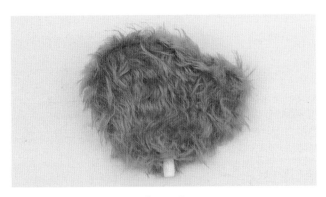

figure 7

figure 8

12. Stuff each part of the bear firmly and ladder-stitch the openings closed with extra-strong brown thread. Pin the ears to the bear, cupping them slightly. (For more on making cupped ears, see lesson 26 on page 93). Ladder-stitch the ears to the head with extra-strong brown thread.

13. For the muzzle, use a piece of thread or yarn to outline the muzzle area that you would like to shear. (For more on outlining an area with yarn see lesson 27 on page 94.) Use small embroidery scissors to trim the fur down to the backing. Iron the Nose pattern piece to a scrap of brown felt and cut it out, adding no seam allowance. Use a dab of craft glue to affix the felt nose pad to the Teddy Bear's face. Satin-stitch the nose with three strands of dark brown embroidery floss. Use six strands of dark brown embroidery floss to form a smile. (For instructions on how to satin-stitch a nose and stitch a smile, see lesson 30 on page 102.)

14. Attach the wire-loop eyes with a 36-inch (91.4 cm) strand of waxed upholstery thread and a doll needle following the instructions in lesson 23 on page 84.

NOTES ON MAKING THIS SOFTIE

Teddy bears are made to withstand many years, even decades, of play. The head, arms, and legs on teddy bears are jointed to allow for movement while maintaining a strong attachment between each part. There are a few jointing options for teddy-bear making, but the goal for all of them is a strong joint that will allow the bear to hold a pose, or even stand on its own.

Artist teddy-bear makers prefer to use a type of hardboard joints for heirloom-quality, collectible bears because these joints can be made very tight. A hardboard joint consists of two hardboard discs joined together by either a steel cotter pin and steel washers, a locknut and bolt, or aluminum rivets and aluminum washers. Toys made with hardboard joints are not washable because the hardboard disks will begin to disintegrate when wet. To install these joints you need some specialized tools and some practice. To learn more about this jointing method, I recommend one of the many books dedicated solely to the art of making teddy bears.

For the purposes of general softie making, we will focus on plastic disk joints, sometimes referred to as doll joints, which don't require any specialized tools or skills to install and can still create a strong, fairly tight joint. The primary disadvantage of plastic disk joints is that they can only be tightened according to the number of grooves on the post, and no tighter. But the advantages for general softie makers are that plastic disk joints are easy to install, they are readily available at most hobby and craft stores, and they are washable.

Excelsior Stuffing

Many artist teddy-bear makers prefer a hard-pack stuffing called excelsior, also known as wood wool. You may find antique teddy bears that are stuffed with excelsior, and stuffing a new toy with this material can help you achieve an antique look and feel.

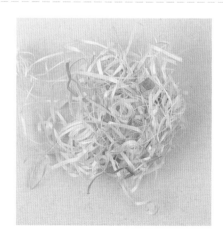

Excelsior can pack into a cavity very firmly, making that area of the Teddy Bear extremely hard. Unlike Teddy Bear parts stuffed with wool or fiberfill, areas stuffed with excelsior can be molded with your fingers and will hold their shape. Excelsior comes in a fine grade for smaller toys and a coarse grade for filling larger areas. To make the excelsior more pliable while you are working you can mist it lightly with water. Some teddy-bear makers only use excelsior in the muzzle, and others use it in the entire bear. A muzzle stuffed with excelsior is very hard, which makes it easier to embroider the nose.

Lesson 40: Plastic Disk Joints

Plastic disk joints are available at many craft stores and through doll- and teddy bear–making supply companies. Each joint consists of three pieces: a post, a washer, and a lock washer. The joints come in a variety of sizes ranging from 15 mm to 65 mm (figure 1). Select a joint that matches the size of the parts you will be attaching together. A joint that is too small will leave the limb wobbly, while a joint that is too large will flatten out the top of the limb where the fabric stretches around the disk.

When designing a toy that will have hard joints, it is really important to make sure you mark the joint placement on the fabric using a marker or a tailor's tack because it is very difficult to remove a joint that is installed in the wrong place. The post on plastic joints is very hard to cut off, even with wire cutters, and if you do manage to cut it, there will be holes left in the fabric. Therefore, it pays to mark carefully and check twice before installing plastic joints! Select a spot well outside of the seam allowance so that you allow enough room for the fabric to curve around the joint before it meets the seam.

All hard joints are installed before the toy is stuffed. When you design the pattern pieces, be sure to mark openings wide enough to slip the joint inside the body.

To install the plastic joint between an arm and the body of the bear, insert the tip of an awl into the fabric between the threads of the backing. Try not to poke a hole in the fabric, which weakens the fabric and eventually leads to a loose joint. Instead, slip the awl between the threads of the fur backing, then pushing the awl in further to widen the hole. If necessary, remove the awl and use your hemostat to widen the hole farther.

Slip the post into the body and push it out through the hole. Then push the post into a hole you've made with the awl in the limb. Slip a washer into the limb and slide it down the post. Make sure no fabric is caught between the post and the washer. Push the lock washer all the way down the post, as far as it can go, to create a tight, permanent joint. It will click as it moves down the post and some force is needed to push it all the way down. Install the joints for the other limbs the same way. When you stuff the body and limbs, be sure to stuff the area around the joints extra firmly so that you won't be able to feel the joint hardware through the bear.

For the head I find it easiest to leave a small opening at the back of the head just below where the head gusset meets the seam between the face pieces. This extra opening allows me to reach my fingers into the bear's head and assemble the joint. Then I add extra stuffing and close the opening with a ladder stitch.

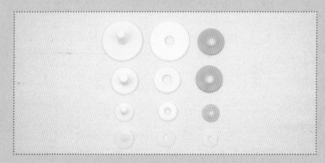

figure 1

Lesson 41: Working with Mohair, Alpaca, and Woven-Back Faux Fur

Mohair and alpaca fabrics are used to create bears of the highest heirloom quality. These natural fibers have a beautiful look and feel and a high sheen, and they are durable and resistant to moisture, stretching, and creasing. They are much more expensive than the faux fur typically used in softie making, costing at least five or six times more per yard. They are only produced in specialty textile mills and are available online through teddy bear–making suppliers. But for a truly fine toy that will become a collector's item or is made for a very special person, it is worth the indulgence to work with these materials.

Mohair and alpaca come in fur lengths from short to long, densities from sparse to thick, and various textures, including straight, matted, and curly (figure 2). They also come in a variety of colors, from traditional to more wild, and color blends in which the strands change color from base to tip. Because they are natural materials, mohair and alpaca take dye very well. You can also stain them with coffee or tea (see opposite page) or paint them using a dye pen or a permanent marker. And don't feel like you need to begin with white fur; try over-dyeing to achieve a unique color.

Store your mohair or alpaca fabrics with care. Hang them in the closet from the clips of a skirt hanger. If the fabric is wrinkled it will likely straighten out while you are making the bear, but if the mohair won't lie flat to be cut, use the steam from an iron held several inches away to relax the wrinkles. (The area you've steamed may look fluffier than the rest, so you may want to steam the entire piece before cutting out your Teddy Bear.) Clean the Teddy Bear as you would clean fine upholstery: very gently with a mild detergent and allow it to air-dry.

Many teddy bear makers shear the fur fiber around the bear's muzzle. Use a wire brush to brush the fur at the muzzle against the nap to make the fibers stand on end. Then use small, sharp scissors to carefully trim the fur. You can trim all the way down so that the backing of the fabric is showing, leaving some fibers in place for a worn-down look, or trim them completely, plucking any stray fibers with tweezers, for a completely bald muzzle. If the backing is a contrasting color to the fur, the area

you shear will show the backing color and stand out. For a somewhat less-expensive, synthetic alternative to mohair or alpaca, try woven-back faux fur. Most faux fur sold in mainstream fabric stores has a knit back, which lends it some stretch. Faux fur with a woven backing has no stretch, so the Teddy Bear will hold its shape even when firmly stuffed. And like mohair or alpaca, the woven backing is often a contrasting color to the fur and will therefore stand out when sheared. Woven-back faux fur can be ordered online through teddy bear-making supply shops.

Paw pads and footpads can be made from any number of sturdy fabrics, including felt, synthetic suede, real suede, or leather. It is especially nice to pair leather with mohair and alpaca because all are luxurious natural materials. Thrift stores can be a source of inexpensive and relatively thin leather gloves that are perfect for Teddy Bear paws.

figure 2

Making Your Own Set of Trial Eyes

The position of the eyes perhaps has the biggest impact on determining the personality of a softie. It helps to use a pair of trial eyes that you can move around the face before committing to sewing your chosen eyes in place. I've used pins for this task (see lesson 3 on page 40), but for larger toys, pinheads are too small to get the full effect of the eyes. Bear-making suppliers sell "trial eyes" that are glass eyes in varying sizes affixed to pin backs. You can make a set of trial eyes yourself by hot-gluing googly eyes to flat thumbtacks. Push the tacks into the Teddy Bear's head where you think the eyes belong, than move them around until you find the eye placement that pleases you.

Lesson 42: Ear Placement

The position of the ears on the Teddy Bear—or on any softie—has a huge effect on the personality of the finished toy. Sew the ears, then play with their positioning on the head, pinning them in place temporarily while you step away and look at the toy from a distance. Depending on the position of the ears the Teddy Bear may look youthful or old, cute or fierce. Although the eyes have a big impact on the overall look of the Teddy Bear, the ears are equally influential, so try out many positions before you decide how your Teddy Bear's ears should be placed (see photos at right).

Tea and Coffee Staining

The fabric faces and bodies on old dolls and toys take on a wonderful dark patina over time from the oils in hands that have touched them. This gives the toy a nostalgic, antique look that you may want to replicate on a new toy. Try tea or coffee staining the fabric before you begin sewing. Select fabric made from natural fibers, such as cotton, wool, or mohair. These fabrics take dye well, and you'll be able to achieve a deeper color. Make a dye bath by boiling enough water to fully submerge your fabrics. Put several tea bags in the hot water—enough to make a dark, strong tea—or mix in enough coffee grounds or instant coffee to make a strong brew. (If you leave coffee grounds in the bath, you will get dark spots; strain them first for an even color.) Then put in your fabric. Stir the fabric every 15 minutes or so for the first hour if you'd like to achieve an even color, or leave it unstirred for a mottled look. The dye color will be lighter once the fabric is dry, so let it sit longer than you may think necessary, from an hour or two to overnight. Rinse the fabric in cold water, then tumble dry and press. Your toy made with tea- or coffee-stained fabric will look naturally aged. A tea bath can also be used to tone down the brightness of fabrics dyed with fabric dye. Or mix a bit of black, brown, or army green fabric dye into a dye bath to achieve an aged look.

KANGAROO

This cheerful Kangaroo, with a Joey tucked in her pocket, is a fun softie to make. Kangaroos have strong, muscular legs; on this softie the legs are sewn to the body using a unique method that involves cutting holes in both the leg and the body. The result is a streamlined leg with neat, sturdy seams. Once you practice this new method of attachment, try incorporating it into your next softie pattern.

Pull the little Joey out of her mother's pocket and you'll see that she is actually a finger puppet. Turning a small softie into a finger puppet is easy to do and adds a new way for children to play with your toy.

Steps

1. Trace the pattern pieces (page 182) with pencil onto freezer paper and cut them out, attaching the Side Body pattern to create one pattern piece.

2. Add a ¼-inch (6 mm) seam allowance to all of the pattern pieces when you cut out the fabric unless otherwise indicated. Fold the brown wool in half, right sides together. Iron the Side Body pattern piece on top. Pin the layers together and cut out. Transfer the markings to the fabric. Use a craft knife to cut directly around the hole and the notch in the Side Bodies (the notches will assist you with aligning the Leg pieces later). Iron the Leg pattern piece to the brown wool and cut out the first set of leg pieces. Use a craft knife to cut directly around the hole and the notch in this set of legs. Cut a second set of legs without holes or notches. Iron the Head Gusset and Ear pattern pieces to the wrong side of a single layer of brown wool and cut out. Pull all of the pattern pieces off the fabric. Cut a second ear that is reverse of the first. Iron the Footpad pattern piece to a double layer of brown wool and cut out. Transfer the markings to the fabric.

3. Fold a piece of cream wool in half, right sides together. Iron the Belly and Pocket on the fold and cut out. Cut two Ear pattern pieces, reversing one. Pull all of the pattern pieces off the fabric and transfer the markings to the fabric.

4. On the belly, fold the arms inward, right sides together, and sew the oval dart on each arm. Fold the pocket in half, wrong sides together, matching the points labeled I to one another. Lay the pocket on top of the belly, right sides together; the pocket is larger than the belly to accommodate the Joey. Align the outer edges of the pocket with the belly, matching the corners as well as points C and I, and pin around. Baste to hold it in place (figure 1). Set aside.

TOOLS & MATERIALS

Basic Sewing Tool Kit (page 11)

½ yard (45.7 cm) of brown wool

¼ yard (23 cm) of cream wool

Scraps of wool-blend felt in gray, cream, and dark brown

All-purpose polyester thread in white, dark brown, and gray

Extra-strong thread in brown and white

Hole punch (optional)

13 ounces (364 g) of fiberfill stuffing

12-inch (30.5 cm) length of dark brown embroidery floss

2 black seed beads

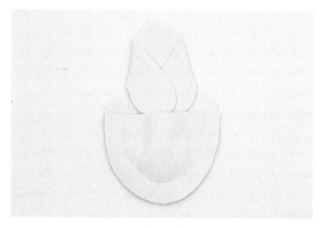

figure 1

figure 2

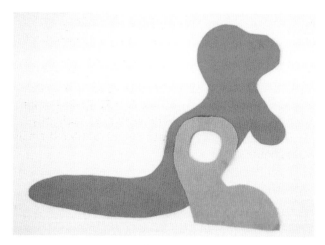

figure 3

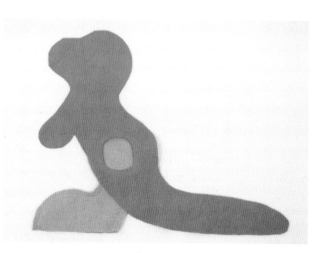

figure 4

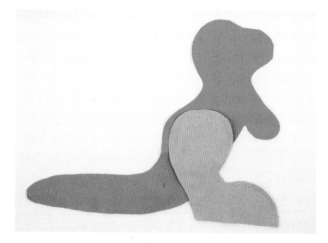

figure 5

figure 6

5. Place one of the legs with a hole in it on top of one side body, right sides together, matching up the notches. Pin well around the hole. Stitch around the hole with a ¼-inch (6 mm) seam allowance (figure 2). Clip the curves inside the seam. Pull the leg through the hole and press it flat (figure 3). Place a matching leg without a hole on top of the sewn leg, right sides together, and pin around the outside edges of the leg. Sew the two leg layers together, beginning at point E at the tip of the toe, and ending at point F at the heel, leaving the bottom of the foot open (figures 4 and 5). Repeat this process with the other side body and the other set of leg pieces.

6. Place one footpad onto the bottom of one leg, right sides together, matching points E and F, and pin well. With the bottom of the leg under the machine needle, stitch one side of the leg first from point E to point F, then stitch the other side. Stitching footpads is fiddly, so pin well and go slowly. You may prefer to sew the footpads on by hand with a small backstitch using extra-strong thread. (For more on stitching footpads see lesson 17 on page 73.) Repeat for the other footpad.

7. Place the belly on top of one side body, right sides together, and pin from point D around the arms to point C. Stitch in place (figure 6). Repeat, stitching the belly to the other side body.

8. Place the head gusset on top of one side body, right sides together, and pin from point A to point B. Stitch in place. Repeat, stitching the head gusset to the other side body.

9. Stitch around the remainder of the Kangaroo's body, from point B down the back and under the tail, to the mark indicating the opening, and from point A under the chin to point D. Clip all the curves and trim the seam allowance at the tip of the tail. Turn the Kangaroo right side out through the opening under the tail. Stuff firmly. Ladder-stitch the opening closed with brown extra-strong thread.

10. Place one cream ear on top of one brown ear, right sides together, and stitch around, leaving the bottom open. Repeat for the other ear. Clip the curves and turn the ears right side out. Turn the raw edges under by ⅛ inch (3 mm) and baste in place. Fold them along the marked fold line with the cream as the inner ear and press. Pin the ears to the Kangaroo's head so that they are sticking straight up. Ladder-stitch the ears in place using extra-strong white thread.

11. Do not add a seam allowance when cutting the facial features on the Kangaroo and Joey. Iron the larger Eye pattern piece to dark brown wool felt twice and cut out, then iron it to cream felt and cut out twice. Use a hole punch or scissors to cut two tiny circles of dark brown wool felt as pupils. From the gray felt cut two circles slightly smaller than the eye. Layer the eyes, offsetting each layer, as follows: dark brown, cream, gray. Use gray all-purpose thread to stitch the gray circle to the others with long stitches radiating from the center. Place the pupil on top and adhere using craft glue. Place the eyes on the Kangaroo and use craft glue to adhere them, using pins to hold the eyes in place until the glue dries (or whipstitch the pupils to the eyes and the eyes to the face with coordinating thread). Iron the Nose pattern pieces to a scrap of dark brown felt and cut them out. Pin the nose and the nose line to the Kangaroo, with the nose overlapping the line slightly, and use dark brown all-purpose thread to stitch them in place (figure 7).

figure 7

14. Iron the Joey Head Gusset pattern piece to the wrong side of a single layer of brown wool and cut it out. Transfer all of the markings. Place the head gusset on top of one body piece, right sides together, matching points G and H. Stitch from point G to point H. Repeat to attach the head gusset to the other body piece.

15. Tuck the arms inside the body and stitch the remainder of the Joey's body from point G to the bottom of the body and from point H to the bottom on the other side, leaving the bottom of the body open so that the Joey can be used as a finger puppet (figure 8). Clip the curves and turn the Joey right side out. Stuff the Joey's head firmly. Use craft glue to adhere a small scrap of felt inside the Joey's head to hold the stuffing in place.

16. Place a scrap of cream wool on top of a scrap of brown wool, right sides together. Iron the Joey Ear pattern piece on top. Use a few pins to hold the layers in place. With the pattern piece still adhered, stitch around the Ear, leaving the bottom open for turning. Pull the pattern piece off and repeat to create a second ear. Trim to within ⅛ inch (3 mm) of the stitching line and turn the ears right side out. Turn the raw edges under by ⅛ inch (3 mm) and baste. Fold the ears in half toward the cream side and press. Pin each ear to the top of the Joey's head so that the ears stick straight up. Ladder-stitch the ears in place using extra-strong white thread.

17. Iron the Joey Nose pattern piece to a scrap of dark brown wool felt and cut it out. Use a 12-inch (30.5 cm) length of dark brown embroidery floss to stitch a mouth on the Joey, then use craft glue to adhere the nose. (For more on stitching a smiling mouth with embroidery floss see lesson 30 on page 102.) Stitch a seed bead to each side of the Joey's head to create eyes.

12. For the Joey, fold a scrap of brown wool in half, right sides together, and iron the Joey Body pattern piece on top. Pin the layers in place and cut out the body pieces, transferring all of the markings. Use a craft knife to cut a slit in each body piece as indicated on the pattern. Fold the bottom edge of each body piece up ⅛ inch (3 mm) toward the wrong side, press, and then fold it up ⅛ inch (3 mm) again and pin it in place. Stitch across the bottom edge of each body piece to create a hem.

13. Iron the Joey Arm pattern piece on top of the folded wool and use a pin to hold the layers in place. With the pattern piece still adhered, stitch around the Arm, leaving the bottom open. Pull the pattern piece off and repeat to create a second arm. Cut out the arms, trimming the seam allowance to ⅛ inch (3 mm). Turn the arms right side and lightly stuff them. Insert the raw edges of one arm into the slit on one body, from the right side, so that the raw edges of the arm are aligned with the slit. Fold the body along the slit, right sides together, and then stitch across the slit to attach the arm to the body. Repeat with the other arm and the other body piece. (For more on attaching limbs by cutting a slit see lesson 10 on page 57.)

figure 8

Lesson 43: Putting in a Pocket

A kangaroo wouldn't be complete without a pocket, but pockets can add an element of fun to any kind of softie. By adding a place for the softie to hold something you are adding functionality and a new way to play with the toy. Think about a monster with a pocket mouth that can gobble up treasures, a daddy seahorse with a pocket full of baby seahorses, or a tooth-fairy softie with a pocket for a lost tooth. (For information on making a zippered pocket see lesson 51 on page 162.)

To add a very simple pocket to a softie cut a shape from felt or another nonfraying material and stitch it in place by machine or by blanket- or whipstitching it in place by hand. The pocket can be added either before the softie is sewn together or after it is sewn and stuffed. If you expect that the pocket will be heavily used, make sure your stitches are very secure and the fabric you choose will not stretch out and become misshapen over time.

A more secure and stronger pocket can be machine-sewn into the body seams at the same time the body itself is sewn together. And if you choose to make the pocket from the same material used on the body, the pocket will blend in as though it really is part of the animal, like the pocket on the Kangaroo.

To design the pattern for an incorporated pocket, begin by tracing the portion of the body pattern piece where you want to place the pocket. In the case of the Kangaroo, I traced the lower half of the belly pattern. Draw a horizontal line across the pattern to indicate the top of the pocket. If you just used this shape as your pattern piece, your pocket would be very tight with little space to tuck anything into it. To make a pocket with some give, widen both sides of the shape (figure 1). The wider you make the pattern piece, the more give the pocket will have.

To cut out the fabric for the pocket, place the pattern piece on folded fabric, with the top of the pocket pattern on the fold. Cut out the pocket, fold it in half with wrong sides together, and press. Place the folded pocket on top of the body piece it will cover, right sides together, matching up the raw edges. There will be extra fabric along the top. That's okay—it's the extra space built into the pocket! Pin or baste the pocket in place to make sure it doesn't shift when the softie is sewn together. Then stitch up the softie's body as you usually would. The edges of the pocket will be sewn into the seams. When you turn the softie right side out, the extra width of the pocket gives you some room to slip something inside.

Whether you are adding a simple or more complex pocket to your softie, remember not to stuff the body too firmly if you want to be able to use the pocket easily.

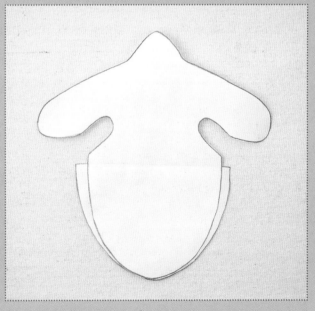

figure 1

Lesson 44:
Cutting a Hole
to Attach Limbs

I am always in search of methods of attaching limbs to my softies that are very strong yet neat. Hard joints are a great option for softies with limbs that will be able to move (like the Teddy Bear on page 128), but for softies with stationary legs, the inventive method that follows is amazing. Essentially, you are sewing the limbs right onto the body before turning and stuffing by creating a circular seam. It can be hard to visualize the first time you do it, so follow the instructions step by step until you get a feel for how it works. Then try applying this method to your own softie patterns.

To begin, locate the spot on the body where you want the limb to be attached. For the kangaroo, this was mid-body, below the arm but above the start of the tail. Draw a circle around that spot. If the circle is large, the limb will be pulled very close to the body. If the circle is small the limb will appear to be more separate (figures 2 and 3). In this case I drew a rather large circle because I needed the legs to stay close to the body in order to better support the animal's weight. Be sure to locate the hole far enough away from the edge of the fabric that you'll still have sufficient room to sew the body together later. Draw a corresponding same-sized hole on the inner leg piece, again locating the hole in toward the center of the fabric, leaving enough room to sew the leg together later.

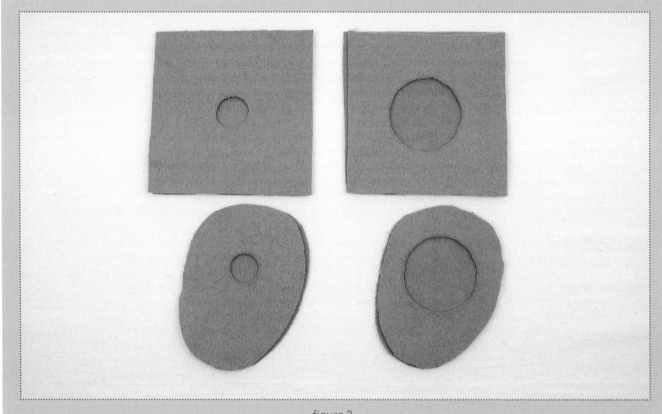

figure 2

Lay the inner leg on top of the body, right sides together, and position it as you'd like. Then cut small notches in the hole on both the inner leg and the body to ensure perfect positioning. Pin and stitch around the hole. Clip the curves and pull the leg through the hole. Press flat. (see figures 2 and 3 on page 138).

The outer leg is left intact with no hole. Place it on top of the inner leg, right sides together. Stitch around the leg (see figures 4 and 5 on page 138). Repeat for the other body and leg pieces, then finish sewing the remainder of the softie. When you turn the softie right side out, the limbs will already be sewn in place and the seam will be neat and strong and ready for stuffing.

This method may feel counterintuitive the first time you use it, but once you try it you'll see that it is an infinitely useful technique for attaching parts, and it results in neat seams that form a strong join and require no hand sewing. A duck's wings could be attached using this method, or a dragon's legs, or even a bunny's haunches.

figure 3

Making a Finger Puppet

You can easily turn the pattern for a small softie into the pattern for a finger puppet. Draw the profile of the head, than extend the lines down several inches. Draw a horizontal line straight across the bottom. A simple pointed oval works well as a head gusset on such a small head. Either sew the puppet from felt or hem the bottom edge for a neat finish. Then add details like ears, arms, a tail, and facial features; insert a little stuffing in the head area, if desired, and hold it in place with a small piece of felt and glue.

MONKEY

A Monkey makes an irresistible companion for any child. Made up in thick brown sherpa fleece and warm wool, this Monkey is especially soft and huggable. Make a fun felt banana and slip it through the elastic on the Monkey's hand so that he has a snack to nibble when he's hungry!

Steps

1. Trace the pattern pieces (on page 184) with pencil onto freezer paper and cut them out.

2. Add a ¼-inch (6 mm) seam allowance to all of the pattern pieces when you cut out the fabric unless otherwise indicated. Fold the cream wool in half, right sides together, and cut two Muzzle Sides, one Muzzle Center (placing this pattern piece on the fold), two Head Front Sides, four Ears, four Hands, two Foot Tops (with the inward-facing curve), and two Foot Bottoms (with the outward-facing curve). Unfold the wool and cut one Belly.

3. Fold the fleece in half, right sides together, and cut two Head Backs, two Head Front Tops, four Arms, two Top Legs (with the inward-curving edge), two Bottom Legs (with the outward-curving edge), and two Tail pieces. Unfold the fleece and cut one Body Back and one Body Front. Cut the Tail Slit with a craft knife as marked in the Body Back. Transfer all the markings to the fabric with chalk or a disappearing fabric marker.

4. Fold the body back and the body front in half, right sides together, and sew up the darts. Place the belly upside down on top of the body front, matching points A (figure 1). Stitch from point A to point B and then from point A to point C (figure 2).

TOOLS & MATERIALS

Basic Sewing Tool Kit (page 11)

1/4 yard (23 cm) of cream wool

1/2 yard (45.7 cm) of brown sherpa fleece

Scraps of wool-blend felt in white, cream, dark brown, and light brown

Pieces of wool-blend felt in white and yellow, 10 x 15 inches (25.4 x 38 cm) each

All-purpose polyester thread in brown, cream, and white

Extra-strong thread in brown and white

Sewing machine needle appropriate for sewing sherpa fleece (14/90)

4 inches (10.2 cm) of elastic, 1/4 inch (6 mm) wide

36-inch (91.4 cm) length of waxed upholstery thread

14 ounces (392 g) of fiberfill stuffing

Ball-point awl

2 black animal eyes, 10 mm in diameter, with wire-loop backings

5-inch (12.7 cm) doll needle

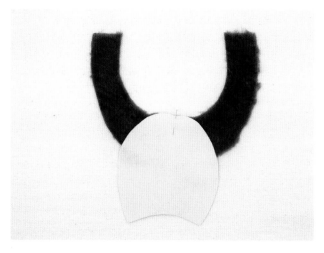

figure 1

figure 2

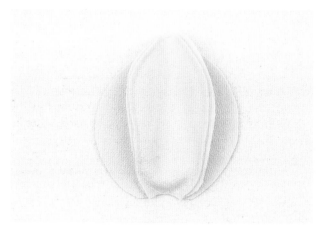

figure 3

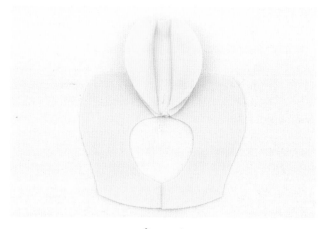

figure 4

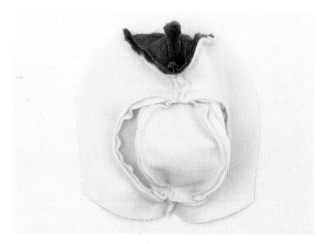

figure 5

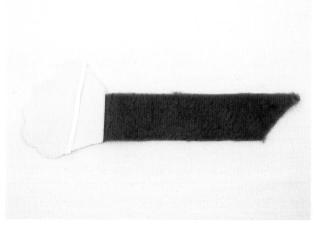

figure 6

5. Place the tail pieces right sides together and stitch around, leaving openings as marked. Turn the tail right side out through the opening. Flatten the tail so that the seam is in the center and the curve of the tail is upward toward the top of the Monkey. From the right side, insert the raw edges of the tail through the slit in the body back. Fold the body back in half over the tail and stitch across the slit (on the wrong side) to sew it up, trapping the raw edges of the tail in the seam.

6. Place one set of ears right sides together and stitch around, leaving the bottom open as marked. Trim the seam allowance to ⅛ inch (3 mm) and clip the curves. Turn the ears right side out and topstitch with white thread as marked. Repeat for the other set of ears.

7. Place one muzzle-side edge marked "center" on top of the muzzle center, right sides together and matching up points D and E. Stitch from point D to point E. Repeat to attach the other muzzle side to the other edge of the muzzle center (figure 3).

8. Place the head front sides on top of each other, right sides together, and stitch from point F to point G and from point H to point I.

9. Place the head front tops on top of one another, right sides together, and stitch from point J to point K.

10. Place the sewn muzzle upside down on top of the sewn head front sides, right sides together, aligning the top center of the muzzle center with point G on the head front side (figure 4). Stitch the muzzle to the head front side, one side at a time, from point G to the bottom center of the muzzle center (point H on the head front side) until both sides are sewn and the entire muzzle is sewn into the head front.

11. Place the head front top upside down on top of the stitched head front sides, aligning point K with point F. Stitch from point K/F to point L/M. Repeat to stitch the other side of the head front top to the other side of the head front side (figure 5).

12. Place the head front upside down on top of the body front, aligning point N on the body with one of the points N on the head front. Stitch the head front to the body front from point N across to point O on the body.

13. Place the head backs on top of one another, right sides together, and stitch down the side marked "center" from point P to point Q. Place the stitched head back upside down on top of the body back, aligning points R. Stitch across from point R to point S.

14. Place one ear on each side of the head back as marked, aligning the raw edges. Baste in place.

15. Place one hand piece on top of one arm piece, right sides together, and stitch across. Repeat, sewing a second hand piece to a second arm piece. Place one arm/hand piece on top of the other, right sides together, and stitch around, leaving the openings as marked; do not topstitch yet. Stitch the other arm/hand pieces the same way, except this time lay the length of elastic across the right side of one hand and baste it in place before stitching the hands together (figure 6). Clip the curves carefully, especially between the thumb and fingers. Turn the arms right side out. Topstitch the fingers on each hand as marked.

16. Place the arms on top of the body back where marked, aligning the raw edges. Check to make sure the thumbs on each hand are pointing upward. Baste in place.

17. Place one foot top on one top leg, right sides together, aligning points T and U. Stitch from point T to point U. Repeat for the other foot top and top leg.

18. Place one foot bottom on one bottom leg, right sides together, aligning points W and X. Stitch from point W to point X. Repeat for the other foot bottom and bottom leg.

19. Place one top leg/foot piece on top of its coordinating bottom leg/foot piece, right sides together, and stitch around, leaving the openings as marked; do not topstitch yet (figure 7). Stitch the other leg/foot pieces the same way. Clip the curves carefully, especially between the slightly separated "big" toe and the others. Turn the legs right side out. Topstitch the toes on each foot as marked.

20. Place the legs on top of the body back where marked, aligning the raw edges. Baste in place.

21. Place the body front on top of the body back, right sides together. There are a lot of body parts to stuff inside the body, so pin every ⅛ inch (3 mm) and stitch slowly around the body, being sure to catch the raw edges of each body part in the seam as you sew the body together. If your machine has an adjustable needle position, moving the needle all the way to the right will help you maneuver more smoothly. Leave an opening as marked. Clip the curves and turn the Monkey right side out.

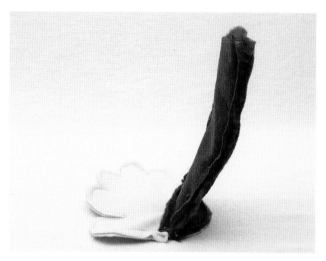

figure 7

22. Through the openings in the arms and legs, stuff each finger, hand, and arm to about 1 inch (2.5 cm) below the elbow, and each toe, foot, and leg to about 1 inch (2.5 cm) below the knee. Topstitch across the elbows and knees with brown thread as marked. Through the opening in the tail, stuff it firmly, leaving a 1-inch (2.5 cm) portion closest to the body unstuffed. Stuff the Monkey's head and body firmly. Ladder-stitch the openings closed with brown extra-strong thread.

23. Cut two eye backs from the cream wool felt, and two eye fronts from white wool felt. Layer an eye back on an eye front and use a glue stick to temporarily adhere the eyes to the Monkey's face. Whipstitch the eye backs with cream thread and the eye fronts with white thread. Stitch the other eye in place the same way.

24. Use an awl to poke a hole in the center of the eye front of each eye, going through the felt and the wool of the Monkey's head. Move the tool back and forth a bit to widen the hole. Attach the wire-loop eyes with a 36-inch (91.4 cm) strand of waxed upholstery thread and the doll needle, following the instructions in lesson 23 on page 84.

25. Cut two nostrils from dark brown wool felt and whipstitch them to the Monkey's face with brown thread. Fold the light brown felt in half and place the Smile pattern piece on the fold. Cut out a smile and whipstitch it to the Monkey's face with light brown thread. (You can coat the backs of the nostrils and smile with a glue stick to hold them in place temporarily while you stitch.)

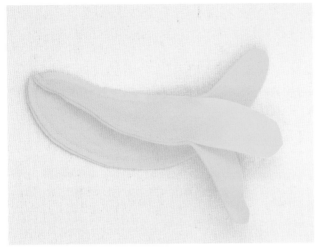

figure 8

26. Use an awl to gently pull the pile out of all of the seams, fluffing up the fleece as you go, to create a seamless look.

27. Cut two Banana pieces and one Banana Gusset from white wool felt. Place one banana piece on top of the other and stitch along the outer edge from Y to Z. Place the banana gusset on top of one banana piece and stitch from Y to Z, leaving an opening as marked. Stitch the other side of the gusset to the other banana piece from Y to Z. Clip the curves and turn the banana right side out. Stuff it firmly and ladder-stitch the opening closed with white extra-strong thread.

28. Adding a ½-inch (1.3 cm) seam allowance, cut two Banana pieces and one Banana Gusset from yellow wool felt. Place one banana piece on top of the other and stitch along the outer edge from Y to the Peel Stitching Line. Place the banana gusset on top of one banana piece and stitch from Y to the Peel Stitching Line. Stitch the other side of the gusset to the other banana piece from Y to the Peel Stitching Line (figure 8). Clip the curves around the seams and turn the banana peel right side out. Slip the banana into the peel, aligning points Y. Take a small stitch at point Y to attach the banana to the peel if you don't want a removable banana. Slip the finished banana under the elastic on the Monkey's palm.

NOTES ON MAKING THIS SOFTIE

● The most important idea to take away from this pattern is the notion of curves and how they work to shape fabric in three dimensions.

● The Monkey's muzzle is made up of three curved pieces. By controlling the arc of the curves on these pieces, you control the degree to which the muzzle protrudes from the Monkey's face. The feet on the Monkey meet the leg at a right angle due to an inward curve at the base of the top of each leg, and an outward curve at the base of the bottom of each leg. These curves are matched by the curves on the feet themselves. Where the two inward curves meet, the foot is pulled up and meets the base of the leg at a right angle. Where the two outward curves meet, the foot is pushed out and forms a heel.

● It can be difficult to imagine the effect a deep or shallow curve may have. Sewing this Monkey will help you see how curves work in pattern design. Then you will be able to use curves in your own soft toy patterns.

Lesson 45: Designing an Incorporated Muzzle

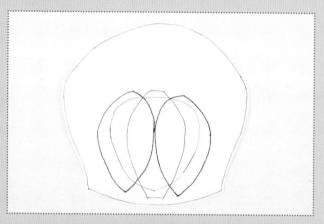

figure 1

Begin by drawing an outline of the head, and then draw in the outline of the muzzle shape. This muzzle shape forms the outer edges of the muzzle pattern you are creating. Now divide the muzzle into three sections: a center and two sides. The center of the muzzle must be symmetrical from left to right. The length of the sides must match the length of the center so that they will match up when they are sewn together (figure 1).

Think about how much you want the muzzle to protrude from the face. If you would like a rather subtle, nearly flat muzzle, draw pieces with subtle curves. If you want the muzzle to protrude dramatically from the face, draw pieces with steep, very rounded curves (figure 2).

Now test your muzzle design by sewing a muslin prototype. Sew the pieces together (see step 6). Put a ball of stuffing inside it so that you can see its shape. Go back and adjust the pattern pieces as needed, making the

curves steeper or shallower, lengthening or shortening the pieces; sew a second muzzle prototype. Experimenting with how curved pattern pieces create three-dimensional shapes is the best way to gain confidence with this aspect of pattern design.

If you think about it, darts shape fabric in the same way that curved pattern pieces do. A very wide, curved dart creates a rounded protrusion in that area of the toy. A narrow, straighter dart creates a more subtle effect. The difference is that curved pattern pieces are cut apart completely so that even more of a steep curve can be added to each piece, resulting in a muzzle that can dramatically protrude from the face.

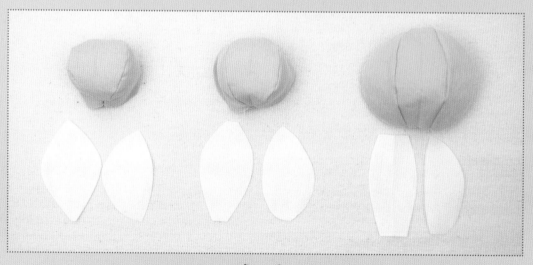

figure 2

Lesson 46: Making Feet at a Right Angle to the Legs

Curves are also responsible for controlling the way the Monkey's foot meets its leg. Where the foot and leg meet, I have drawn rather steep inward curves on both pattern pieces. When these two inward curves are sewn together, the foot is pulled upward so that it meets the leg at a right angle. The heel, on the other hand, juts out. Where the back of the leg meets the bottom of the foot I have drawn steep outward curves on both pattern pieces (figure 3). When these two outward curves are sewn together, a protruding heel shape is formed (see figure 7 on page 148).

figure 3

Lesson 47: Topstitching for Dimension and Jointing

Simple rag dolls often have lines of topstitching for joints. A row of stitching across the limbs at the knee and the elbow allows the arms and legs to bend easily at those points. On the Monkey, the areas above the topstitching (the upper arms and the thighs) are left unstuffed, but you could stuff them, topstitch across at the joint, and then stuff the calves and forearms, too. Topstitched joints are especially nice for a toy that will sit on a shelf: the thighs rest horizontally while the lower calves and feet dangle. Be sure to backstitch at the beginning and end of the lines of stitching to hold the stitches in place. And remember, the stitches will show, so be sure to stitch neatly!

Hands That Can Hold and Hug

Toys that sit up and have arms and hands can hold or hug something or someone. The Monkey's banana is slipped under a band of ¼-inch (6 mm) elastic that was sewn into the hand when it was stitched together. (Alternatively, use a hair elastic that you have cut through.) Another possibility is to sew a square of hook-and-loop tape on the palm and a coordinating piece on the banana, or sew the corresponding piece of hook-and-loop tape to the other palm to create a Monkey that can form a hug. A third method is to insert a very strong magnet in the Monkey's hand after the toy is turned right side out, before stuffing. Place the magnet right up against the palm fabric, then use small bits of stuffing to nestle it firmly in place. Test a corresponding magnet to make sure it has the opposite polarity, then insert it into the banana, or into the other palm for a Monkey that can hug. Keep in mind, though, that small magnets are not safe for toys that will be given to children who might swallow them.

HIPPO

Hippos may appear big and lazy, but they are in fact fast runners regarded by many to be one of the most dangerous animals in Africa! A squishy fleece toy Hippo, though, is soft, sweet, and ready for a snuggle. Making this Hippo helps you practice sewing a toy with an open mouth; the same technique can be used to design a hand puppet. And its nostrils and toes are defined with needle sculpting, a finishing detail used to bring out a toy's features.

Steps

1. Trace the pattern pieces (page 187) onto freezer paper with a pencil. Cut them out, transferring all of the markings. Assemble the Side Body and Underbody pattern pieces.

2. Be sure to place all of the pattern pieces parallel to the selvage when working with fleece to ensure that the toy retains its shape once stuffed and does not stretch too much. Fold the gray fleece in half, right sides together. Iron the Side Body, Footpad, Head Gusset, and Underbody pattern pieces onto the fleece. Pin the layers of fleece together. Add a ¼-inch (6 mm) seam allowance to all of the pattern pieces and cut them out. Iron the Footpad pattern onto the fleece again and cut out two more Footpads. Use a disappearing fabric marker or chalk to transfer all of the markings to the fabric. Iron the Eyelid pattern piece to the doubled fleece and cut them out without adding any seam allowance.

3. Fold the legs of one underbody upward, right sides together, along the fold line and pin in place. Stitch the oval darts on each leg. Repeat for the other underbody and place them on top of one another, right sides together, and stitch across the top from point A to point B, leaving the opening for turning and stuffing as marked (figure 1).

4. Iron the Tail pattern piece to the folded fleece. Pin the layers together. With the pattern piece still adhered, stitch around the Tail without adding any seam allowance, leaving the bottom open as marked. Cut the tail out to within ⅛ inch (3 mm) of the stitching line and turn it right side out. Place the tail against one side body where marked, lining up the raw edges of the tail with the raw edges of the side body so that the tail is pointing down. Baste in place.

5. Cut two squares of fleece and two squares of pink flannel, each a bit larger than the Ear pattern piece. Layer one square of fleece on one square of flannel, right sides together, and iron the Ear pattern piece on top. Use a few pins to hold the layers together. With the pattern piece still adhered, stitch around the Ear, leaving the bottom open as marked. Cut around the ear to within ⅛ inch (3 mm) of the stitching line and turn it right side out. Repeat for the second ear. Fold the sides of each ear inward to the center, with the pink flannel as the inner ear, and baste to hold.

TOOLS & MATERIALS

Basic Sewing Tool Kit (page 11)

½ yard (45.7 cm) of gray fleece

Piece of pink flannel, 12 x 14 inches (30.5 x 35.6 cm)

Scraps of wool-blend felt in white, dark blue, and black

All-purpose polyester thread in gray and white

Extra-strong thread in light gray

6½ ounces (182 g) of fiberfill stuffing

1 white felted-wool ball, 15 mm in diameter

12-inch (30.5 cm) length of white perle cotton

5-inch (12.7 cm) doll needle

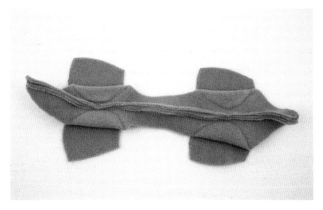

figure 1

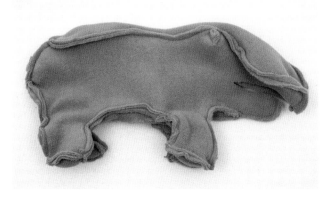

figure 2

6. Place one ear, pink side down, against one side body in the ear dart on the frontmost dart edge, aligning the raw edges of the ear with the edge of the dart. Fold the dart over the ear, pin, and stitch across the dart, closing it and catching the raw edges of the ear in the seam. Repeat for the other ear dart.

7. Place one side of the underbody against one side body, right sides together, lining up points A and B. Pin well. Stitch from point A down to the bottom of the front leg, leaving the foot open. Continue stitching up the other side of the front leg, under the belly and down the back leg, leaving the foot open. Stitch up the other side of the back leg and all the way to point B. Repeat for the other side of the underbody and the other side body.

8. Place the head gusset against one side body, right sides together, lining up points C and D. Stitch from point C to point D. Place the other side of the head gusset against the other side body and stitch from point C to point D (figure 2).

9. Iron the Tooth pattern piece to a double layer of white felt. With the pattern piece still adhered, stitch around the Tooth, leaving the bottom open as marked. Repeat to create a second tooth. Trim around each tooth to within ⅛ inch (3 mm) of the stitching line. Turn the teeth right side out and press. Place the teeth against the lower portion of the right side of the inner mouth where marked, lining up the raw edges of the teeth with the raw edges of the inner mouth. Baste in place.

10. Fold the pink flannel in half, right sides together, and iron the Inside Mouth pattern piece on top. With the pattern piece still adhered, stitch around the inward curve of the mouth from point E to point F. Cut the mouth out ¼ inch (6 mm) away from the pattern piece. Remove the pattern piece. Turn the mouth right side out and press. Fit it into the Hippo's body, aligning points E/F and C. Pin well (figure 3). Stitch the mouth to the upper jaw from point C to point E and from point C to point F. Stitch the mouth to the

Making a Hand Puppet

Making a hand puppet with a mouth that opens is very similar in concept to making a softie with a mouth that opens. To make a Hippo hand puppet I took the Hippo pattern and removed the legs and the behind. I widened the side body a bit to make room for my hand and arm. After I sewed it up, I made a double-fold hem on the bottom edges. Time for a puppet show!

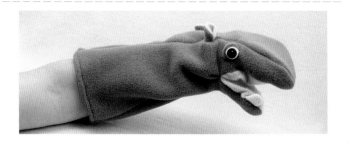

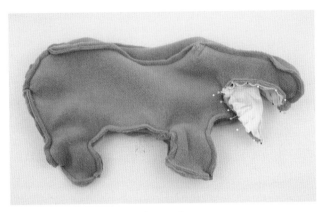

figure 3

lower jaw from point C to point E and from point C to point F, catching the raw edges of the teeth in the seam.

11. Stitch the remainder of the body together from point D to point B. Clip all of the curves and turn the Hippo right side out through the opening between the underbody pieces. Stuff the Hippo lightly so that it remains squishy. The lower jaw should be very lightly stuffed. Ladder-stitch the opening closed with gray extra-strong thread. To pull the teeth upward, tack them to the inner mouth with a few stitches using white thread.

12. Slice the felted-wool ball in half with a craft knife. Iron the Eye pattern piece to a scrap of dark blue felt and cut it out, adding no seam allowance. Repeat to create a second eye. Iron the Pupil pattern piece to a scrap of black felt and cut it out, adding no seam allowance. Repeat to create a second pupil. To create a highlight, thread a needle with a 12-inch (30.5 cm) length of perle cotton. Insert the needle through the pupil, leaving a 2-inch (5 cm) thread tail. Take two straight stitches right next to one another in the pupil. Take the needle off and tie the ends of the perle cotton in a double knot. Rethread the needle with the remaining length of perle cotton and repeat for the other pupil. Use a dab of craft glue to glue the pupil to the eye and then to glue the eye to the halved felted-wool ball (or whipstitch the pupils to the halved wool balls with coordinating thread). Use craft glue to adhere each of the halved wool balls to each side of the Hippo's face (or whipstitch them using coordinating thread). Pin an eyelid to each eye and stitch in place with gray all-purpose thread and whipstitch.

13. To needle-sculpt the nostrils, thread a 5-inch (12.7 cm) doll needle with a single strand of extra-strong light gray thread and tie a knot at the thread end. Insert the needle through a head gusset/side body seam, pulling the knot so that it slips between two of the stitches

Tail Options

A tail is a whimsical detail that can really add appeal to your toy's overall look. When designing a toy, consider various textures and shapes for the tail. The tail on the Hippo is fairly straightforward: a curved triangle that's been sewn, turned, and then stitched into the side body seam. But tails can be made in all kinds of ways.

A tail can have an interesting texture. A pompom creates a fluffy tail (see the Bunny on page 66). Make a tail with a fur tip by piecing scraps of long-pile faux fur to the end of the tail pieces. A tassel, strands of rickrack, long lengths of yarn, or torn fabric strips can be a tail. For a fringed tail, cut a square or rectangle of a nonfraying fabric and roll it up. Ladder-stitch or whipstitch the edge to hold the roll in place, than make small snips all along one of the short ends of the roll.

To create a curly tail, make a pattern piece like a spiral. A pipe cleaner inserted into a tail helps hold its shape.

Prepare the pipe cleaner by forming a loop on the end before inserting it into the tail so that the wire does not poke through the fabric.

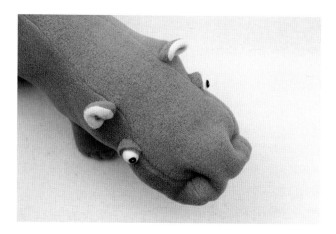

figure 4

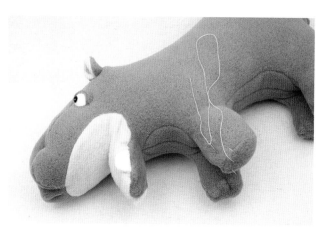

figure 5

of the seam and into the body. Bring the needle up at one nostril as marked on the Head Gusset and reinsert the needle right next to where you came up, making a small stitch. Bring the needle up through the second nostril, make a small stitch, and go back through the first nostril. Squeeze the nostrils inward with your finger, making an indentation, then pull the thread taut to hold the shape. Go back and forth as many times as needed until you are satisfied with the sculpting. Make a knot by wrapping the thread around the needle once or twice, then insert the needle through the sculpting stitch and come out a little ways away. Pull the thread end taut and snip it off so that the tail gets buried inside the stuffing (figure 4).

14. To needle-sculpt the toes, thread a 5-inch (12.7 cm) doll needle with a single 24-inch (61 cm) strand of light gray extra-strong thread. Tie a knot in

one end. Insert the needle through the heel of one leg at the point where the leg seams meet one another and the footpad. Bring the needle through the foot, coming out at the first dot on the footpad. Pull the thread taut so the knot slips inside the body. Insert the needle into the first dot on the leg, exiting through the second dot on the footpad (figure 5). Use your fingers to pinch the toe together, then pull the thread taut. This is the first toe. Continue sculpting the toes by entering through the dot on the leg and out the corresponding dot on the footpad until all five toes have been defined, pinching them each time with your fingers. Bring the thread out through the back of the leg where it originally entered. Tie a knot and insert the needle back into the same spot, exiting a little ways away. Pull the thread taut and cut it, burying the thread tail inside the leg. Repeat on the other feet.

Lesson 48: Creating an Open Mouth

A toy with an open mouth makes you wonder what it might say—it really gives a softie a personality, and it is a great technique to have in your repertoire. To add an open mouth to your toy pattern, draw a line on the side body where you'd like the mouth to be. The length of

the line equals the depth of the mouth. On the Hippo I chose to start the mouth at the point where the tip of the head gusset meets the side body to create a neat conglomeration of seams. You may want to widen the line a little bit above and below, curving upward or downward to control the shape of the mouth (figure 1).

Next, you need to create a pattern for the inside of the mouth. If the upper and lower jaws are the same length, you can create just one pattern piece and use it for both; otherwise, measure the length of each jaw to determine the length of each pattern piece. To get the width and outer curve of the pattern, I actually sewed up the rest of the Hippo's body, then inserted a piece of freezer paper between the upper and lower jaws, spread the jaws out as far as they would go, and traced them. It may not be the most elegant way to get the shape of a pattern piece, but it works! Where the pattern pieces meet at the back of the mouth, draw an inward curve (figure 2). This eliminates the excess fabric that would otherwise bunch up on the inside of the mouth.

Go easy when stuffing a toy with an open mouth. You may want to leave the lower jaw unstuffed, or stuff it very lightly. Firmly stuffing this area will distort the shape of the mouth.

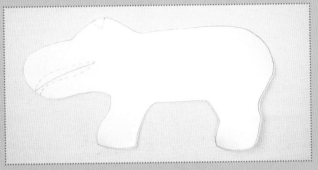

figure 1

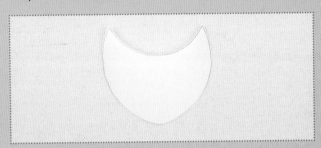

figure 2

Lesson 49: Needle Sculpting

Needle sculpting is a technique in which you define a toy's features by passing a needle and thread through parts of the body as you mold the face or body with the tips of your fingers. Then you tie off the thread to hold the shape of the molded area. The Hippo's nostrils are needle-sculpted, as are its toes. Try needle sculpting to make a bulge for a nose by alternately taking tiny stitches on either side of the nose, passing your needle under the stuffing, and pinching the nose with each stitch. Dimpled cheeks, kneecaps, or a furrowed brow can all be defined using needle sculpting.

Lesson 50: Darted Ear Slits

The ears on this softie are machine sewn. I like machine-sewn ears because they are quicker and neater to attach and are held on more strongly than hand-sewn ears. I knew I needed to cut a slit in the Hippo's side body to machine-sew the ears, and I decided that instead of just a slit, I would create a dart at the same time. Remember, any time there is a seam there is an opportunity to create shape and to attach parts, and darted ear slits do both! The dart helps round the Hippo's head and delineate where the head ends and the body begins, and by slipping the ears into the dart, I get machine-sewn ears, too!

To create a darted ear slit, mark where on the body you want the ears to be placed. Draw a slit that is at least a ¼ inch (6 mm) longer than the ear to account for the seam allowance. Now think about the shape of the dart. A very wide dart with sides that curve away from one another creates a significant rounded protrusion, whereas a small, straight dart provides more subtle shaping. Draw the dart and cut it away. When you are ready to sew, simply slip the ears into the dart, lining up the raw edges of the ears with the edges of the dart before you sew it up.

DINOSAUR

Roar! The power and mythic quality of dinosaurs make them eternally popular with young children. And after making a toy with an open mouth like the Hippo (page 152), this pattern takes things to the next level by inserting a zipper so that the mouth can be zipped up! Whenever people get close to this Dino they can't help but to zip and unzip his mouth. The zipper makes him an irresistible toy!

Steps

1. Trace the pattern pieces (page 189) onto freezer paper with a pencil. Cut them out, transferring all of the markings. Tape together the two Side Body pieces and the two Spine pieces where indicated.

2. Adding a ¼-inch (6 mm) seam allowance to all of the pattern pieces unless otherwise indicated, cut out from the green fleece one Head Gusset, one Lower Jaw, two Head Sides (reversing one), four Footpads, two Underbodies (reversing one), and two Side Bodies. Cut two Mouth pieces from red velveteen (reversing one). Transfer all the markings to the fabric with disappearing fabric marker or chalk.

3. Fold the yellow fleece in half, right sides together. Iron the Spine pattern piece on the wrong side of the fleece and stitch from point A, around each spike, to point B at the base. Trim to within ⅛ inch (3 mm) of the stitching line, then pull the pattern piece off.

4. On the underbody pieces fold each leg up, right sides together, on the fold line and stitch each oval dart. Place the two underbody pieces on top of one another, right sides together, and stitch from point C to point D, leaving an opening as marked.

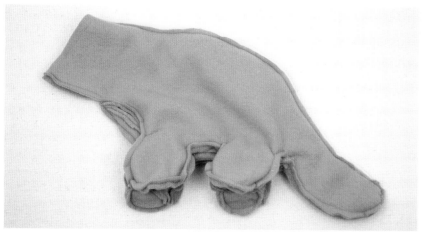

figure 1

figure 2

figure 3

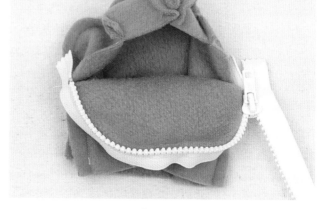

figure 4

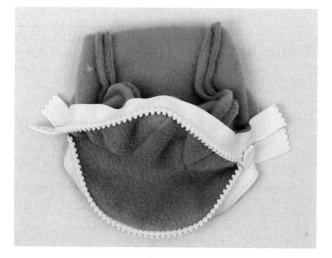

figure 5

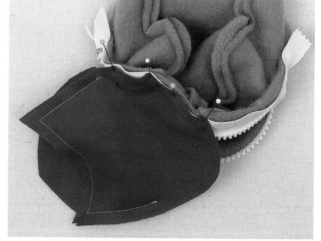

figure 6

5. Place one underbody against one side body, right sides together, and stitch from point C down to the base of the front leg. Leave the base of the leg open as marked. Stitch from the back part of the leg, up under the belly, and down to the base of the back leg. Leaving the base of the back leg open as marked, stitch from the back part of the back leg up to point D. Repeat for the other side of the underbody and the other side body.

6. Place one footpad against one foot, right sides together. Pin and stitch. (For more on footpads, see lesson 17 on page 73.) Repeat for the remaining feet.

7. Place the spine against one side body, aligning the raw edges of the spine with the raw edges of the side body. Baste in place. Pin the side bodies together and stitch from point C to point E and from point D around the tail up to point A. Remove the basting stitches on the spine. Clip all of the curves on the body and set it aside (figure 1).

8. Stitch the triangular darts on each head side closed. Place one head side on top of one side of the head gusset, right sides together, aligning points F and G, and stitch. Repeat for the other head side. Set aside.

9. Place the two mouth pieces right sides together and stitch from point H, along the inner portion of the mouth, to point I as marked (figure 2).

10. Stitch the triangular dart on the lower jaw closed. Place the lower jaw against the now-constructed upper portion of the head, right sides together, and stitch from point J to point K, and from point J1 to point K1 (figure 3).

11. Attach the zipper foot to your sewing machine and adjust the needle position so that you can sew very close to the zipper as it slides next to the foot on the left. Open the 7-inch (17.8 cm) sport zipper most of the way and place it against the lower jaw piece, right sides together, aligning the outer edge of the zipper with the edge of the lower jaw, beginning at point K and extending to K1. Make sure the zipper is on top of the fabric, right sides together. Pin every ¼ inch (6 mm). Stitch from K to K1, pausing to move the zipper pull out of your way as you go (figure 4). Stitch the other outer edge of the zipper to the upper portion of the head from point K, around the nose, to the other point K. Now you have an upper jaw and a lower jaw with a zipper in between (figure 5)!

12. Open the red mouth and place one side of the mouth against one unsewn edge of the zipper, right sides together. Pin every ¼ inch (6 mm) (figure 6). Stitch from point H to point I, pausing periodically to move the zipper pull out of your way. Pin and stitch the lower part of the mouth to the other unsewn zipper portion, right sides together, from point H to point I. Clip all of the curves on the head and turn it right side out (you don't need to clip the curve of the zipper).

13. Insert the head into the body, aligning the dart seam on the lower jaw with point E on the body. Pin and stitch in place. (For more on inserting a presewn head into a presewn body, see lesson 21 on page 82.)

14. Clip all the curves and trim the seam allowance at the tip of the tail. Pull the Dinosaur right side out through the opening between the underbodies. Stuff the Dinosaur firmly, leaving the lower jaw only very lightly stuffed. Ladder-stitch the opening closed with green extra-strong thread.

15. Cut four Large Spots, two Medium Spots, and four Small Spots from dark green felted wool, adding no seam allowance. Pin the spots to the Dinosaur's back and whipstitch them in place with dark green all-purpose thread.

16. Cut two white Eyes, two dark brown Eyeballs, two light brown Eyeballs, and two black Pupils from the wool-blend felt, adding no seam allowances. Using a 12-inch (30.5 cm) strand of perle cotton, make two closely spaced straight stitches in each pupil to create highlights, tying the thread ends in a double knot on the back of each pupil to secure. Layer the pupils on the dark brown eyeballs and affix with a dab of craft glue (or whipstitch in place). Layer the dark brown eyeballs on the light brown eyeballs, offsetting slightly, and affix with a dab of craft glue (or whipstitch in place). Whipstitch the dark brown eyeballs to the eyes with dark brown all-purpose thread. Pin the eyes on the Dinosaur and whipstitch the whites in place with white all-purpose thread.

Lesson 51: Creating a Zippered Mouth

"Zip your lips!" was the expression that inspired this toy's design. A zipper is a fun, interactive element to add to a toy. To install it you stitch the outer edges of the zipper tape to the toy's body and the inner edges to a presewn pocket. It isn't tricky to sew the zipper as long as you have the right tool: you need to attach a zipper foot to your sewing machine. This allows you to stitch right up next to the zipper teeth (figure 1). If your machine has an adjustable needle position, shift the needle all the way over, close to the zipper teeth.

I chose a white sport zipper for this toy because it has large, exposed plastic teeth that look like . . . teeth! Zippers come in all different colors, lengths, and styles, though, so choose one that will work well for your particular toy's design. A 7-inch (17.8 cm) opening was a good length for the mouth on this Dinosaur.

To design the pattern pieces I employed the same method used in the Hippo (page 152), whose mouth is an open pocket; see lesson 48 on page 156. The difference here is that instead of sewing the head to the mouth pocket, I sewed the head to the outer edges of the zipper and the mouth to the inner edges of the zipper.

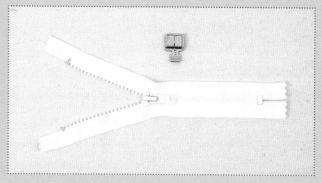

figure 1

To prepare the head before inserting the zipper I wanted to first close up the sides of the face and the sides of the mouth. I stitched the upper portion of the head to the lower portion, leaving a 7-inch (17.8 cm) opening between them for the zipper. This gives me a clear starting and stopping point for sewing in the zipper, and it neatly encloses the ends of the zipper, too. To prepare the red inside of the mouth I stitched the mouth pieces together along the last inch (2.5 cm) or so of the edges and along the back wall, leaving 7 inches (17.8 cm) in the front open to stitch to the zipper. Once the jaws and mouth are prepped, it's time to sew in the zipper. Attach the zipper foot and move the needle position over.

Next, it is just a matter of stitching the outer edge of the zipper along the 7-inch (17.8 cm) opening on first the upper then the lower portions of the head, right sides together. The zipper pull will get in the way, so you'll need to pause halfway through and unzip or zip up

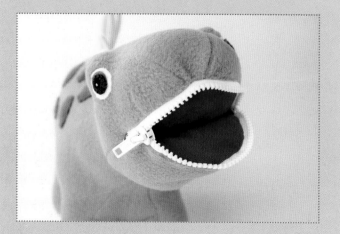

the zipper to move it out of the way. The zipper pull will get in the way, so you'll need to pause halfway through and unzip or zip up the zipper to move it out of the way. Stitch one inner edge of the zipper to one side of the mouth, right sides together, and then stitch the other inner edge of the zipper to the other side of the mouth, right sides together.

Unzip the zipper and turn the head right side out. Open and close the zipper and examine the seams. If your stitching isn't quite straight or any repairs need to be made, turn the head inside out and fix it. Once you are satisfied, turn the head right side out and insert it into the neck opening to stitch it in place.

When stuffing a toy with a zippered mouth, like a toy with an open mouth, stuff the lower jaw very lightly or leave it unstuffed. Too much stuffing can make it difficult to zip the zipper and distorts the shape of the mouth.

Lesson 52: Compensating for a Top-Heavy Design

One thing that appeals to me about this Dinosaur is his outsize head. A big head gives him a cute, babyish appearance, but it also makes him top heavy. I didn't want to reduce his head size, but I did want him to be able to stand up on his own. There are a few tweaks you can make to a pattern if you want to make a top-heavy design work. First, you can shorten the back legs. Front legs that are longer than back legs tip the Dinosaur backward a bit, helping to maintain balance (figure 2). Second, you can shorten the neck, shifting the center of gravity toward the middle of the toy and away from the front end. If all else fails, you can sew a weight into the back end of the toy. Some possible weights include glass pellets (see lesson 36 on page 119 for more on glass pellets), steel fishing weights (also called "sinkers") found at sporting goods stores, or even smooth stones. Whatever weight you choose, enclose it in a muslin bag that you stitch closed and tack in place inside the toy to prevent it from drifting during play or washing.

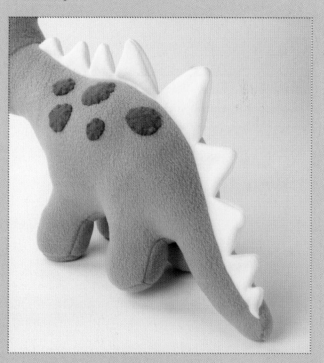

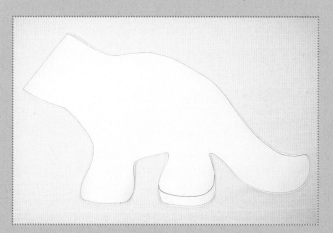

figure 2

TEMPLATES

Every template in this book is printed at full-size except for the Dinosaur's templates. The Dinosaur's templates are all printed at 90% size, which means all pieces will need to be enlarged 110%.

In order to include full-sized templates, some of the individual pieces are layered on top of one another. Although this may seem confusing at first glance, once you look a bit closer you'll see templates with colored outlines overlaying templates with black outlines. To trace a particular template piece, simply follow its outline and transfer its markings to your paper pattern. Or, if you are using a copier, make two copies (one for the colored layer and one for the black layer). Again, the Dinosaur on page 189 caused problems with his size—he will need three copies.

For your convenience, the templates for all of the patterns in this book are also available in a single layer online. When you print them out, be sure it is set to print "size at 100%" or "actual size." Do not set the document to print "to fit." To download these full-sized, single layer templates visit: www.LarkCrafts.com/bonus

For the patterns in this book you'll need to add $1/4$-inch (6 mm) seam allowance. The quickest way to do this is to simply eyeball it. Trace around the pattern piece on the fabric, or iron it on if the pattern has been copied onto freezer paper, then cut the fabric $1/4$ inch (6 mm) away from the edge of the pattern piece measuring it by eye. With a little practice, cutting a $1/4$ inch (6 mm) away becomes easy. If you aren't comfortable eyeballing it, use a sliding gauge (page 12) set at $1/4$ inch (6 mm). Line it up with the edge of the pattern piece and use a disappearing fabric marker or chalk to make a dot $1/4$ inch (6 mm) away. Move the gauge over $1/2$ inch (1.3 cm), and make another dot. Continue all the way around the pattern piece, making dots $1/4$ inch (6 mm) away from the edge of the pattern piece every $1/2$ inch (1.3 cm). Connect the dots to create a $1/4$-inch (6 mm) seam allowance, then cut the fabric along this line.

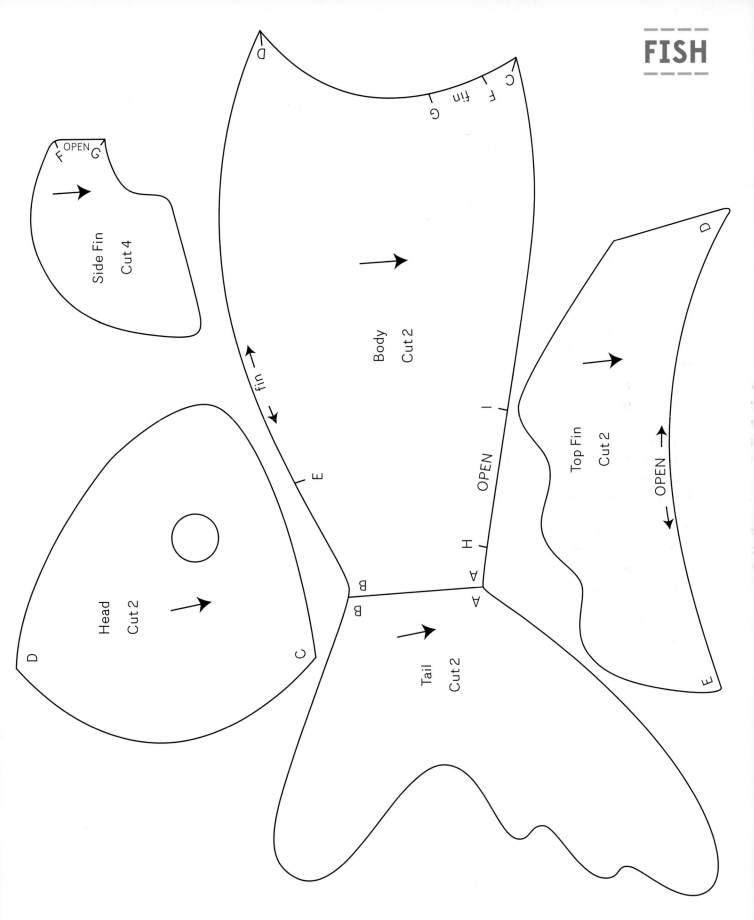

FISH

Side Fin
Cut 4

F OPEN G

Body
Cut 2

D

C fin F G

fin
E

Head
Cut 2

D

C

Top Fin
Cut 2

D

OPEN

E

I

OPEN

H

A

A

B

B

Tail
Cut 2

BUMBLEBEE

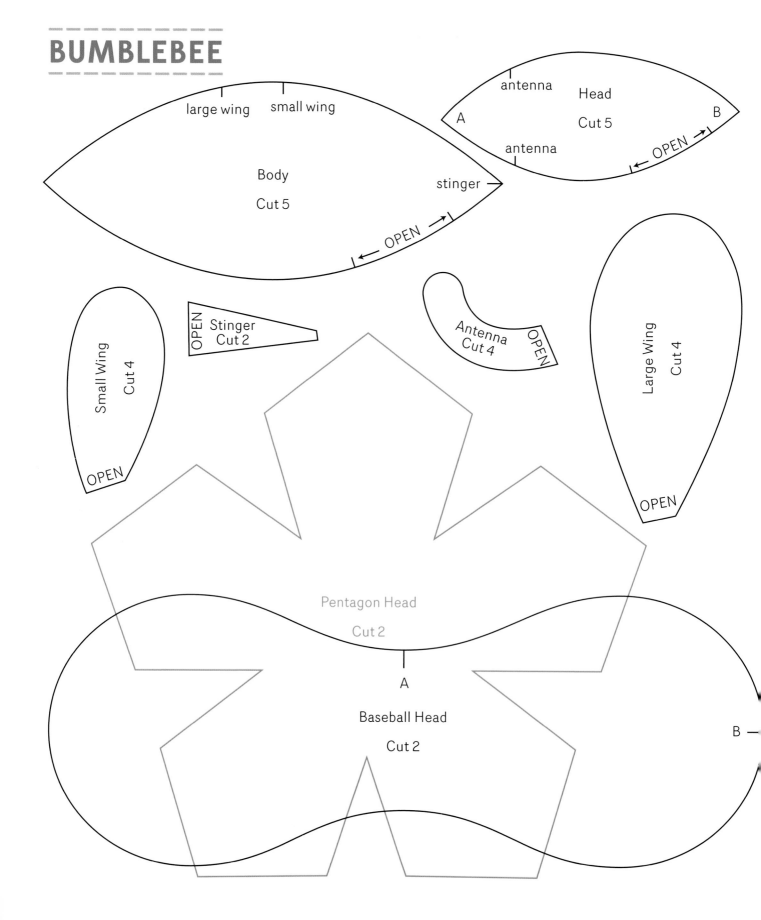

large wing   small wing

antenna   Head
Cut 5

A   B

antenna

Body
Cut 5

stinger

OPEN

OPEN

Small Wing
Cut 4

OPEN   Stinger
Cut 2

Antenna
Cut 4

OPEN

Large Wing
Cut 4

OPEN

OPEN

Pentagon Head

Cut 2

A

Baseball Head

Cut 2

B

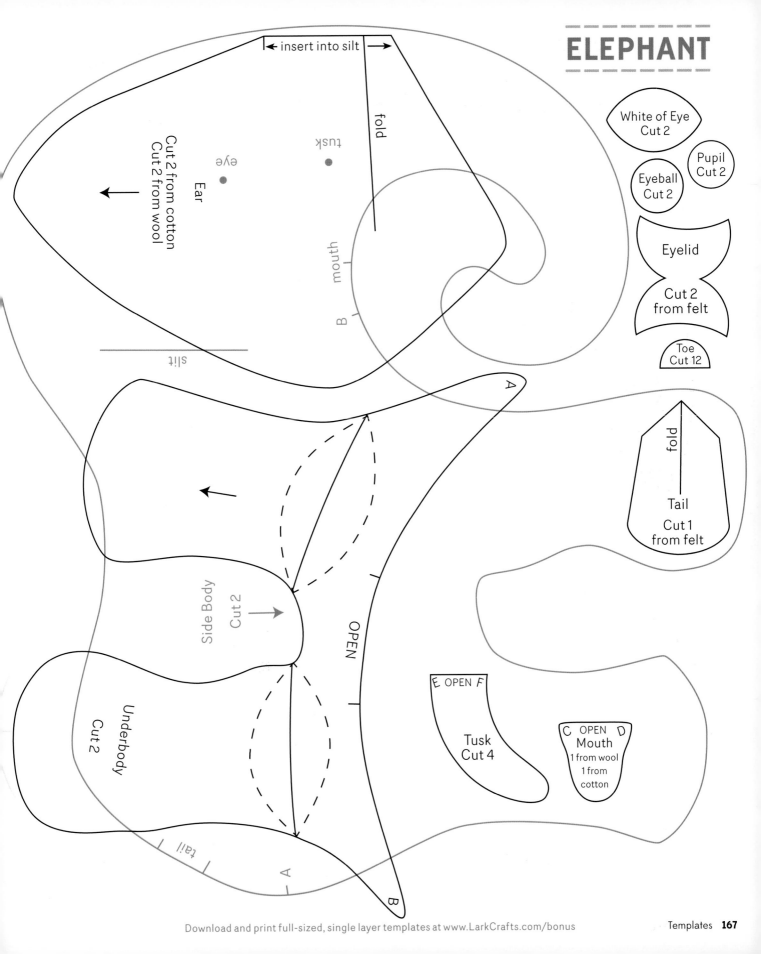

ELEPHANT

White of Eye
Cut 2

Pupil
Cut 2

Eyeball
Cut 2

Eyelid

Cut 2
from felt

Toe
Cut 12

fold

Tail
Cut 1
from felt

insert into silt

fold

tusk

eye

Ear

Cut 2 from cotton
Cut 2 from wool

mouth

B

silt

A

Side Body
Cut 2

OPEN

Underbody
Cut 2

tail

A

B

E OPEN F

Tusk
Cut 4

C OPEN D
Mouth
1 from wool
1 from
cotton

RAM

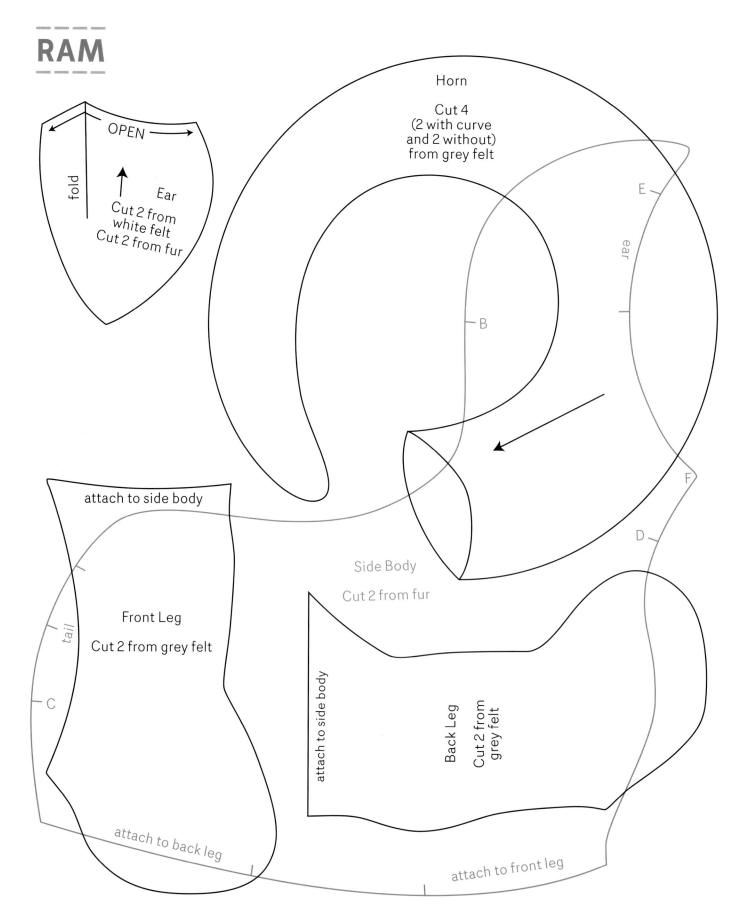

OPEN

fold

Ear
Cut 2 from
white felt
Cut 2 from fur

Horn

Cut 4
(2 with curve
and 2 without)
from grey felt

E

ear

B

F

D

attach to side body

Side Body

Cut 2 from fur

Front Leg

Cut 2 from grey felt

tail

C

attach to side body

Back Leg

Cut 2 from
grey felt

attach to back leg

attach to front leg

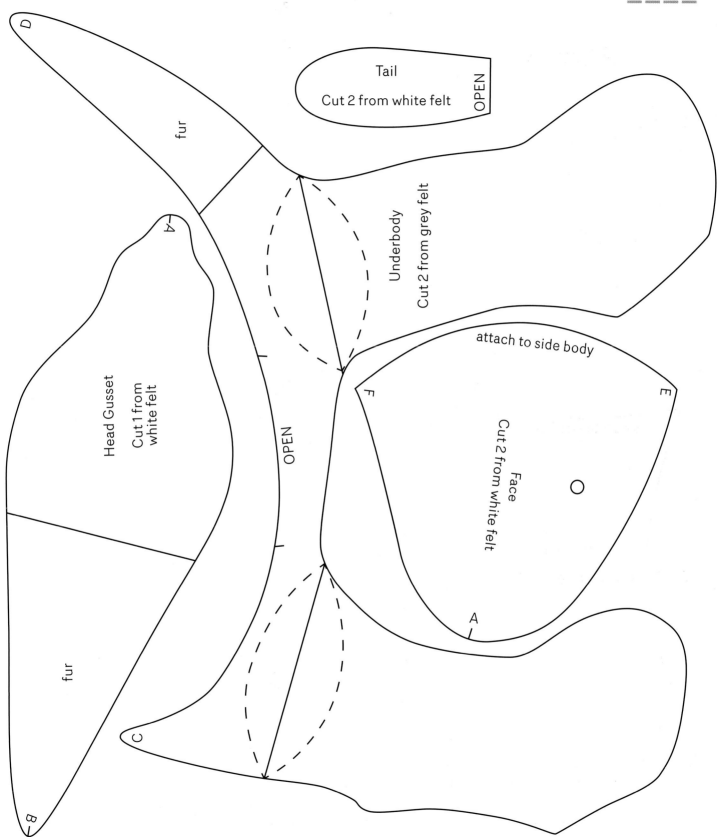

Tail

Cut 2 from white felt

OPEN

fur

D

A

Underbody
Cut 2 from grey felt

attach to side body

F

E

Head Gusset

Cut 1 from white felt

OPEN

Face
Cut 2 from white felt

fur

A

C

B

BUNNY

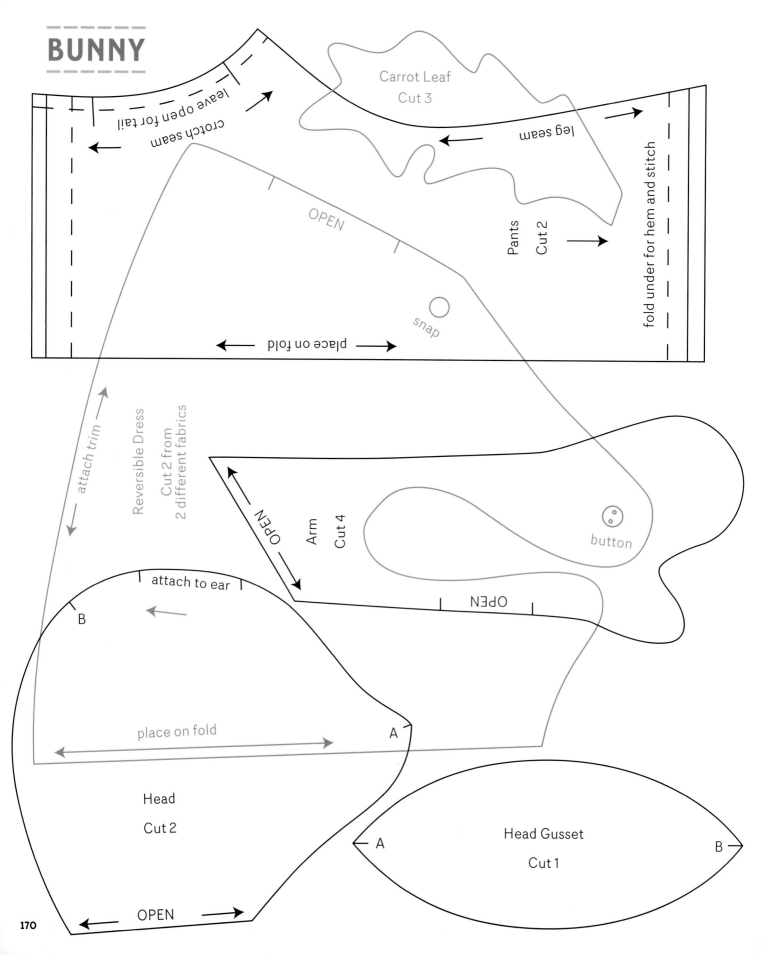

Carrot Leaf
Cut 3

leave open for tail

crotch seam

leg seam

OPEN

Pants
Cut 2

fold under for hem and stitch

snap

place on fold

attach trim

Reversible Dress
Cut 2 from
2 different fabrics

OPEN

Arm
Cut 4

button

OPEN

attach to ear

B

place on fold

A

OPEN

Head

Cut 2

A

Head Gusset

Cut 1

B

BUNNY

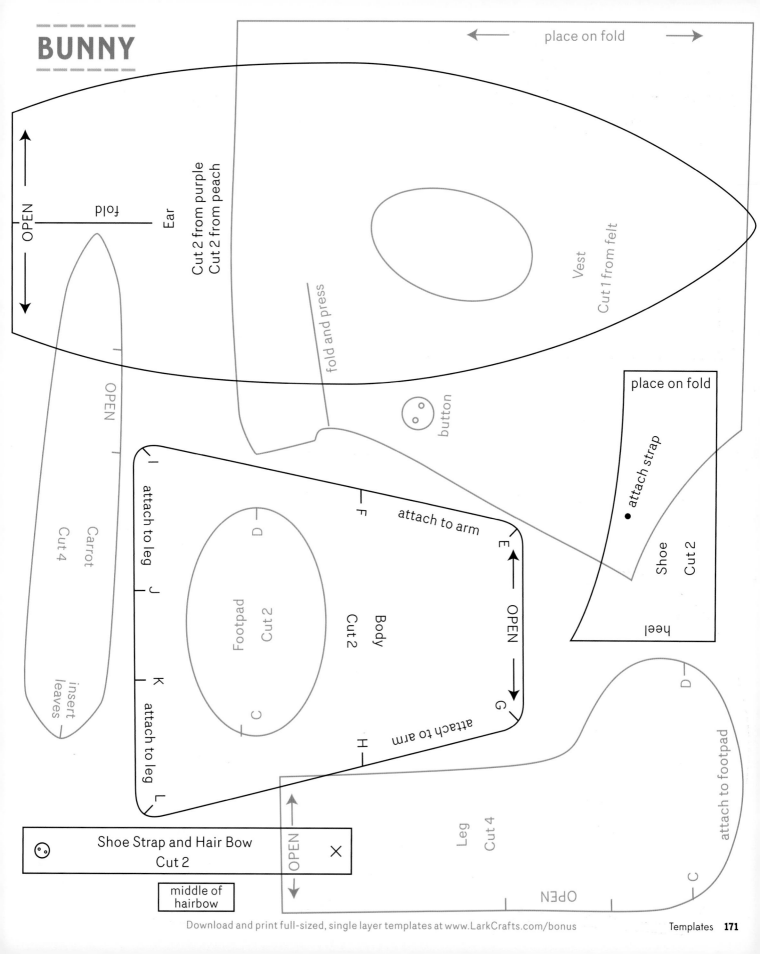

place on fold

OPEN

fold

Ear

Cut 2 from purple
Cut 2 from peach

Vest
Cut 1 from felt

fold and press

button

place on fold

attach strap

Shoe
Cut 2

heel

OPEN

Carrot
Cut 4

insert leaves

I

attach to leg

J

attach to leg

K

L

D

Footpad
Cut 2

C

F

Body
Cut 2

E

OPEN

G

attach to arm

attach to arm

H

D

attach to footpad

Leg
Cut 4

OPEN

C

OPEN

X

Shoe Strap and Hair Bow
Cut 2

middle of
hairbow

PUPPY

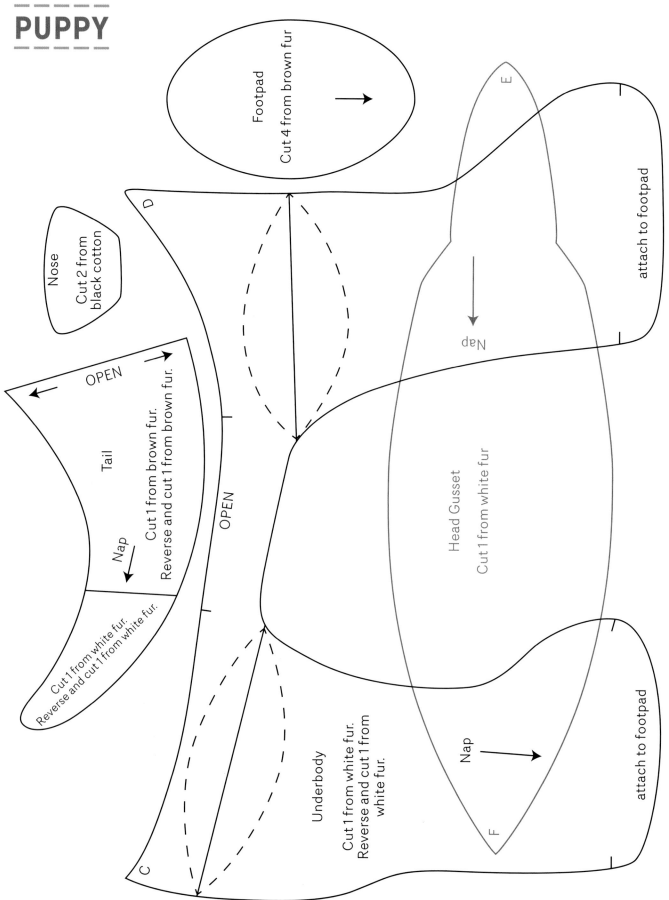

Footpad
Cut 4 from brown fur

Nose
Cut 2 from black cotton

D

OPEN

Tail
Cut 1 from brown fur.
Reverse and cut 1 from brown fur.

Nap

OPEN

OPEN

Cut 1 from white fur.
Reverse and cut 1 from white fur.

E

attach to footpad

Nap

Head Gusset
Cut 1 from white fur

Underbody
Cut 1 from white fur.
Reverse and cut 1 from white fur.

Nap

F

attach to footpad

C

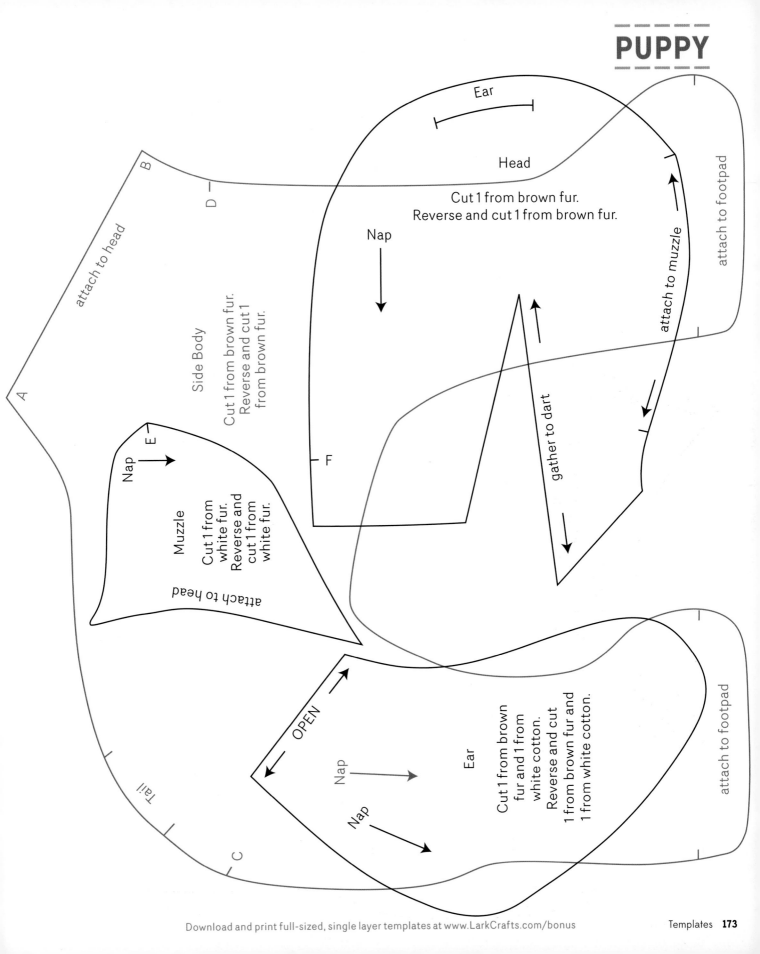

PUPPY

Ear

Head

Cut 1 from brown fur.
Reverse and cut 1 from brown fur.

Nap

attach to head

attach to footpad

attach to muzzle

B

D

Side Body

Cut 1 from brown fur.
Reverse and cut 1
from brown fur.

Nap

F

A

gather to dart

E

Nap

Muzzle

Cut 1 from
white fur.
Reverse and
cut 1 from
white fur.

attach to head

Tail

C

OPEN

Nap

Nap

Ear

Cut 1 from brown
fur and 1 from
white cotton.
Reverse and cut
1 from brown fur and
1 from white cotton.

attach to footpad

LION

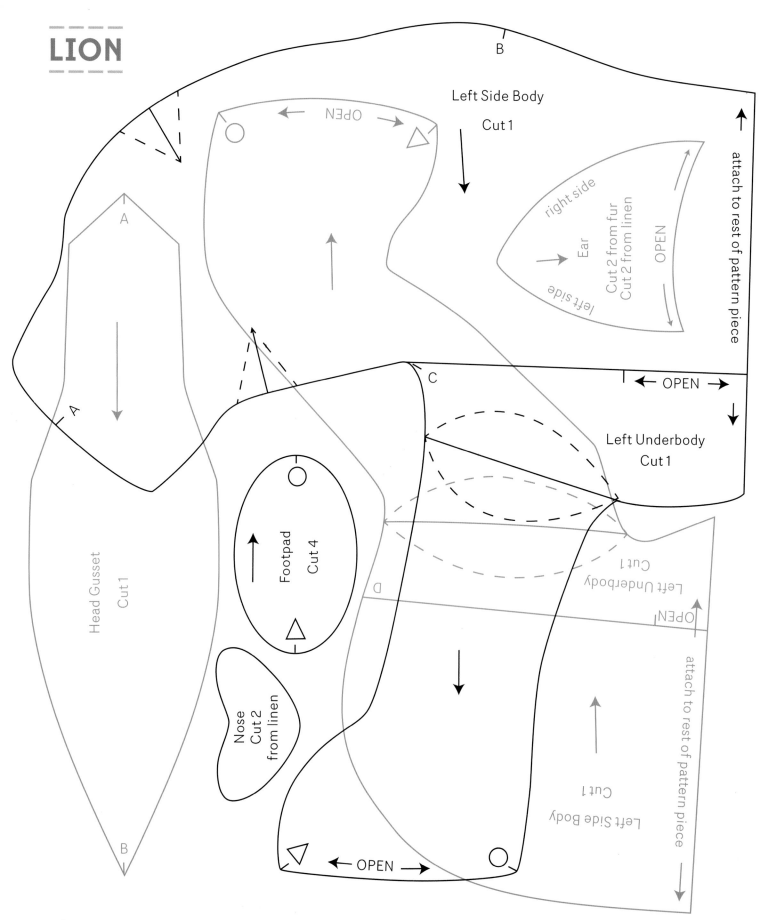

Left Side Body
Cut 1

B

right side

Ear
Cut 2 from fur
Cut 2 from linen

OPEN

left side

attach to rest of pattern piece

OPEN

C

Left Underbody
Cut 1

A

A

Head Gusset
Cut 1

Footpad
Cut 4

Left Underbody
Cut 1

OPEN

attach to rest of pattern piece

D

Nose
Cut 2
from linen

Left Side Body
Cut 1

B

OPEN

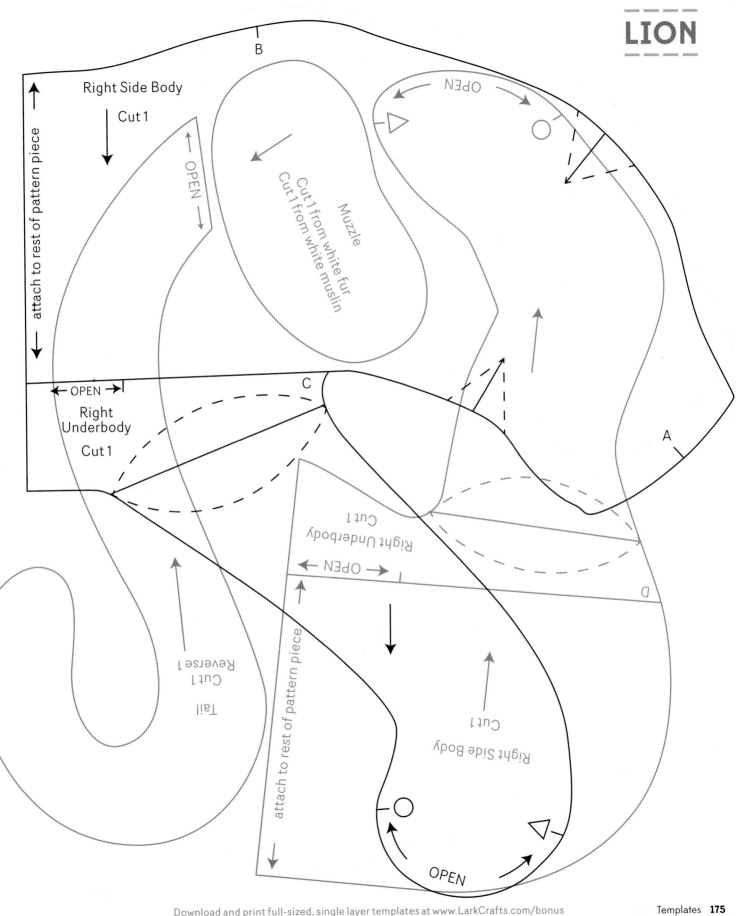

Right Side Body

Cut 1

attach to rest of pattern piece

OPEN

OPEN

B

Muzzle

Cut 1 from white fur
Cut 1 from white muslin

OPEN

C

OPEN

Right
Underbody

Cut 1

Right Underbody
Cut 1

OPEN

D

A

Tail
Cut 1
Reverse 1

attach to rest of pattern piece

Right Side Body

Cut 1

OPEN

CAT

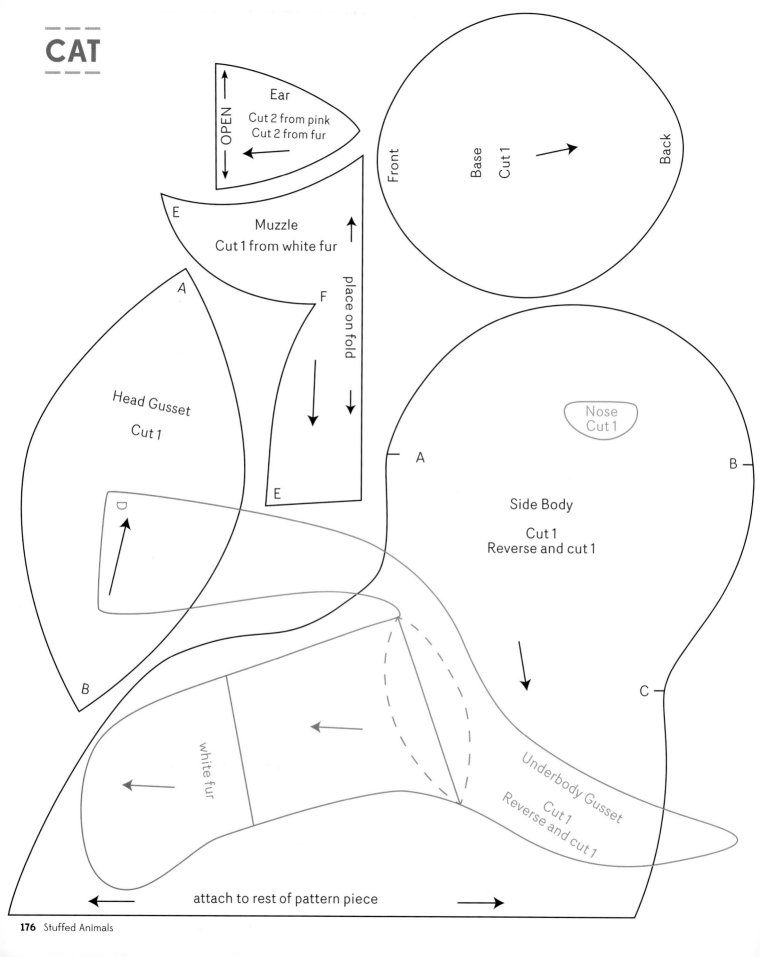

Ear
Cut 2 from pink
Cut 2 from fur

OPEN

Base
Cut 1

Front

Back

Muzzle
Cut 1 from white fur

E

F

place on fold

E

A

Head Gusset
Cut 1

D

B

Nose
Cut 1

A

Side Body

Cut 1
Reverse and cut 1

B

C

white fur

Underbody Gusset
Cut 1
Reverse and cut 1

attach to rest of pattern piece

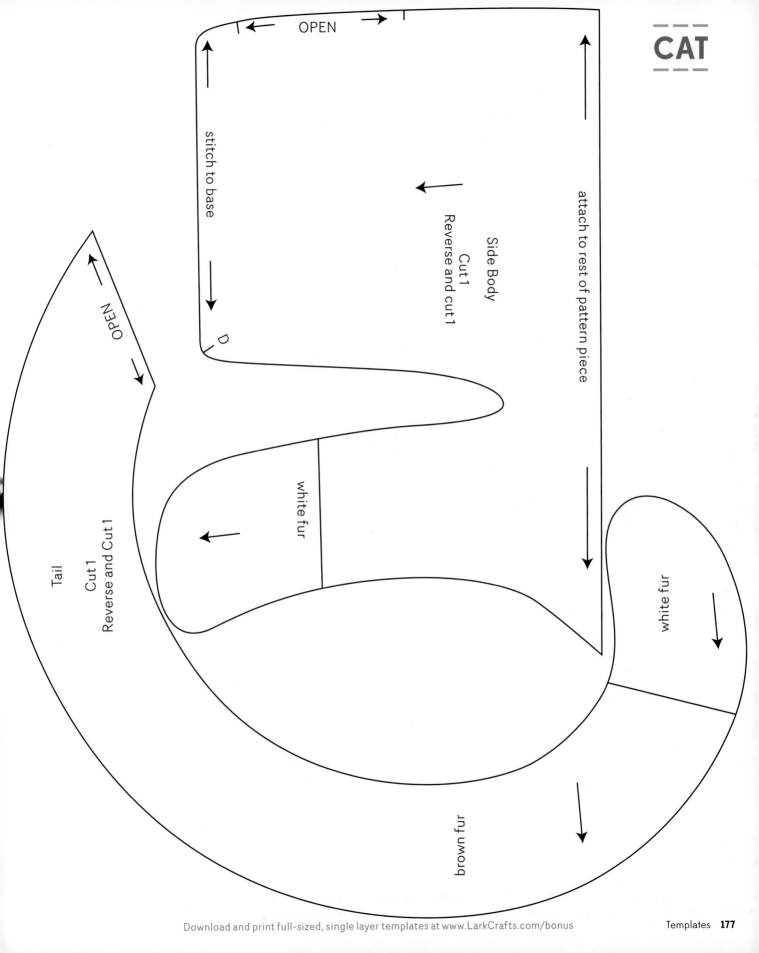

OPEN

CAT

stitch to base

Side Body

Cut 1
Reverse and cut 1

attach to rest of pattern piece

OPEN

Tail

Cut 1
Reverse and Cut 1

white fur

white fur

brown fur

CAMEL

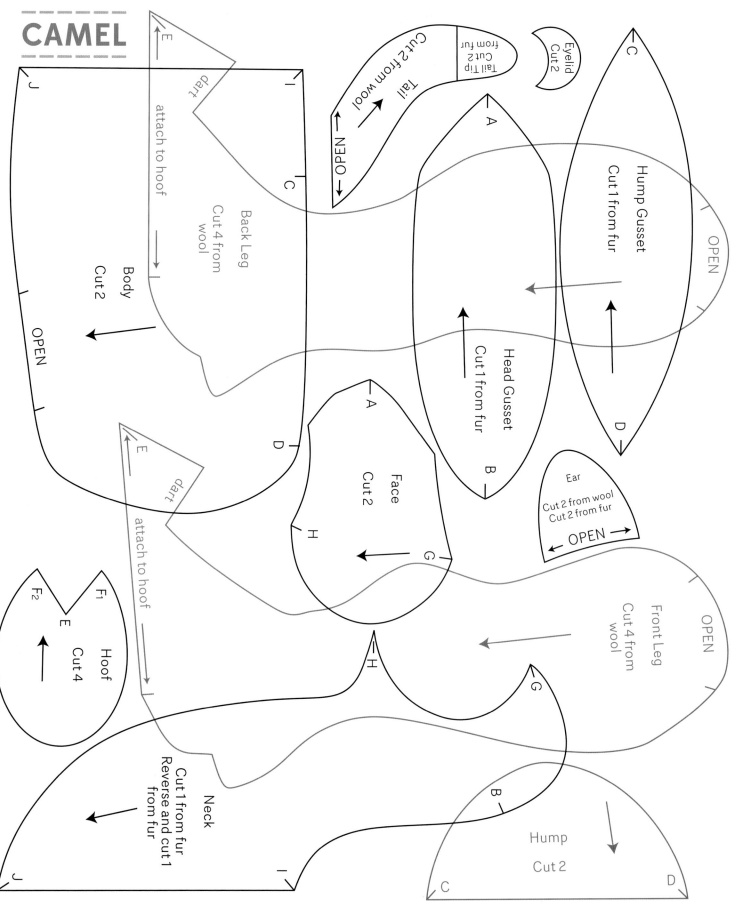

Hump Gusset
Cut 1 from fur

Head Gusset
Cut 1 from fur

Back Leg
Cut 4 from wool

Body
Cut 2

attach to hoof

dart

OPEN

Tail
Cut 2 from wool

Tail Tip
Cut 2 from fur

Eyelid
Cut 2

OPEN

Face
Cut 2

Ear
Cut 2 from wool
Cut 2 from fur
OPEN

Front Leg
Cut 4 from wool

OPEN

Hoof
Cut 4

attach to hoof

dart

Neck
Cut 1 from fur
Reverse and cut 1
from fur

Hump
Cut 2

MONSTER

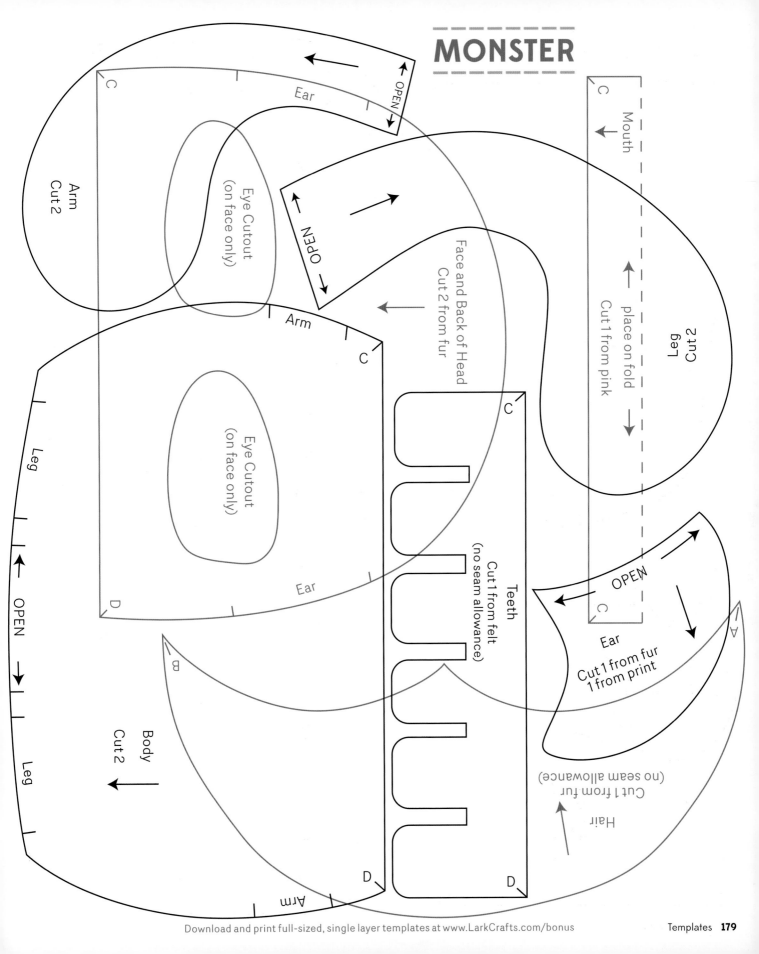

Ear

OPEN

Arm
Cut 2

Eye Cutout
(on face only)

OPEN

Arm

C

Mouth

place on fold
Cut 1 from pink

Leg
Cut 2

Face and Back of Head
Cut 2 from fur

C

Eye Cutout
(on face only)

Ear

D

Teeth
Cut 1 from felt
(no seam allowance)

C

OPEN

C

Ear
Cut 1 from fur
1 from print

A

Leg

OPEN

B

Body
Cut 2

Leg

Hair
Cut 1 from fur
(no seam allowance)

D

D

Arm

CRAB

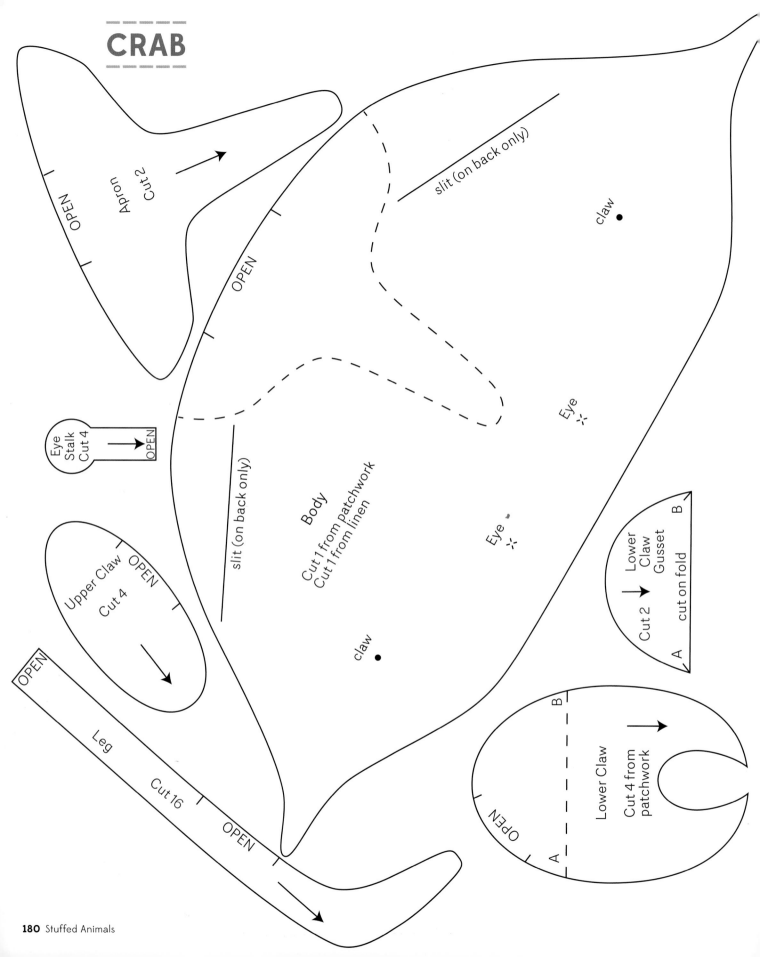

Apron
Cut 2

OPEN

OPEN

slit (on back only)

claw

Eye

Eye

Eye Stalk
Cut 4

OPEN

Body
Cut 1 from patchwork
Cut 1 from linen

slit (on back only)

claw

Lower
Claw
Gusset

Cut 2

cut on fold

A

B

Upper Claw

OPEN

Cut 4

OPEN

Leg

Cut 16

OPEN

B

Lower Claw
Cut 4 from patchwork

OPEN

A

TEDDY BEAR

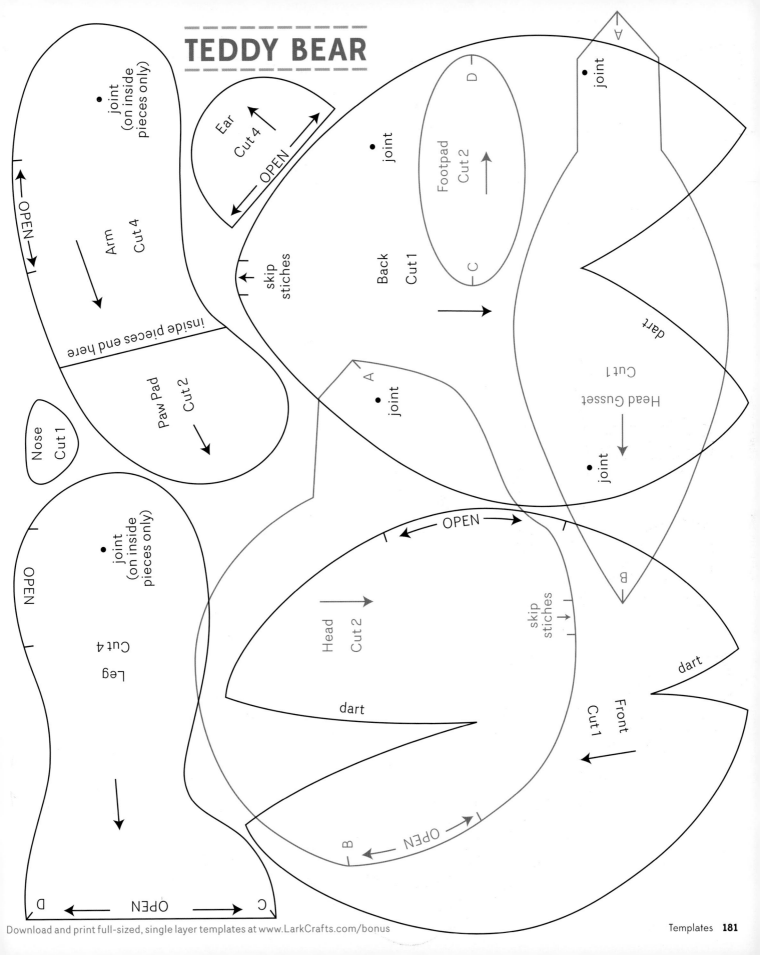

joint (on inside pieces only)

Arm
Cut 4

OPEN

inside pieces end here

Nose
Cut 1

Paw Pad
Cut 2

Ear
Cut 4

OPEN

skip
stiches

Back
Cut 1

Footpad
Cut 2

D

C

joint

A

joint

A

joint

D

Head Gusset
Cut 1

dart

joint

joint

OPEN

Head
Cut 2

dart

skip
stiches

B

Front
Cut 1

dart

OPEN

B

joint (on inside pieces only)

OPEN

Leg
Cut 4

OPEN

D

C

KANGAROO

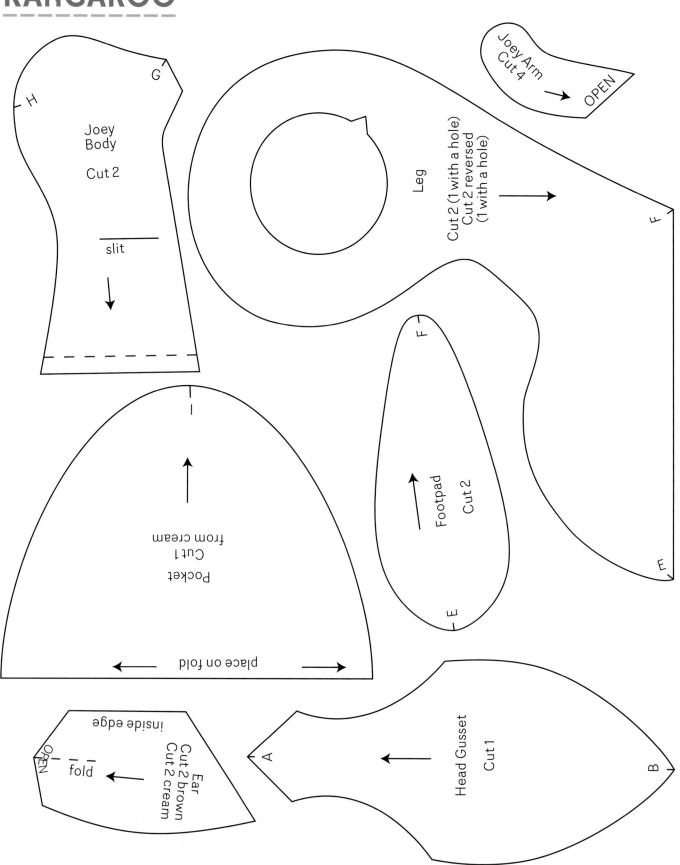

Joey Arm
Cut 4 → OPEN

Joey
Body

Cut 2

slit

Leg
Cut 2 (1 with a hole)
Cut 2 reversed
(1 with a hole) →

F

E

F

Footpad
Cut 2 ↑

E

Pocket
Cut 1
from cream

place on fold

Ear
Cut 2 brown
Cut 2 cream

inside edge

fold

OPEN

A

Head Gusset
Cut 1 ←

B

KANGAROO

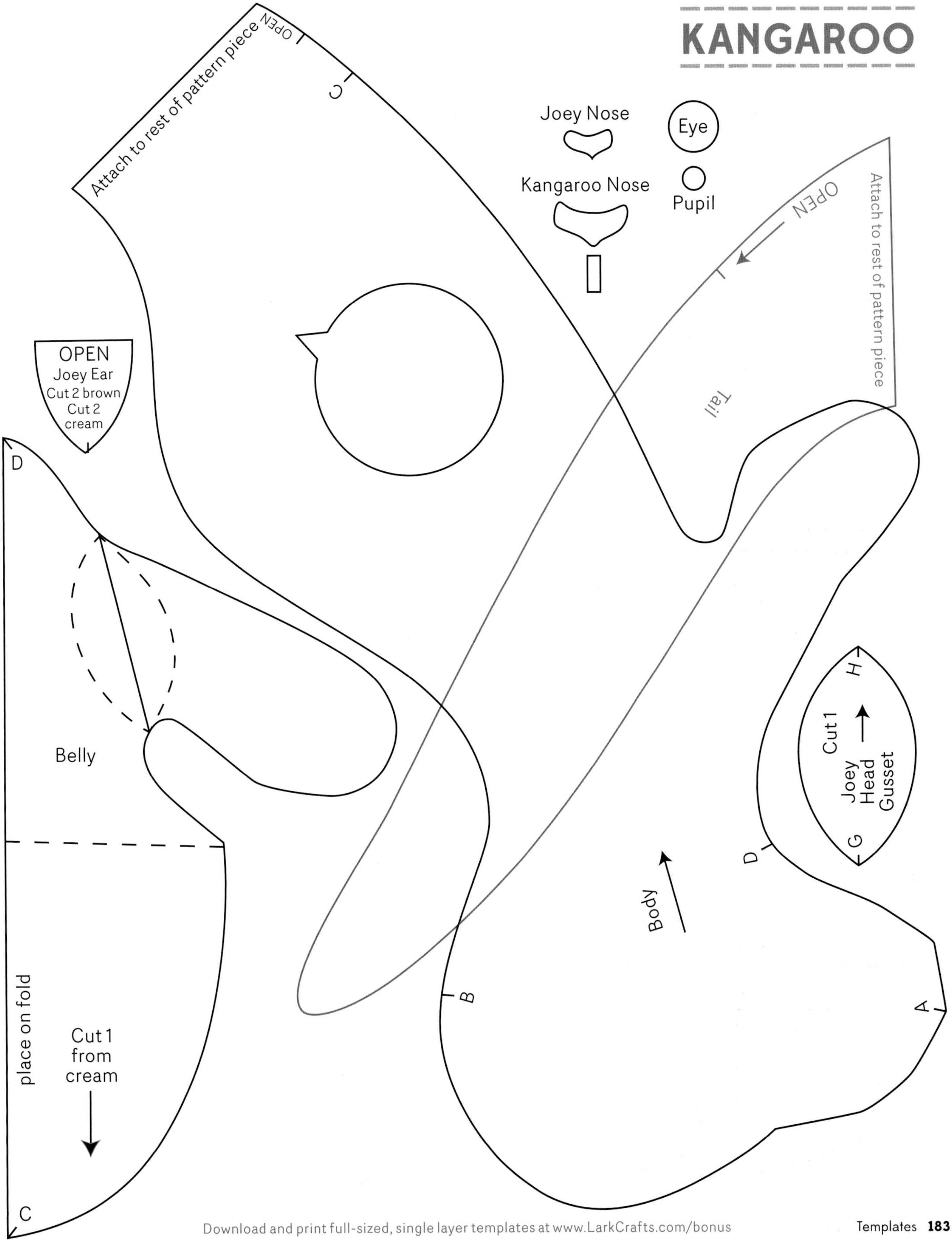

Joey Nose

Kangaroo Nose

Eye

Pupil

Attach to rest of pattern piece

OPEN

C

Attach to rest of pattern piece

OPEN

Tail

OPEN
Joey Ear
Cut 2 brown
Cut 2
cream

D

Belly

place on fold

Cut 1
from
cream

C

B

Body

D

H

Cut 1
Joey
Head
Gusset

G

A

MONKEY

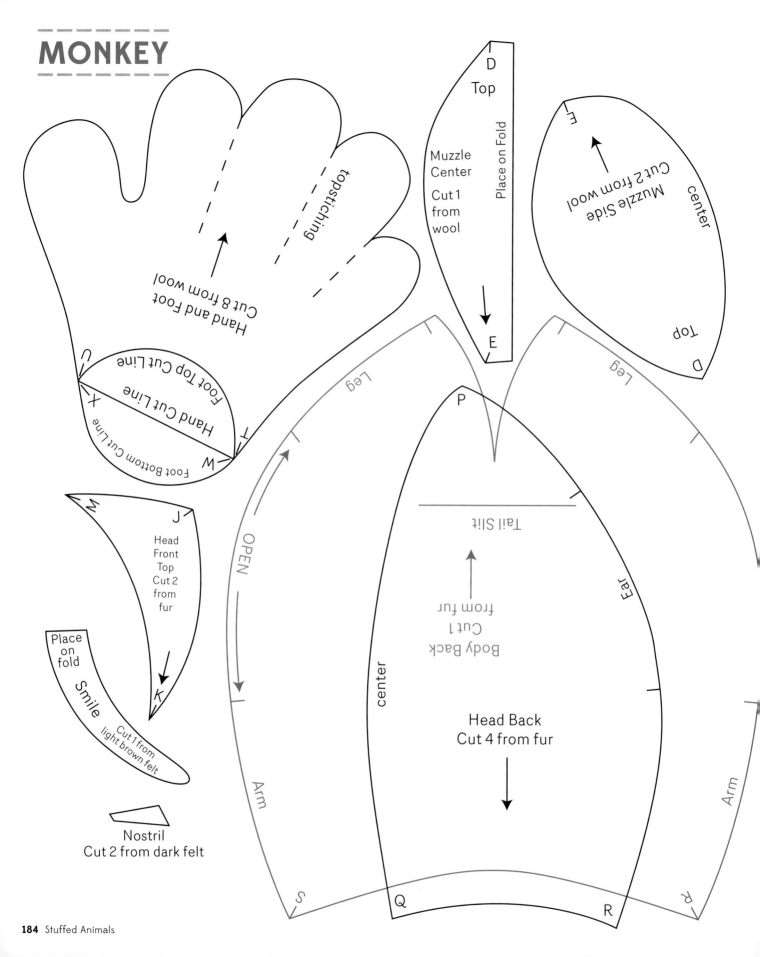

Hand and Foot
Cut 8 from wool

topstiching

Hand Cut Line
Foot Top Cut Line
Foot Bottom Cut Line

D
Top

Muzzle
Center
Cut 1
from
wool

Place on Fold

E

Muzzle Side
Cut 2 from wool
center

Top
D

Leg

Leg

OPEN

P

Tail Slit

Body Back
Cut 1
from fur

Ear

center

Head Back
Cut 4 from fur

Arm

Arm

S

Q

R

Head
Front
Top
Cut 2
from
fur

J

K

Place
on
fold

Smile
Cut 1 from
light brown felt

Nostril
Cut 2 from dark felt

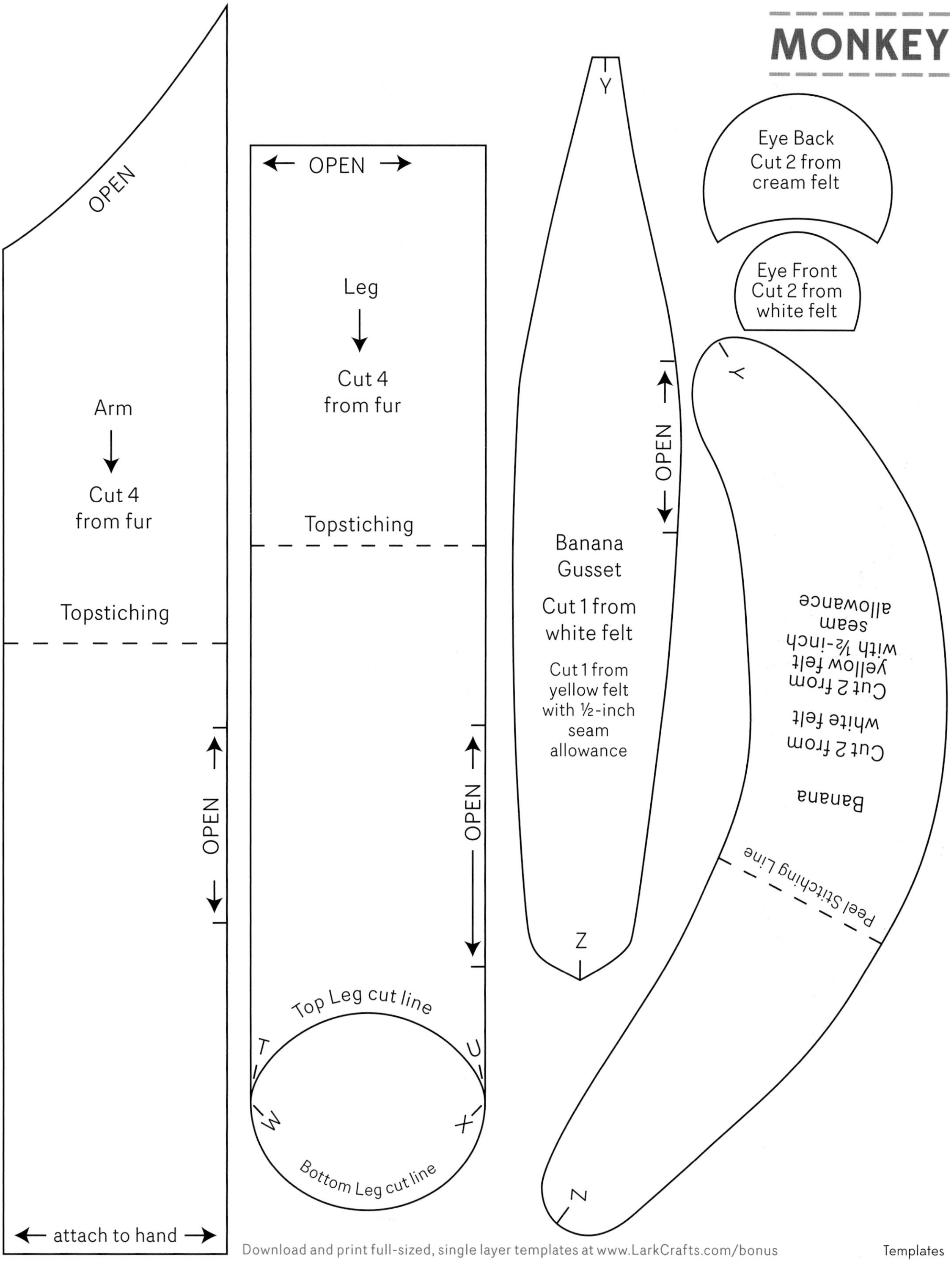

OPEN

Arm

↓

Cut 4
from fur

Topstiching

↑ OPEN ↓

← attach to hand →

← OPEN →

Leg

↓

Cut 4
from fur

Topstiching

↑ OPEN ↓

Top Leg cut line

T   U

W   X

Bottom Leg cut line

Y

Banana
Gusset

Cut 1 from
white felt

Cut 1 from
yellow felt
with ½-inch
seam
allowance

↑ OPEN ↓

Z

Eye Back
Cut 2 from
cream felt

Eye Front
Cut 2 from
white felt

Y

seam
allowance
with ½-inch
yellow felt
Cut 2 from

white felt
Cut 2 from

Banana

Peel Stitching Line

Z

MONKEY

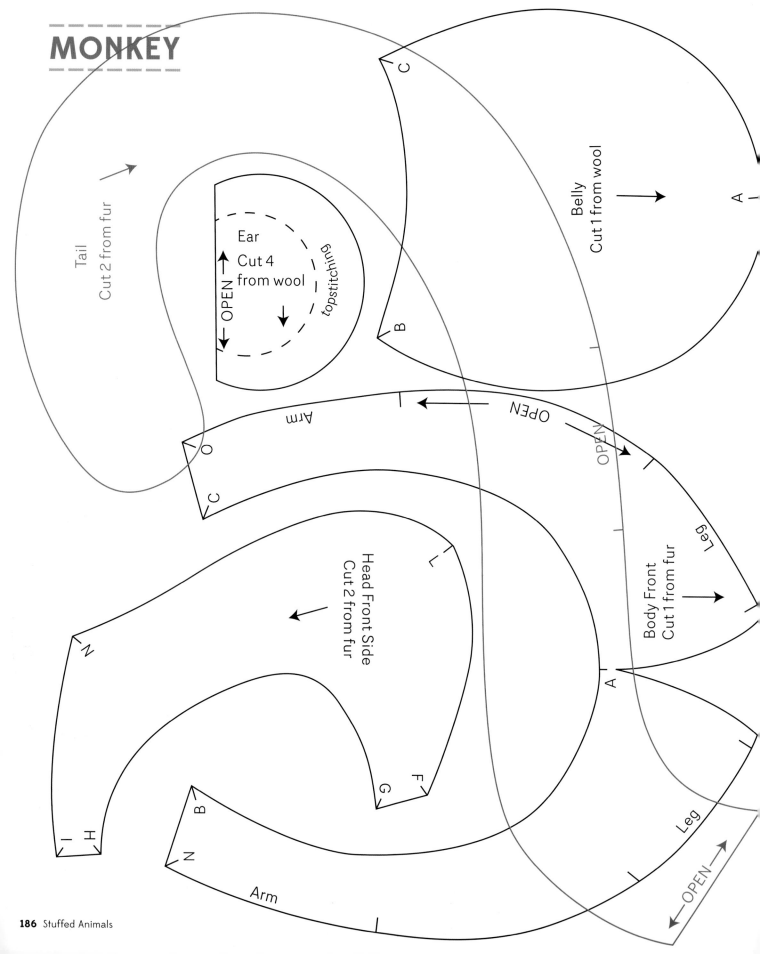

Tail
Cut 2 from fur

Ear
Cut 4
from wool

OPEN

topstitching

Belly
Cut 1 from wool

A

C

B

Arm

C

O

OPEN

OPEN

Leg

Body Front
Cut 1 from fur

A

Head Front Side
Cut 2 from fur

L

N

F

G

H

B

N

Arm

Leg

OPEN

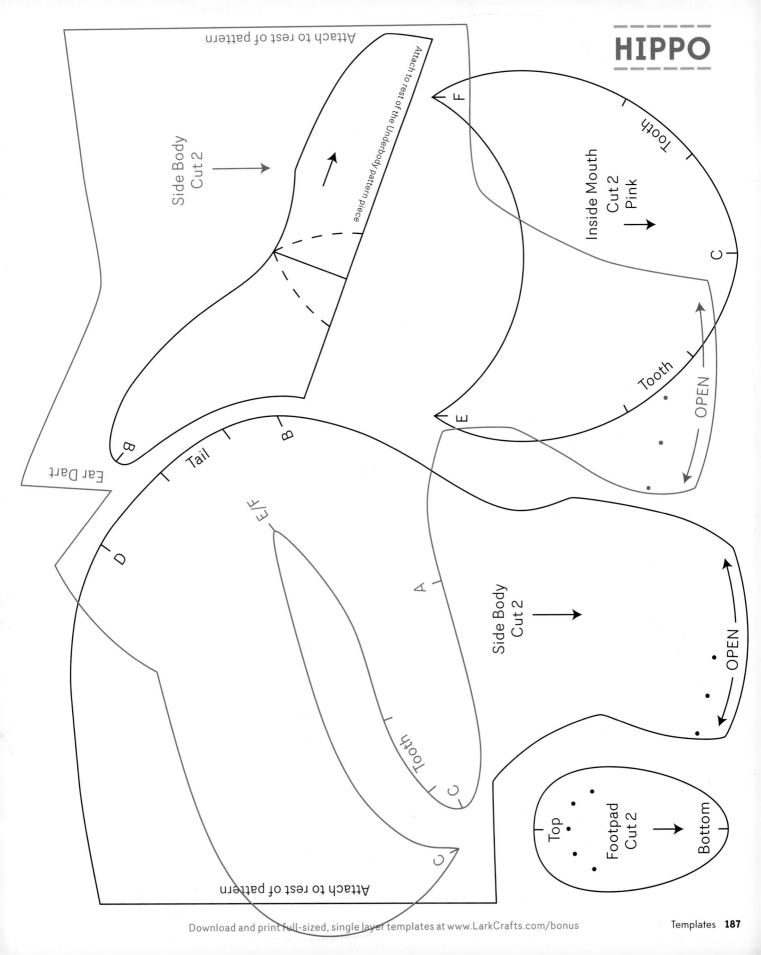

HIPPO

Side Body
Cut 2

Attach to rest of pattern

Attach to rest of the Underbody pattern piece

Ear Dart

Side Body
Cut 2

Inside Mouth
Cut 2
Pink

Tooth

Tooth

OPEN

F

E

C

Tail

B

B

D

E/F

A

Tooth

C

OPEN

C

Attach to rest of pattern

Footpad
Cut 2

Top

Bottom

HIPPO

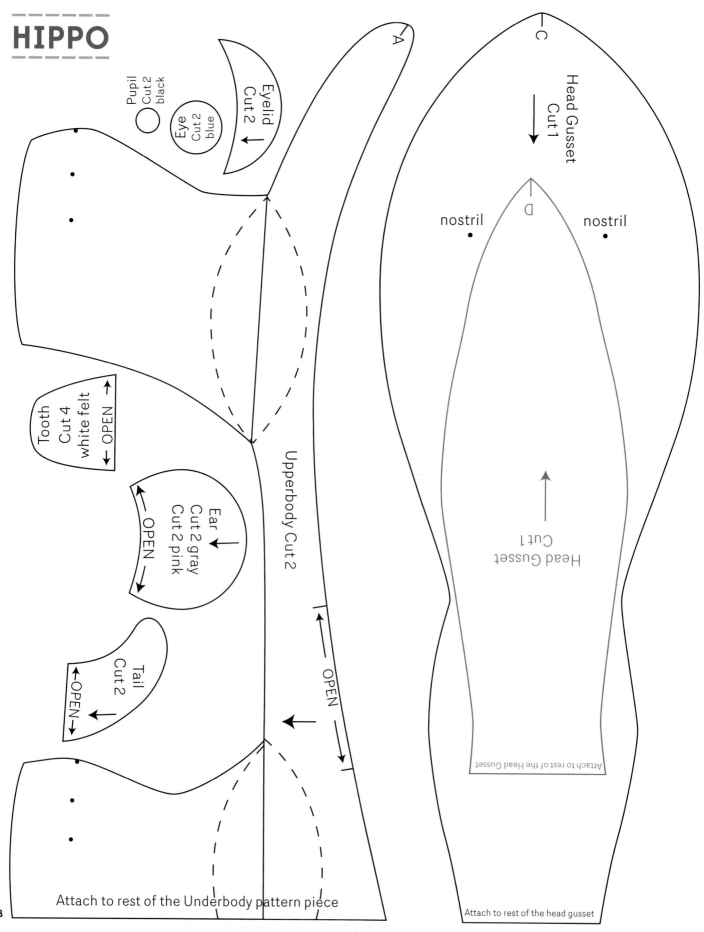

Pupil
Cut 2
black

Eye
Cut 2
blue

Eyelid
Cut 2

A

Head Gusset
Cut 1

C

D

nostril   nostril

Tooth
Cut 4
white felt
OPEN

Ear
Cut 2 gray
Cut 2 pink
OPEN

Upperbody Cut 2

OPEN

Tail
Cut 2
OPEN

Head Gusset
Cut 1

Attach to rest of the Head Gusset

Attach to rest of the Underbody pattern piece

Attach to rest of the head gusset

DINOSAUR

ENLARGE 110%

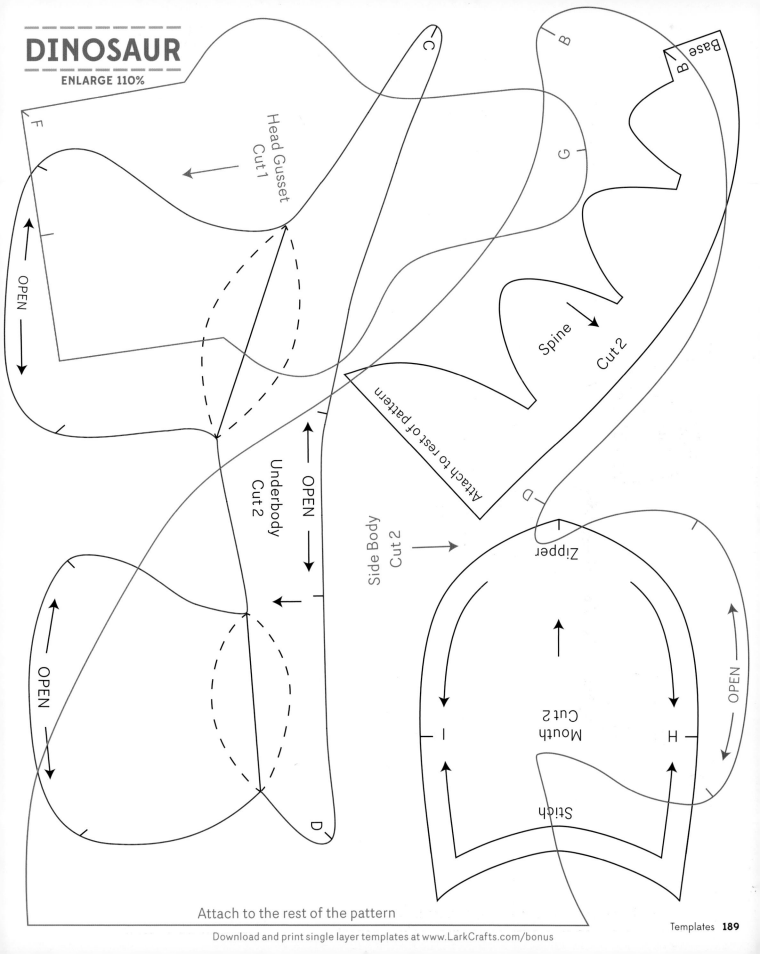

Head Gusset
Cut 1

F

OPEN

C

B

Base

B

G

Spine

Cut 2

Attach to rest of pattern

OPEN

Underbody
Cut 2

Side Body
Cut 2

D

Zipper

OPEN

OPEN

Mouth
Cut 2

I

H

Stich

D

Attach to the rest of the pattern

Download and print single layer templates at www.LarkCrafts.com/bonus

DINOSAUR

ENLARGE 110%

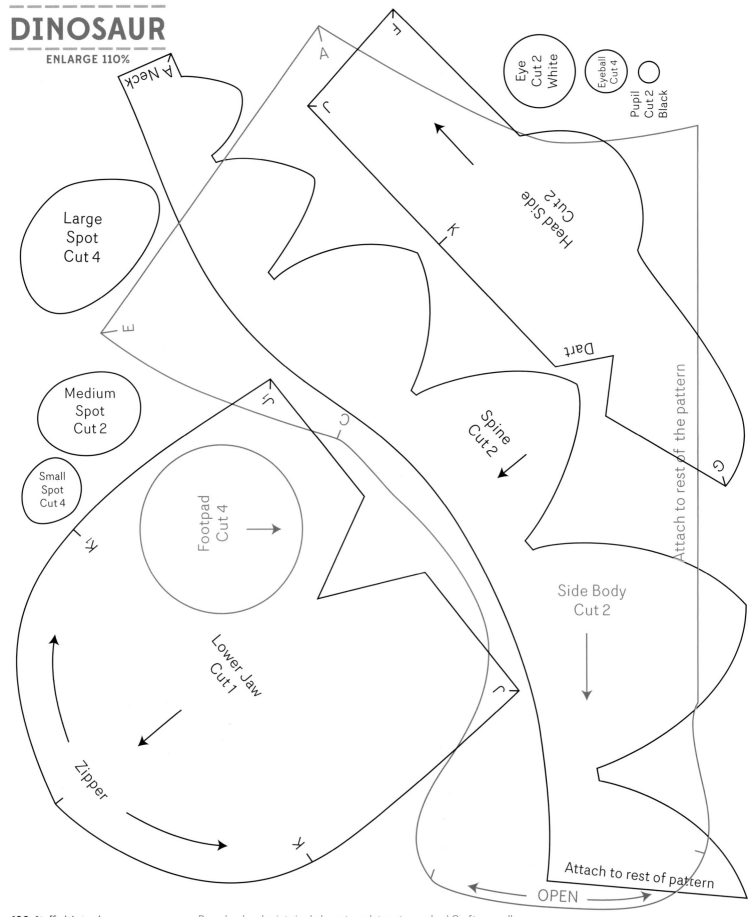

Eye
Cut 2
White

Eyeball
Cut 4

Pupil
Cut 2
Black

A Neck

A

F

C

K

Head Side
Cut 2

Dart

G

Attach to rest of the pattern

Large
Spot
Cut 4

E

Medium
Spot
Cut 2

F

C

Spine
Cut 2

Small
Spot
Cut 4

Footpad
Cut 4

Lower Jaw
Cut 1

Side Body
Cut 2

K

Zipper

K

J

Attach to rest of pattern

OPEN

Download and print single layer templates at www.LarkCrafts.com/bonus

RESOURCES

Most supplies for softie making can be found at a regular fabric store. There are a few specialty supplies you will need.

Felt

Wool felt and wool-blend felt come in a huge array of colors. For the best selection I order online from www.woolfeltcentral.com. Their felt is manufactured by National Nonwovens, who generously supplied me with felt for the projects in this book.

Freezer Paper

I buy freezer paper at the grocery store or big box store. It can be found near the aluminum foil.

Hemostats

Hemostats are my most essential softie-making tool. The cheapest hemostats are free from suture kits at hospitals (where they are thrown away after every patient, even if unused). If you don't know a doctor who can save them for you, buy them online through a medical supply company; I like www.allheart.com.

Mohair

Mohair is produced by three different European mills (Helmbold, Norton, and Schulte) and is very difficult to find in retail stores. I buy mohair online from www.intercaltg.com or from various Etsy sellers (www.etsy.com).

Needle-Felting Supplies

If you want to try incorporating needle felting into your softies, shop for supplies at www.woolery.com.

Squeakers

If you are going to make several toys that squeak, buy a pack of squeakers from a dog-toy supply company. I buy them from www.sitstay.com.

Various Softie-Making Specialty Supplies

For faux fur, animal eyes and noses, joints, excelsior and other specialty stuffing, music boxes, and growlers I shop online at doll- and teddy bear–making supply companies, including www.crscraft.com and www.edinburghimports.com.

Wool Stuffing

Wool stuffing is not much more expensive than polyester fiberfill, but it can be very hard to find. I order wool stuffing from the Amish at West Earl Woolen Mill. They do not have a website, but if you call (717) 859-2241 and say you'd like to order wool for stuffing dolls, they'll know just what you are talking about.

DEDICATION

This book is dedicated to my daughters, Roxanne, Stella, and Josephine, and to their special softies, Plush USA, Pink Kitty, and Mr. Purples.

ACKNOWLEDGMENTS

I owe a tremendous thank you to all of the women who tested my patterns while I was working on the manuscript. Their feedback made each pattern clearer and made the whole book stronger. Thanks to the team at Lark for helping me realize the dream that became this book, and most especially to my editor, Thom O'Hearn, who shared my vision of what this book could be. To Charlie, my husband and best friend, who has put up with having softies staring at him from all corners of our bedroom for many years.

ABOUT THE AUTHOR

Abigail Patner Glassenberg creates unique patterns for stuffed animals from her home studio in Wellesley, Massachusetts. Since 2005 she has shared her creations and her ideas on design, technique, and the online culture of craft through her blog (www.whileshenaps.typepad.com). Her work has been featured on the websites *Sew Mama Sew*, *Design*Sponge*, *WhipUp*, and *CRAFT* as well as in numerous print publications, including *Stitch* magazine, *Cloth Paper Scissors*, and the *Boston Globe*. She has contributed to half a dozen craft books and is the author of *The Artful Bird* (Interweave, 2011). Abby has a master's degree in education from Harvard and taught middle school social studies in Mississippi and Massachusetts before becoming a textile artist and the mother of three girls. Today Abby enjoys teaching people to sew and opening their eyes to the joy of designing their own stuffed animals.

INDEX